Reprints of Economic Classics

FAIRS, *PAST & PRESENT*

FAIRS

PAST & PRESENT

A CHAPTER IN THE HISTORY OF

COMMERCE

BY

CORNELIUS WALFORD

[1883]

Reprints of Economic Classics
AUGUSTUS M. KELLEY PUBLISHERS
New York 1968

First Edition 1883

(London: Elliot Stock, *62 Paternoster Row, E. C.,* 1883)

Reprinted 1968 by

AUGUSTUS M. KELLEY · PUBLISHERS

New York New York 10010

LIBRARY OF CONGRESS CATALOGUE CARD NUMBER

68 - 16699

PRINTED IN THE UNITED STATES OF AMERICA
by SENTRY PRESS, NEW YORK, N. Y. 10019

FAIRS, PAST AND PRESENT.

FAIRS,

PAST AND PRESENT:

A

CHAPTER IN THE HISTORY OF

COMMERCE.

BY

CORNELIUS WALFORD, F.I.A., F.S.S.,

Barrifter-at-Law, and Vice-Prefident of Royal Hiftorical Society.

LONDON: ELLIOT STOCK,
62, PATERNOSTER ROW, E.C.
1883.

PREFACE.

T feems a little remarkable that an inftitution at once fo popular and fo
univerfal as fairs fhould not heretofore
have found an hiftorian. The fact
may perhaps be accounted for in the circumftance
that fairs, as now regarded, are affociated with
notions of frivolity. Many of the circumftances
connected with their origin are certainly not generally known. They were the product of a blending
of Religion with Commerce, fuited to the genius of
former ages, but finding little fympathy now. They
have been affociated with the development of commerce in the nations of Europe—perhaps in the
nations of the world.

The materials for fuch a hiftory are reafonably
abundant upon diligent fearch. They do not lie
upon the furface. Prolonged inveftigation revealed
fo much, that for the purpofe of this work fome
felection became neceffary. I had to confider
whether it would be more inftructive to prefent
the incomplete outline of a number of fairs ranging
throughout the world, or to felect fome of the prin-

cipal ones at home and abroad, paft and prefent, and trace minutely their origin, their development, and their decadence. I determined upon the latter courfe; and this, too, notwithftanding that Mr. Henry Morley had already traced in much detail one of the great fairs whose records it would become neceffary for me to traverfe.

I was chiefly led to the decifion ftated from the faft that the greateft fair ever held in this country, and held for many centuries—that of *Sturbridge*, by Cambridge—had hitherto found no hiftorian; yet many of its annals are on record in a form of undoubted authenticity. It feemed to me that it would be more inftructive to follow fuch a hiftory through its fucceffive phafes than to prefent a feries of minor fketches, however varied the details fhould be. I truft it may be felt that I have felected the right courfe. The other materials brought together are not loft; they are only held over, and will receive the benefit of fome additions and corrections. They can be had when called for, and they will reveal much that is new, even after this work fhall have been read.

The greateft fair in England was that of STUR-BRIDGE; the greateft fair in London that of ST. BARTHOLOMEW, Smithfield. Their hiftories are here given. They have fome points of refemblance; but on the whole they reprefent two really diftinct pictures of old Englifh manners.

The fairs of Continental Europe required fome elucidation. I have given therefore an outline of feveral of the more notable fairs of FRANCE, including thofe moft famous gatherings of the middle ages at Champagne and Brie. Concerning thefe latter I have been able to prefent fome original documents, forming part of the records of the City of London, and now for the firft time printed. Many of thefe fairs are things of the paft. I have added an outline of the fairs of RUSSIA, including the great fair of *Nijni-Novgorod*, becaufe thefe are inftitutions of the prefent. I think the hiftory of this laft-named fair has not previoufly been written in fuch detail.

I truft that the work will be found reafonably free alike from author's and from printer's errors.

C. W.

BELSIZE PARK GARDENS,
LONDON, *February*, 1883.

ERRATA.

Page 17, firſt line, read *dieta* for *dicta*.

Pages 20, 21, 22, for *Magna Carter* read *Magna Charta*.

Page 21 (note), ſixth line, after "Saxon" read *Tholl*, Low Latin.

Page 245, nine lines from bottom, for "A.D. 427," read *in the fifth century.*

CONTENTS.

x   *Contents.*

CHAPTER I.

ORIGIN OF FAIRS.

HE origin of Fairs, like that of many other ancient inftitutions, is involved in much obfcurity. The almoft univerfal belief is that they were affociated with religious obfervances; or, as Mr. Morley poetically puts it : " the firft fairs were formed by the gathering of worfhippers and pilgrims about facred places, and efpecially within or about the walls of abbeys and cathedrals, on the Feaft days of the Saints enfhrined therein." The facred building and its furroundings being too fmall to provide accommodation, tents were pitched ; and as the refources of the diftrict would no more fuffice to victual than to lodge its throngs of vifitors, ftalls were fet up by provifion dealers; and later thefe were turned to more general purpofes of trade. This incidental origin feems, in fome cafes, hardly fufficient to account for the refults which followed ;

but then it has ever been the genius of commerce to follow clofe upon the wants of the people.

The eftablifhment of fairs as a fource of revenue to religious houfes was probably a later development. The Church has always been keenly alive to its temporal interefts.   And while it was one of its principal functions to adminifter hofpitality to the needy and decrepit, there was juftice in drawing contributions from thofe who too foon might have to rely upon its bounty.   Certain it is that nearly all the early charters which I fhall have to notice in the progrefs of this work were fhaped in view of granting tolls and revenue to the purpofes of religion and charity.

The fignification of the word Fair (French *foire*) is in the Latin *forum* a market-place, or *feriæ* holidays. But the German defignation *Meffen* feems ftill more fignificant, as being a word employed to denote the moft folemn part of the Church fervice—the mafs (Latin *miffa*).   The affociation of ideas here implied ftrengthens with every ftep of inveftigation. In the time of Conftantine the Great (fourth century of Chriftian era) Jews, Gentiles, and Chriftians affembled in great numbers to perform their feveral rites about a tree reputed to be the oak mambre under which Abraham received the angels.   At the fame place, adds Zofimus, there came together many traders, both for fale and purchafe of their wares.   St. Bafil, towards the clofe of the fixth century, complained (*De Afcetifis*) that his own Church was profaned by the public fairs held at the martyr's fhrines.   While Michaud ("Hiftory of

Crufades," i., 11) records that under the Fatimite Caliphs, in the eleventh century, a fair was held on Mount Calvary on the 15th September every year, in which were exchanged the productions of Europe for those of the Eaft. Gibbon implies an earlier date, in ftating that it was promoted by the frequent pilgrimages between the feventh and the eleventh centuries. This Fair was of fpecial importance in the commerce of the Italians with the Eaft. *Vide* Cunningham's " Growth of Englifh Induftry and Commerce," 1882, p. 120, n.

Thefe notes are but preliminary and introductory : the inquiry has now to take a wider range.

Greece.—The affociation of commerce with re-ligious obfervances feems indeed not to have origi-nated in or with the Chriftian Church. It is fup-pofed for inftance that at the celebrated Greek games, fuch as thofe at Olympia, &c., trade was no entirely fubordinate object; and this idea gains confirmation from various paffages in the ancient claffic authors. Cicero expreffly ftates that even fo early as the age of Pythagoras, a great number of people attended the religious games for the fpecial purpofe of trading. At Delphi, Nemæa, Delos, or the Ifthmus of Corinth, a fair was held almoft every year. The Amphyctionic fairs were held twice a year. In the time of Chryfoftom, thefe fairs were infamoufly diftinguifhed for a traffic in flaves, def-tined for public incontinence.[1] The Amphyctionic

[1] We fhall find that at a later period the fale of flaves was introduced into the fairs and markets of England and the north of Europe generally.

fpring fair was held at Delphi, and the autumn
fair at Thermopylæ: in fact at the fame times that
the deputies from the States of Greece formed the
Amphyctionic Council—another proof that wher-
ever large affemblies of people took place in Greece,
for religious or political purpofes, advantage was
taken to carry on traffic. At the fairs of Thermopylæ medicinal herbs and roots, efpecially hellebore,
were fold in large quantities.

It may be taken for granted that one principal
reafon why the religious games or the political
affemblies of the States were fixed upon to hold the
fairs was that during thefe, *all hoftilities were fufpended:* and every perfon might go with his merchandife in fafety to them, even through an enemy's
country. The priefts, fo far from regarding thefe
fairs as a profanation of the religious ceremonies,
encouraged them; and the priefts of Jupiter, in
particular, advanced large fums on intereft to fuch
merchants as had good credit, but had not fufficient
money with them, *vide* Stevenfon's "Hiftorical
Sketch of the Progrefs of Difcovery, Navigation
and Commerce," vol. 18 of Kerr's "Travels,"
1824.

Early Eaftern Nations.—By reference to " The
Books of the Prophets," we are enabled to realize
the importance of the fairs in the ancient commerce of the great city of Tyre (probably B.C. 597-
74) "the crowning city whofe merchants were
princes, whofe traffickers the honourable of the
earth " (Ifaiah xxiii. 8). Thus in Ezekiel xxvii.:—

" 12. Tarfhifh was thy merchant by reafon of

the multitude of all kinds of riches; with filver, iron, tin and lead, they traded in thy fairs. . . .

" 14. They of the houfe of Togarmah traded in thy fairs with horfes and horfemen and mules. . . .

" 16. Syria was thy merchant by reafon of the multitude of the wares of thy making : they occu- pied in thy fairs with emeralds, purple and broide- red work, and fine linen and coral and agate. . . .

" 19. Dan alfo and Javan going to and fro occupied in thy fairs : bright iron, caffia, and cala- mus, were in thy market. . . .

" 22. The merchants of Sheba and Raamah, they were thy merchants : they occupied in thy fairs with chief of all fpices, and with all precious ftones and gold. . . .

" 27. Thy riches, and thy fairs, thy merchandife, thy mariners fhall fall into the midft of the feas in the day of thy ruin."

The merchant traders mentioned here claim anceftry from families mentioned Genefis x. 3-7. The expreffion " they occupied " may be ren- dered " they inhabited." In the fame chapter, in alternate verfes, there are many references to markets.

Rome.—It is afferted by learned writers (Fof- broke and others) that fairs, as fuch, took their origin in ancient Rome. Romulus, Servius, Tullius, and the Republic, at its commencement, are feve- rally faid to have inftituted fairs, in order that the country people might come in every ninth day (*nundinae*) to hear the laws proclaimed, or the decrees of the people delivered.[1]   Other public bufinefs was tranfacted thereat.   Booths, tents, and wooden ftands for fhows were always ufual in fuch places.   The fairs were frequently held in the public ftreets ; and one of the moft conftant objects of fale or barter was that of indulgences !   Dogs, and efpecially greyhounds, were fold at thefe Roman fairs.   It is further faid that the fairs were appointed to be held on Saints' days *in order that trade might attract thofe whom religion could not influence.*   The monafteries fold goods, probably fuch as their inmates and furrounding dependents could manufacture.

Courts for the purpofes of adjudicating upon queftions of difpute arifing out of the dealings at the fairs were held alike in Greece and Rome ; thefe being fimilar to the Pie-powder Courts of the middle ages, and moft likely their precurfors.   In time of war, fairs were guarded by foldiers, attempts at plunder being frequent.   Bells were provided in fairs for the purpofe of giving fpeedy alarm.

It has been generally admitted that the Romans introduced the practice of holding fairs into the north of Europe.   I think I fhall make it abundantly clear that they introduced them into England.

Italy.—It is towards the clofe of the fifth century of the Chriftian era that we firft find any authentic account of fairs fpecially defigned as marts for

---

[1] Suetonius records that Claudius Cæfar made fuit unto the Confuls for a licence to hold fairs and markets for his own private manors and lands.—*Sueton.*, ch. xxii.

commerce. Like many other incidents affociated with the hiftory of commerce, the firft traces are found in Italy. The Weftern Roman Empire had become extinguifhed ; but Italy had fallen into good hands. Theodoric the Chief or King of the Oftro-Goths had done much to revive its agriculture, and fomething for its commerce. Foreign merchants began to vifit it again ; and about A.D. 493 feveral *fairs* were appointed for the purpofe of exchanging its redundant produce with the merchandife of other countries. Many rich Jew traders fettled in Rome ; and by means of thefe fairs a wide interchange of commodities was effected.

Germany.—We next turn to *Germany*. We know that the Emperor Charles the Great (Charlemagne) towards the clofe of the eighth century paid great attention to the commerce of weftern Europe—a fact indeed which feems difficult to be reconciled with the circumftance that he allowed the priefts to make a canon declaring all intereft for the ufe of money to be finful ! It may be that he yielded this point in the hope that commercial dealings would foon explode the fallacy. He recognized in fairs a means of exchange of commodities well fuited to the times. The great fairs of his period were thofe of Aquisgranum (*Aix la Chapelle*) and of *Troyes*. Thefe were frequented during his reign by traders from moft parts of Europe. The weight ufed at the latter fair for dealings in coin—then often accepted by weight only on account of its battered condition—became

adopted as the weight for bullion in all parts of
Europe—the pound troy.

Flanders.—Our attention is next directed here.
The woollen manufactures commenced probably in
the latter half of the tenth century (960). At firft
the fales were moftly to the French, whofe thrifty
habits enabled them to purchafe fine woollen cloths
for wear. On account of the fcarcity of coin the
trade was moftly carried on by barter, to facilitate
which Baldwin, Earl of Flanders—who feems to
have exceeded moft of the fovereigns of that period
in defiring the real intereft of himfelf and his fubjects—fet up weekly markets, and eftablifhed
regular fairs at *Bruges, Courtray, Torhout* and *Mont-
Cafel,* at all which he exempted the goods fold or
exchanged from paying any duties on being brought
in or carried out. The new trade was thus greatly
extended, and it continued to flourifh for feveral
centuries—largely due to its being widely known
through the fairs of Europe.

France.—Much of the European commerce of
the middle ages was tranfacted at the celebrated
fairs of Champagne and Brie. There the merchants of Italy, Spain and France congregated.
From far diftant climes the Genoefe tranfported
thither bales of goods; and bufy traders came to
meet in open market the infant efforts of Belgian
manufacturers from Yprès, Douai, and Bruges.
Burgundy fent cloth, Catalonia leather, and the
Genoefe and Florentines brought filks; while at
all the feaports along their coafts vaft cargoes
were unfhipped and placed on the backs of mules

to wend their way to the place appointed for the fair.

Thefe fairs would begin with the fale of cloth, perhaps for feventeen days; the cloth merchants would fettle their accounts prior to the filk merchants entering upon their bargains. In the middle of it all the great cry " Ara " was raifed, as a fignal for the money-changers to take their feats, and for four weeks they fat for the benefit of the various nationalities who wifhed to realize their gains in their native coin.

After the conclufion of the fair a bufy time of fifteen days was fet apart for thofe who had not yet fettled their accounts, and to rectify difputes; which time was extended in favour of the reprefentatives of more diftant people who wifhed to go home and return before finally completing their books. The Genoefe burfar at thefe fairs had always a month allowed him before fettling his accounts.

Bent (in his " Genoa : how the Republic Rofe and Fell," 1881) from whom we have drawn fome of the preceding details fays (p. 106) thefe fairs in fouthern France were not without their political fignificance. Befides bringing hither their merchandife, the Italian traders imported into thefe towns their fpirit of independence and their love of republicanifm. It was from the fouth of France that the feeds of liberty, equality, and fraternity fpread northwards. No greater ftronghold of the rights of the third eftate exifted than at Marfeilles. To this day the influence of this fact is ftrong on

the politics of France. And the principles incul-
cated by the independent traders of Italy took deep
root here under the eyes of defpotifm, and found a
truly favourable foil in which to develop. The
French revolution, and the ftate of France as it is
to-day, may owe their firft fource to thefe very
times when a Genoefe merchant would repair to
thefe fairs, proud and boaftful of his own freedom,
of his vote in the General Council, and of a government which owned no royal mafter ; and all this
could be faid with a fneer at the people over whom
the banner of the lilies held defpotic fway.

North of Europe.—Towards the clofe of the tenth
century periodical public markets or fairs were
eftablifhed in the northern portions of Europe, and
were ufed for a purpofe altogether new in thefe
higher latitudes, but arifing out of the rapine and
hoftilities peculiar to the period. In feveral of the
North German towns the merchandife brought to
them confifted of flaves taken in the wars—many of
which were believed to have been fermented for the
fimple purpofe of carrying off captives. Helmold
relates that he faw 7,000 Danifh flaves at one time
expofed for fale in the market at Meklenberg. The
common price of ordinary flaves of either fex was
about a mark (or 8 oz.) of filver ; but fome female
flaves for their beauty or qualifications were rated
as high as three marks. (*Vide* Thorkelin's " Effay
on the Slave Trade," pp. 4-9.)

We arrive at the clofe of the fixteenth century.
The city of *Antwerp* had at this period arrived very
nearly at the fummit of its wealth and glory, which

Anderſon ("Hiſt. of Commerce," ii., p. 25) conſiders it had acquired by two principal means :—

I. By the grants of free fairs for commerce, made formerly by the ſovereigns of the Nether-lands—two of which fairs laſted each time ſix weeks —whither merchants reſorted from all parts of Chriſtendom with their merchandiſe, cuſtom free. *At theſe fairs vaſt concerns were managed, not only in merchandiſe, but in bills of exchange with all parts of Europe.*

II. It had become the entrepot of the commerce between the ſouthern and northern ports of Europe, and eſpecially of the Portugueſe merchants. This drew the German and other merchants to ſettle there ; and the merchants of *Bruges* largely removed thither after the Archduke Maximilian had (about 1499) reduced their city. The fairs were aided by, and themſelves aided, this development.

ENGLAND.

CHAPTER II.

ORIGIN AND LAWS—ENGLAND.

N the preceding furvey I have intentionally omitted any mention of *England*. Hiftorians of the ordinary type have thought it beneath their dignity to refer to anything fo common-place as fairs. The real mainfprings of our commerce feem in fact very generally to have efcaped them. The greateft commercial nation of the world has found no hiftorian willing to record the true caufes of its greatnefs. The intrigues of fovereigns, the machinations of ecclefiaftics; the trickeries of ftatefmen and diplomatifts, have alone commanded their attention and abforbed their limited energies. The Statute-book, the one great ftorehoufe of our national hiftory, has efcaped their obfervation. I propofe to devote a fpecial chapter to the origin and development of fairs in England.

It has been claimed that the Anglo-Saxons

founded alike fairs and markets in England. To
Alfred the Great the honour is ufually affigned. I
have no doubt whatever that the Romans firft introduced the practice of holding markets and fairs
in England. I find very diftinct traces of fairs of
Roman origin at *Helfton* (Cornwall), at *Barnwell*
(by Cambridge), at *Newcaftle-upon-Tyne*, and at
feveral places along the line of the Roman wall in
Northumberland. But affuming that the inftitutions of the country were largely recaft during the
Anglo-Saxon period, we may take note of the fuppofed re-inftitution of markets and fairs in the
ninth century. The tithings held their fittings in
their tithing or free-borough once a week, and
many people coming thither to have their matters
adjudicated upon, brought alfo their garden produce, corn, beafts, and *id genus omne*, for fale : becaufe there they could meet one another, and buy
and fell as their needs required, hence the commencement of a market weekly. From the Courts juft
mentioned there lay an appeal, if either plaintiff or
defendant were not fatisfied, to a County Court,
held about Eafter and Michaelmas, and over thefe
a bifhop and ealderman prefided. To this fuperior
Court alfo came numbers who, at the various inter-
mediate Court-leets were not fatisfied. And as large
numbers came together, a greater and better opportunity was afforded for felling their wares and
goods, corn, beafts, ftuffs, linens. " *In this we
can trace the origin of fairs,* which were generally
held twice a year, on or about the times mentioned."
This is the dictum of Mr. G. Lambert, F.S.A., in

a paper read before the London and Middlefex Archæological Society in 1880, the fubftance of which is publifhed in the "Antiquary," ii., pp. 102-3. The fairs here are feen to be purely fecular inftitutions.

It was by the *Normans* that the fairs of England were moulded into the fhape with which we are moft familiar. The Norman kings placed themfelves largely under the influence of the Papal throne; and it was to the Church, or in the intereft of the Church, that nearly all fairs were granted after the Norman Conqueft in the eleventh century. It was under John, early in the thirteenth century, that the power of the Church became moft pronounced in England, and it is during this reign that moft of the exifting charters of fairs date.

Trying to harmonize thefe fomewhat conflicting views, it may be fuppofed that fome of our fairs at leaft were eftablifhed during the Roman occupation. Thefe were probably largely added to during the Anglo-Saxon period. The Normans admittedly encouraged fairs in the intereft of the Church. The fairs of the firft and fecond category were moftly fairs eftablifhed by prefcription, the latter were chiefly eftablifhed by charter. But in the courfe of centuries the identity of origin becomes loft. Shepheard, in his "Corporations, Fraternities, and Guilds" (publifhed 1659), fays : "It is very ufual in thefe Charters to confirm the old markets and fairs, and to grant new markets and Fairs. Or to change the dayes of the old markets or Fairs. And to grant to the Corporation the

Py-powder Court and Incidents and profits of the Fair." (P. 69.)

I am difpofed to believe that many of the early fairs affociated with religious obfervances and ceremonies, were in their inception fairs of prefcription only : that is to fay, fairs which took their origin in paffing events, without any fpecial authority, and that upon later occafions charters were obtained. Bailey fas that in ancient times amongft Chriftians, upon any extraordinary folemnity, particularly the anniverfary dedication of a church, tradefmen ufed to bring and fell their wares even in the churchyards, efpecially upon the feftival of the dedication; as at Weftminfter, on St. Peter's Day; at London, on St. Bartholomew's; at Durham, on St. Cuthbert's Day, &c.; but riots and difturbances often happening, by reafon of the numbers affembled together, privileges were by royal charter granted, for various caufes, to particular places, towns, and places of ftrength, where magiftrates prefided, to keep the people in order. ("Pop. Antiq.," Brand.)

Blackftone fays:—Fairs and markets, with the tolls belonging to them, can only be fet up by virtue of the royal grant, or by long and immemorial ufage and prefcription, which prefuppofes fuch a grant. The limitation of thefe public reforts to fuch time and fuch place as may be moft convenient for the neighbourhood forms a part of economics, or domeftic polity, which, confidering the kingdom as a large family, and the fovereign as the mafter of it, he clearly has a right to difpofe and order as he pleafes.

Again, a man may have a right to hold a fair or market, or to keep a boat for the ferrying of paffengers; and this either by royal grant or by prefcription, from which a royal grant may be prefumed to have been at fome time conferred. But (unlefs under an Act of Parliament) no other title than thefe will fuffice; for no fair, market, or ferry can be lawfully fet up without licenfe from the Crown. On the other hand, a man may, under fuch titles, lawfully claim to be lord of a fair or market, though he be not the owner of the foil on which it is held.

The right to take toll is ufually (though not neceffarily) a part of the privilege; and the tolls of a fair or market are due either in refpect of goods fold there (that is, from the feller, not the buyer), or for ftallage or pickage, or the like, in refpect of ftalls or polls fixed in the foil.

I have feen it ftated that before the granting of a fair it was cuftomary to iffue a writ of *ad quod damnum*, to inquire whether the grant would be prejudicial to any; but I doubt if the practice was at all general.

If I am entitled to hold a fair or market, and another perfon fets up a fair or market fo near mine that he does me a prejudice, it is a nuifance to the freehold which I have in my market or fair. But in order to make this out to be a nuifance it is neceffary (1) That my market or fair be the elder, otherwife the nuisance lies at my own door. (2) That the market be erected within the third part of twenty miles from mine. Sir M. Hale conftrues the *dicta* or reasonable day's journey mentioned by Bracton, to be twenty miles; as, indeed, it is usually understood, not only in our own law, but also in the civil law, from which we probably borrowed it. So that if the new fair or market be not within seven miles of the old one, it is no nuisance; for it is held reasonable that every man should have a market within one-third of a day's journey from his own home; that the day being divided into three parts, he may spend one part in going, another in returning, and the third in transacting his necessary business there. If such market or fair be on the same day with mine, it is *primâ facie* a nuisance to mine, and there needs no proof of it, but the law will intend it to be so; but if any other day it *may* be a nuisance; but of this there must be proof.

The statute of Gloucester (1278) conferred the right of inquiring into the title of all who claimed rights usually exercised by the Crown. Where such rights were questioned, the judicial process of *quo warranto* was set in motion. One of the principal matters about which inquisition was frequently made under this statute was the right of holding markets and fairs. This right could (as we have seen) only be conferred by royal grant, where prescription could not be pleaded. In many cases it had been assumed by those who had bought land on which fairs had usually been held, and who were then taking tolls from merchants which should in justice have gone to the King. Much curious information was obtained by means of the inquisitions conducted under this Act. This was originally recorded in the

Hundred Rolls, and it is made free ufe of in this work.

It has been afferted that it is not in the King's power to refume a franchife that has been once granted : fo that a fair once authorized by royal grant, is, by the common law of England, good againft the King. I have found no cafe wherein this principle is declared ; but there is an inftance which points in a contrary direction : for in 1446-7 (25 Hen. VI.) it was enacted " that all grants of franchifes, markets, fairs, and other liberties to buy or to fell within the towns of North Wales made to any Welfhman before this time, fhall be void and of no effect." Here it was parliament, not the King, revoking the grants. For further legiflation regarding Welfh Fairs, fee Chapter V., anno 1534.

Brady (in his famous work on " Boroughs ") feemed to be of opinion that every free borough had the privilege of a market and fair, with free right to come and go thereto and therefrom, as of courfe (p. 33, ed. 1777). But I difcover no such inherent right, and where this privilege is fuftained it has ufually been included in one of its early charters. Certainly the converfe is not the cafe : that is to fay, it was in no way cuftomary that fairs fhould be limited to boroughs free or otherwife. Many were, indeed, granted to fmall towns, frequently to lords of manors, and commonly to religious houfes; and in various cafes to individuals.

In the next chapter I fhall examine more in detail the regulations upon our ftatute rolls regarding fairs.

CHAPTER III.

EARLY REGULATIONS AFFECTING FAIRS—
ENGLAND.

T has been attributed to Alfred the Great that amongſt the many wiſe and beneficial meaſures he took for the advancement of this kingdom, was the eſtabliſhment of fairs and markets. I have already ſhown that this is not quite ſo; but certain it is that the firſt general meaſures for the regulation of commerce in England, are dated back to his reign. Hence it was then provided that alien merchants ſhould come only to the "four fairs," and ſhould not remain in England more than forty days. This was in the latter half of the ninth century. But I have already ſhown that fairs were held in other parts of Europe, and in Aſia, centuries earlier than this date. The point of importance in the regula-tion of Alfred is that foreign merchants were per-mitted by royal authority to attend theſe Engliſh fairs.

King Ethelred II. (end of tenth and commence-

ment of eleventh centuries) proclaimed that the *ſhips
of merchants, or of enemies from the high ſeas, coming
with goods into any port ſhould be at peace.* The
principle here enunciated, of commerce being deemed
an act of peace, is believed to be of high antiquity
in Great Britain; but whether it originated here is
by no means clear, nor is it material to determine.
At later periods the practice has not been con-
tinuouſly upheld.

Henry I. granted to the citizens of London (*inter
alia*) that they ſhould be free throughout England
and the ſea ports from *toll*, paſſage through towns,
ports, gates, and bridges; *and leſtage, or a toll paid
for freedom to ſell at Fairs.*

Magna Carter (1215).—The demand of the
Barons preſented to King John embodied the following: " That merchants ſhall have ſafety to go
and come, buy and ſell, without any evil tolls, but
by antient and honeſt cuſtoms."   In the completed
Charter the actual grant took the following ſhape:

All merchants ſhall have ſafety and ſecurity in
coming into England and going out of England, and
in ſtaying and in travelling through England, as well
by land as by water, to buy and ſell without any
unjuſt exactions, according to ancient and right
cuſtoms, excepting in time of war, and if they be of
a country at war againſt us: and if ſuch are found
in our land at the beginning of a war, they ſhall be
apprehended without injury of their bodies and goods
until it be known to us, or to our Chief Juſticiary,
how the merchants of our country are treated who
are found in the country at war againſt us; if ours

be in fafety there, the others fhall be in fafety in our land.

The doctrine of international reciprocity is here very clearly ftated.

Macpherfon ("Annals of Commerce") is of opinion, after an examination of the trading of the chief commercial ports of Great Britain, that by the middle of the twelfth century (A.D. 1156) "the foreign trade was almoft entirely conducted by foreign merchants;" indeed he declared it to be "evidently" fo. I expect to be able to fhow that the great centres of trade at this period were the fairs held in various parts of the kingdom. The cafe of *Sturbridge Fair* (Cambridge) is a remarkable inftance.

1216.—The firft Great Charter of Henry III. confirmed the provifions of *Magna Carter* as to merchants, except in the cafe of thofe *who had been before publicly prohibited.* The privileges thus accorded to foreign merchants were feven. (1) To come into England (2) To depart thereout (3) To remain (4) To travel by land or water (5) To buy and fell (6) To be free of evil tolls [1] (7) To

---

[1] The protection from "evil tolls" was alfo a matter of great confequence. It was to be regarded as a fecurity from paying fo large a cuftom or impofition upon any goods that the fair profit is loft therein, and the trade thereby prevented. The original term expreffive of this is *Mala Tolneta*, the word toll or tolt being derived from the Saxon *Tolnetum*, or *Theolonium*, which fignifies a payment in markets, towns, and fairs, for goods and cattle bought and fold. It alfo ftands for any manner of cuftom, fubfidy, impofition, or fum of money taken of the buyer for the importing or exporting of any wares ; and

enjoy the ancient cuftoms.   This laft was of material confequence, and implied privileges not common to ordinary perfons.   The promife of freedom from " evil tolls " hardly lefs fo, as will hereafter appear.

Thefe early privileges accorded to foreign merchants who vifited our fhores feem fo natural to us, in thefe free-trade times, that we have a difficulty in realizing at the firft glance the full meafure of their fignificance.   It may aid us in doing fo if I review the general regulations regarding foreigners which prevailed (reciprocally) in moft of the countries of Europe prior to this period (thirteenth century) and in many cafes long thereafter.   Every foreigner was anfwerable to the debts, and even crimes of all other foreigners of his own nationality [1]

it may be affumed that the words in *Magna Carter* were ufed in their evident fenfe.   The compound word *Mala-tolneta*, which appears in the original text, fignifies bad or evil tolls, or unjuft exactions.   In the later ftatutes it is rendered into French by the ancient term *Maletout* (*Vide* R. Thomfon's " Notes on the Great Charters," 1829).

[1] In illuftration of the early cuftom of holding foreigners living or trading in England refponfible for the offences and crimes of other foreigners, the following inftance may be given.   In 1301 a perfon belonging to the houfe of the Spini, of Florence, was killed in a fquabble with fome other people belonging to the fame houfe in England, and the guilty perfon having abfconded, the officers of juftice feized the bodies and goods of other perfons belonging to the company, and alfo (luckily for the merchants), a fum of money collected by them in Ireland for the *Pope*, and fome merchandife purchafed on his account.   He (the Pope) immediately fent a Bull to England requiring the liberation of the people and property arrefted (" Fœdera," v. ii., p. 891).

—and the queſtion of nationality was very freely in-terpreted in ſome ſuch caſes. And in the caſe of the death of a foreign merchant his property in poſſeſſion was either forfeited to the King or fell a prey to the rapacity of the lord of the ſoil in whoſe territory the death occurred.[1] Further, by an early cuſtom of London, merchants giving reference for ſtrangers, who purchaſed goods on the credit of ſuch references, were held liable to pay for the goods ſo obtained. Thus under the cuſtom of merchants, two perſons of the ſame nationality being found in arrear, the whole debt might be charged to one of them—as the creditor might ſelect!

Theſe reſtrictions removed, or greatly modified, it is no wonder that fairs greatly increaſed in numbers and importance.

1235. This ſame monarch Henry III. gave ſpe-cial permiſſion to the merchants of *Cologne* to attend fairs in all parts of England. This was probably in conſequence of ſome claim from the branch of the Hanſeatic League eſtabliſhed in London, to trade in its corporate capacity excluſively for the cities which belonged to the confederacy. There was another aſſociation of German merchants ſettled in London at this date.

1275. The Firſt Statute of Weſtminſter (c. 23) was intended to remedy the ſtate of primitive juſtice already ſpoken of, and which to a large degree aroſe out of local juriſdictions. Under it no foreign perſon—that is to ſay, one who was not

---

[1] This practice remained in force in France from the age of Charlemagne down to our own times.

free of the town he vifited—which is of this realm (*i.e.* of England) was to be diftrained for any debts but his own in any city, burgh, town, market or fair.

1283. The Statute *de Mercatoribus* (11 Edw. I.) was intended to affift merchants in the recovery of their debts, and thus to encourage them to trade in England. When they fupplied goods and the debt was acknowledged before royal officers in fpecified towns, they could be empowered under the King's feal to diftrain for debt in default of payment. At Acton Burnel this new fcheme was determined on, for trial in London, York, and Briftol; and after two years it was decreed (*Statutum Mercatorum*, 1285, 13 Edw. I.) that it fhould be brought into much more extenfive operation by giving fimilar facilities in many other places, efpecially in *fairs*, and a much greater number of royal officers were empowered to act in the matter. Thefe privileges were not limited to men from particular towns or countries: all foreign merchants could avail themfelves thereof, except when this kingdom was at war with their native land. The claufe relating to the "Seal of the Fair" was as follows:—

" And a Seal fhall be provided that fhall ferve for Fairs, and the fame fhall be fent unto every Fair under the King's Seal, by a Clerk fworn, or by the Keeper of the Fair, and the Seal fhall be opened before them, and the one piece fhall be delivered unto the aforefaid merchants, and the other fhall remain with the Clerk; and before them, or one of the merchants, if both cannot attend, the Recognizances fhall be taken as before is faid."

In the cafe of London two merchants of the Commonalty fhould be chofen that fhould fwear compliance with this law.

And by a charter of the following year granted to foreign merchants then refident in England, it was ordained, "that one weight fhall be kept in every fair and town; that the weigher fhall fhow the buyer and feller that the beam and fcales are fair, and that there fhall be *only one weight and meafure* in our dominions, and that they be ftamped with our ftandard mark." All ftudents of hiftory, know how well this ordinance has been obferved!

By the Statute of Wynton [Winchefter] attributed to the reign of Edw. I., but probably of earlier date it is enacted (c. 6) "And the King commandeth and forbiddeth that from henceforth neither Fairs nor markets be kept in the *Churchyards* for the Honour of the Church."[1]

1321. About this date—reign of Edw. II.—there is fuppofed to have been enacted "Articles of the Office of Efcheatry." Amongft the duties of this officer of the crown, he was to hold inqueft (*inter alia*) of markets, fairs, tolls, paffage-monies, and cuftoms, unjuftly levied without licenfe of the King; alfo where, when, and from what time, and how much they are worth by the year. Under the power fo granted various inquifitions regarding fairs, and the tolls charged, and the privileges afferted, were conducted.

---

[1] It had before this time been quite cuftomary to hold fairs in churchyards.

CHAPTER IV.

HESE have been already referred to, and will arife in various other parts of this work, as being clofely affociated with fairs.

Thefe Courts, defignated in the Latin tongue *curia pedis pulverizati*, in the Old French *pied puldreaux*, alike in each cafe, it is fuppofed, in reference to, or as typical of the dufty feet of the fuitors. Some indeed fay becaufe "juftice is there done as fpeedily as duft can fall from the feet." But without reference to fuch fanciful derivations they may be fpoken of as a rough-and-ready mode of adminiftering juftice at fairs, markets, &c. There is no record or ordinance by which any fuch Court was called into exiftence in this country. They came to us with fairs; they paffed away with the decay of the commercial ufages of fairs.

Thofe curious in matters of archæology may confult a paper hereon by Dr. Pettingall, which appears in "Archæologia," i. pp. 190-203.

Barrington, in his " Obfervations on the Statutes," obferves that " In the Burrow Laws of Scotland, an alien merchant is called Piedpuldreaux, and likewife ane Farand-man, or a man who frequents fairs. The Court of Piepowder is, therefore, to determine difputes between thofe who refort to fairs and thefe kind of Pedlars who generally attend them. *Pied puldreaux* in Old French fignifies a Pedlar, who gets his livelihood by vending his goods where he can, without any certain or fixed refidence."

In the " Regiam Majeftatem," 1609, there is the following : " Gif ane ftranger merchand travelland throw the Realme, havand na land, nor refidence, nor dwelling within the fchirefdome, bot vaigand fra ane place to ane other, quha therefore is called Pied Puldreaux, or duftifute."

Hence then the Court of Pie Powder fignifies in fimple language a *Court of Pedlars*.

Such Courts were held in the markets of the Romans, as they were in the markets of the Normans, and probably all through the old Roman Europe. But they had yet an earlier origin. Demofthenes makes it plain that all caufes relating to the feftival of Bacchus were heard on the fpot. Fairs were affociated with the Olympic games; and it feems clear defcended from the feftivities of the Greek Church.

The neceffity in all fairs of a tribunal which could promptly deal with the differences arifing amongft a fleeting population were the fame, quite irrefpective of where the fair might chance to be held. Again the merchants attending the principal fairs of diffe-

rent countries were in a large degree the fame.
They travelled from country to country. What
they found beneficial in one part of the globe was
equally fo in another, and hence became adopted as
of courfe. The tribunals of commerce which once
exifted in England, and which ftill exift in various
parts of Continental Europe, are analagous to the
Courts of Piepowder held at fairs.

In an account of a fair held in the northern
region of Lapland as far back as two centuries ago
(1681), a Court of Piepowder is recorded as one of
its features.

The peculiar conftitution of the Court has to be
kept firmly in view. It had jurifdiction only in
commercial queftions. It tried them before a jury
of traders formed on the fpot. It could entertain a
cafe of flander, if of merchandife or wares exhibited,
but not of the merchant or trader who vended the
fame. It could fit only during fair time; could
take cognizance only of things happening during
fair time, and within the fair. It could try a thief
who had committed robbery in the fair only when
he had been captured within its bounds. It might
hold pleas for amounts, in later times, above forty
fhillings; and its judgments could be deferred and
enforced at the next fair. So firmly indeed had
cuftom defined the powers of thefe Courts, that it
has been well faid, even the King himfelf if he were
fitting as judge in fuch a Court, could not extend
them.

Specific Legiflation.—1478. There having been
many abufes committed in the Courts *Piepowder*

held at the fairs in England, chiefly by the avarice and injuftice of their ftewards, bailiffs, and others, whofe province it was to hold the courts and ad-minifter impartial juftice in all cafes arifing during the continuance, and within the jurifdiction, of the fairs : but who took cognizance of contracts and trefpaffes unconnected with the fairs, and frequently having no foundation in truth. Thefe abufes began to have the effect of preventing merchants from attending the fairs : whereby the people of the country were deprived of the convenience of pur-chafing goods; and the lords of the fairs loft their cuftomary profits. The entire fubject came before parliament, and a meafure intended for relief refulted, which I fhall now review in detail :

17 Edw. IV. c. 2.—*Item*, Whereas divers Fairs be holden & kept in this Realm, fome by Prefcription allowed before Juftices in Eyre, & fome by grant of our Lord the King that now is, & fome by the grant of his noble Progenitors & Predeceffors, & to every of the fame Fairs is of right pertaining a Court of Pypowders, to minifter in the fame due Juftice in this behalf; in w^h Court it hath been all times accuftomed, that every perfon coming to the f^d Fairs fh^d have lawful remedy of all manner of Con-tracts, Trefpaffes, Covenants, Debts, & other Deeds under or done within any of the fame Fairs, during the time of the fame Fairs, & within the jurifdiction of the fame, & to be tried by merchants being of the fame Fair; w^h Courts at this day be mifufed by Stewards. . . .

And fometimes, by the device of evil difpofed

people feveral fuits be feigned to trouble them to whom they bear evil will, to the intent that they for Lucre may have favorable Inquefts of thofe that come to the f^d Fairs, where they take their actions . . . whereby the Lords of the fame Fairs do lofe great profit by the not coming of divers merchants to the fairs . . . & alfo the Commons be unferved of fuch ftuff & merchandife as w^d other-wife come to the faid Fairs

For remedy whereof it was Ordained & Eftablifhed that from the firft day of May then next enfuing no Steward, Under-fteward, Bailiff, Commiffary, nor other minifter of any fuch Courts of Pypowders fhould hold plea upon any action at the Suit of any perfon or perfons, unlefs the Plaintiff or plaintiffs, or his or their attorney, in the prefence of the de-fendant or defendants do fwear upon the holy Evangelifts, upon the Declaration, that the Con-tract or other Deed contained in the f^d Declaration was made or committed within the Fair & within the Time of the f^d Fair where he taketh his action, & within the bounds & jurifdiction of the fame Fair. The Defendant might plead that the caufe did not arife out of the Fair. If the plaintiff refufed to fwear the defendant fh^d be quit. The penalty on a Steward for holding a Court contrary to this act 100$\frac{1}{2}$ fhillings. This act to be Proclaimed, & was to continue until the firft day of the next Parliament " Provided always, That this act nor anything com-prifed in the fame act be hurtful & prejudicial to William now Bifhop of Durham, nor to his fuccef-fors within the Liberty & Franchife of the Bifhoprick of Durham." This act was amended in flight details by 1 Rich. III. c. 6 (1483). See Chap. V.

Appeal.—1779. By the 19 George III. c. 70 right of appeal was given againſt the judgments of any of the inferior courts—and hence againſt thoſe of the Courts of Piepowder—by means of a writ of error to the ſuperior courts at Weſtminſter ; and ſuch courts were to have the right of iſſuing writs of execution in aid of their proceſſes after judgment not appealed againſt. This largely extended the efficacy of this particular court, as goods of the defendant—not in the fair, and therefore beyond the ancient juriſdiction of this court—could now be levied upon.

CHAPTER V.

LEGISLATION FOR FAIRS IN ENGLAND.

Duration of Fairs.

1328.

HERE was enacted 2 Edwd. III. c. 15. " No perfon fhall keep a Fair longer than he ought to do," which was as follows :

Item, it is eftablifhed That it fhall be commanded to all the Sheriffs of England & elfewhere, where need fhall require to cry and publifh within Liberties & without, that all the Lords [of the foil] w^h have Fairs, be it for yielding certain Ferm [Rent?] for the fame to the King or otherwife, fhall hold the fame for the time that they ought to hold it, & no longer; that is to fay, [1] fuch as have them by the King's Charter granted them, for the time limited by the f^d Charters (2) and alfo they that have them without Charter, for the time that they ought to hold them of Right. (3) And that every Lord at the beginning of his Fair fhall there do cry & publifh how long the fair fhall endure, to the intent that merchants fhall not be at the fame

Fairs over the time fo publifhed, upon pain to be grevioufly punifhed towards the King (4) Nor the f^d Lords fhall not hold them over the due Time upon pain to feize the Fairs into the King's hands, there to remain till they have made a fine to the King for the offence, after it be duly found, that the Lords held the fame Fairs longer than they ought, or that the merchants have fitten above the time fo cried & publifhed. See 1331.

1331. The 5 Edw. III. c. 5—"The Penalty if any do fell Ware at a Fair after it is ended" was as follows:

Item, Where it is contained in the Statute made at Northampton [1328] . . . that the Lords w^h have Fairs by Charters or otherwife, fhall hold them during the Time that they ought to do, & no longer upon Pain to feize fuch Fairs into the King's hands (2) & that every Lord at the Beginning of his Fair *fhall proclaim how long the fair fhall endure;* (3) and in the fame Statute is no certain punifhment ordained againft the merchants if they fell after the time, (4) it is accorded, That the f^d merchants after the f^d time fhall clofe their Booths & Stalls without putting any manner of Ware or Merchandife to fell there. (5) And if it be found, that any merchant from henceforth fell any Ware or merchandife at the f^d Fairs after the f^d Time, fuch Merchant fhall forfeit to me Lord the King the double value of that w^h is fold (6) and every Man that will fue for our Lord the King, fhall be received, & fhall have the fourth part of that w^h fhall be loft at his fuit.

Macpherfon ["Hift. of Commerce"] commenting upon this act fays *Fairs were "the feats of moft
of the inland trade of the kingdom."*

1448. The 27 Henry VI. c. 5 was directed againft
"the Scandal of holding Fairs & markets on Sundays & upon High Feaft Days." This practice
had in earlier times been very general.

Attempted Limitation of the Commerce of Fairs.—
1487. The Common Council of London, in order to
oblige the people to refort to the City for their purchafes, had made an ordinance that no citizen fhould
carry goods for fale to any fair or market out of
the city. The affortment of goods in London (fays
Macpherfon) appears to have been fo commanding
that thofe interefted in fairs of Salifbury, Briftol,
Oxford, Cambridge, Nottingham, Ely, Coventry,
and other places, and alfo the people of the country
in general, were alarmed, and reprefented to Parliament the deftruction of the fairs, and the great
hardfhip of being obliged to travel to London to
procure chalices, books, veftments, and other church
ornaments, and alfo victuals for the time of Lent,
linen cloth, woollen cloth, brafs, pewter, bedding,
ofmond, iron, flax, wax, and other neceffaries. The
London ordinance was thereupon annulled by Parliament; and the citizens were permitted to go
with their goods to the fairs and markets in every
part of England. ("Hift. of Com." i. p. 708.)

The act by which this was effected is 3 Hen.
VII. c. 9—*Freemen of London may carry their wares
to any Fairs or Markets*—which recites as follows :

"Humbly fhowen and prayen unto your High-

" neſs, your true & faithful Commons of this your
"your Realm of *England*, That where the Citizens
" & Freemen of the City of London have uſed out
" of time & mind to go, carry & lede their mer-
" chandiſe & ware unto all Fairs & markets at their
" Liberty of the ſᵈ City; now of late time the Mayor,
" Aldermen, & Citizens of the City of *London* have
" made & enacted an Ordinance within the ſame City,
" upon a great Pain, that no man that is a freeman or
" a Citizen of the ſᵈ City ſhall go or come to any Fair
" or Market out of the ſame City of London, with
" any manner of ware or merchandiſe to ſell or to
" barter, to this Intent, that all Buyers & merchants
" ſhould reſort to the ſᵈ City to buy their ware
" & merchandiſes of the ſᵈ Citizens & Freemen of
" London aforeſaid, becauſe of their ſingular Lucre
" & Avail; wʰ Ordinance, if it ſhould hold as is
" before expreſſed, *ſhall be to the utter deſtruction of*
" *all other Fairs & markets within this your Realm,*
" wʰGod defend: for there be many fairs for the com-
" mon weal of your ſaid liege People, as at *Saliſbury,*
" *Briſtol, Oxenforth, Cambrigge, Netyngham, Ely,*
" *Coventre,* & at many other places *where Lords*
" *Spiritual, & Temporal, Abbots, Priors, Knights,*
" *Eſquires, Gentlemen, & your ſaid Commons of Every*
" *Country hath their common reſort, to buy & purvey*
" *many things that be good & profitable,* as Ornaments
" of Holy Church, Chalice, Books, Veſtments, &
" other ornaments of Holy Church aforeſᵈ, & alſo
" for Houſehold, as victual for the time of Lent,
" & other ſtuff, as Linnen Cloth, Woollen Cloth,
" Braſs, Pewter, Bedding, Oſmonde, Iron, Flax, &

" Wax, & many other neceſſary Things, the wᴴ
" might not be forborn amongſt your ſaid liege
" People ; but, by the fᵈ Ordinance every man
" willing to buy any of the premiſſes, ſhall be courted
" to come to the fᵈ City of London, to their import-
" able Coſts & Charges, wᴴ if the fᵈ act ſhould en-
" dure, ſhall grow great hurt & prejudice to the
" common weal of this your Realm, & ſhall cauſe
" many pernicious ſtrifes & debates between your
" ſaid liege people, & the ſaid Mayor, Aldermen &
" Citizens in time to come, by the making the fᵈ
" Ordinance, the wᴴ is thought may not continue
" & ſtand with good charity, the premiſſes con-
" ſidered, wherefore it may pleaſe your ſaid High-
" neſs moſt noble & abundant Grace, in conſidera-
" tion of the Hurt likely to grow of & by the
" premiſes, that it may be enacted :

The King Lords and Commons therefore enacted
that every freeman and citizen of London then
or thereafter, might go with his victual ware or
merchandiſe, at his or their liberty to any fair or
market that ſhould pleaſe him within the realm of
England, any act, ſtatute or ordinance to the contrary notwithſtanding. Any diſregard of the ſtatute
to incur a penalty of £10 to the King.

1496. The Company of Merchant-Adventurers
of England which was ſaid to have been in exiſtence for nearly two centuries—although not actually chartered until 1505—took ſteps about this
period calculated to interfere with the freedom of
Britiſh merchants to attend fairs and marts in
foreign countries.

The merchants who traded on their own indivi-
dual account reſiding in various parts of England
and of the City of London, ſent up a petition to
the Houſe of Commons, (as againſt the claims of
the ſaid Company of Merchant-Adventurers) wherein
it was ſet forth that they traded beyond the ſea with
their goods and merchandiſe, as well into Spain,
Portugal, Bretagne, Ireland, Normandy, France,
Seville, Venice, Dantzic, Eaſtland, Friſeland and
many other parts—the geography is often a little
hazy in theſe early documents—there to buy and
ſell and make their exchanges, according to the laws
and cuſtoms of thoſe parts: every one trading as
ſeemed moſt to his advantage, without ſanction,
fine, impoſition or contribution, to be had or
taken of them, or any of them, to for, or by, any
Engliſh perſon or perſons. And in like ſort they,
before this time had uſed, and of right ought to
have and uſe the like commerce into the coaſts of
Flanders, Zealand, Holland, Brabant, and other adjacent parts, under the obedience of the Archduke
of Burgundy; in which places are uſually kept the
univerſal marts or fairs, four times in the year; to
which marts all Engliſhmen, and divers other nations
in times paſt, have uſed to reſort, there to ſell their
own commodities, and freely to buy ſuch merchandiſe as they had occaſion for: till now of late, the
Fellowſhip of Mercers, and other merchants and ad-
venturers, dwelling and being free within the City
of London by confederacy amongſt themſelves, for
their own ſingular profit, contrary to every Engliſhman's liberty, to the liberty of the ſaid mart there,

and contrary to all law, reaſon, charity, right and
conſcience have made an ordinance among themſelves to the prejudice of all other Engliſhmen, that
no Engliſhman reſorting to the ſaid mart, ſhall either
buy or ſell any merchandiſe there, unleſs he ſhall
firſt have compounded and made fine with the ſaid
Fellowſhip of Merchants of London, at their pleaſure; upon pain of forfeiture to the ſaid Fellowſhip
of ſuch their ſaid merchandiſe. Which fine, impoſition, and exaction, at the beginning, when firſt
taken, was demanded by colour of the *Fraternity
of St. Thomas Becket;* at which time it was only an
old noble ſterling. And ſo by colour of ſuch feigned
holineſs, it hath been ſuffered to be taken of a few
years paſt: it was afterwards increaſed to 100 ſhil-
lings, Flemiſh; but now the ſaid Fellowſhip of
London take of every Engliſhman or young merchant, being there, at his firſt coming £40 ſterling
for a fine, to ſuffer him to buy, and ſell his own
goods. By reaſon whereof, all merchants not of
the ſaid Fellowſhip, do withdraw themſelves from
the ſaid marts : whereby the woollen cloth of this
realm, which is one of the greateſt commodities of
the ſame, as well as ſundry other Engliſh commodities of the ſame, as well as ſundry other Engliſh
commodities, are not ſold and got off as in times
paſt, but are for want of ſale thereof, in divers parts,
where ſuch clothes are made, conveyed to London,
and there ſold at an undervalued price, even below
what they coſt the makers. Moreover the merchandiſe of thoſe foreign parts, imported by the
ſaid Fellowſhip, is ſold to your complainants and

other fubjeċts at fo high a price that the buyers cannot live thereupon ; by reafon whereof all the cities
and towns of the realm are falling into great
poverty, ruin and decay : and the King's cuſtoms
and fubſidies, and the navy of the land greatly
decreaſed.

It was therefore enaċted (12 Hen. VII. c. 6) that all
Englifhmen from henceforth fhould and might freely
refort to the Coaſts of *Flanders*, *Holland*, Zealand,
Brabant, and other parts adjoining, under the obedience of the Archduke ; and at their marts or fairs
there, fell their merchandife freely, without exaċtion,
fine, impofition, or contribution taken or received of
any of them by the faid Fraternity or Fellowfhip,
excepting only the fum of ten marks [£6 13s. 4d.]
fterling, on pain of forfeiting £20 for every time
they take more ; and fhall alfo forfeit to the perfon
fo impofed on ten times fo much as contrary to this
aċt was taken of him. See 1554.

Welſh Fairs.—1534. There was enaċted 26
Hen. VIII. c. 6—*The Bill concerning Councils in
Wales*—which recited : " Forafmuch as the people
" of *Wales*, & the marches of the fame, not dread-
" ing the good & wholefome Laws & Statutes
" of this Realm, have of long time continued &
" perfevered in Perpetration & Commiffion of divers
" & manifold Thefts, Murthers, Rebellions, wilful
" Burning of Houfes & other fcelerous Deeds &
" abominable malefaċts, to the high difpleafure of
" God, Inquietation of the Kings well-difpofed fub-
" jeċts, & Diſturbance of the Public Weal, wʰ
" malefaċts & fcelerous Deeds be fo rooted &

" fixed in the ſame People, that they be not like to
" ceaſe unleſs ſome ſharp correction & Puniſhment
" for Redreſs & Amputation of the Premiſes be
" provided, according to the Demerits of the
" offenders." Whereupon it was enacted (*inter
alia*) :

That no perſon or perſons dwelling or reſident
within *Wales* or the Lordſhips marches of the ſame,
of what Eſtate, Degree, or Condition ſoever he or they
be of, coming, reſorting, or repairing unto any
Seſſions or Court to be holden within *Wales* or any
Lordſhips, marches, of the ſame ſhall bring or bear,
or cauſe to be brought or born to the ſame Seſſions
or Court or to any place within the diſtance of two
miles from the ſame Seſſions or Court, nor to any
Town, Church, *Fair*, Market or other congregation,
except it be upon a Hute or Outcry made of any
Felony or Robbery done or perpetrated, nor in the
Highways in affray of the King's Peace, or the
Kings liege People, any Bill, Long-bow, Croſs-bow,
Hand-gun, Sword, Staff, Dagger, Halbert, More-
ſpike, Spear, or any other manner of weapon,
Proof-coat or Armour defenſive, upon pain of forfeiture of the ſame and of impriſonment and fine,
except permiſſion by given by the proper authori-
ties authoriſed thereto.

Robberies in Fairs.—1552.   The 5 and 6 Edw.
VI. c. 9—*An Act for the taking away of the Benefit of Clergy* for certain offenders recites : (3) " And
" where alſo it hath been in queſtion & doubted,
" that if ſuch Robberies & Felonies happen to be
" committed & done in any Booth or Booths, Tent

" or Tents in any Fair or market, the Owner of the
" ſame, his wife, Children or Servants happening
" to be within the ſame at the time of the com-
" mitting of ſuch Felonies, & put in fear & dread,
" the offenders therein being found guilty after the
" Laws of this Realm, ſhould not loſe the Benefit
" of Clergy."

Whereupon it was enaċted that perſons ſo offending ſhould not be entitled to benefit of Clergy, but
ſhould ſuffer death in ſuch manner and form as was
mentioned in the aċt 23 Hen. VIII. c. 1, for Robberies and Felonies committed and done in Dwelling
houſes and Dwelling places, the Owner and Dweller
in the ſame, his wife children or ſervants being
within the ſame, and put in fear and dread, without
having any reſpeċt or conſideration whether the
owner or dweller in ſuch booths and tents his wife,
children or servants being in the ſame Booths or
Tents at the time of ſuch Robberies and Felonies
committed, ſhall be ſleeping or waking.

Reſtriċting the dealing in Fairs. —1554. By the
1ſt and 2nd Philip and Mary, c. 7 —*An Aċt for that
Perſons dwelling in the Country ſhall not ſell divers
Wares in Cities or Towns Corporate by retail*—it is
recited : Where before this time the ancient Cities,
Boroughs, Towns Corporate and market Towns
(within this Realm of *England*) have been very
populous, and chiefly inhabited with merchants,
Artificers, and Handicraftſmen, during which time
the Children in thoſe Cities were civilly brought up
and inſtruċted, and alſo the ſaid cities &c. kept in
good order and obeſience, and the inhabiters of the

fame well ſet on work and kept from idlenefs. (2)
By reafon whereof, the faid Cities &c. did then
profper in riches and great wealth, and were as then
not only able to ferve and furniſh the King and
Queens majeſties, and their noble progenitors, Kings
of this Realm, as well with great numbers of good
able perſons and well furniſhed, meet for the wars,
as alfo then charged, and yet chargeable with great
fee-farms, *Quindifmes*, Taxes, and divers other
payments to the King and Queen's Majeſties, which
at this prefent they be not able to pay and bear, but
to their utter Undoing, being few in number to pay
and bear the fame; but alfo the fame Cities &c.
are likely to come very ſhortly to utter deſtruction,
ruin and decay; (3) by reafon whereof the occupiers, Linendrapers, woollen-drapers, Haberdaſhers
and Grocers dwelling in the Counties out of the
faid Cities &c. do not only occupy the art and
myſtery of the faid Sciences in the places where
they dwell and inhabit, but alfo come into the faid
Cities &c. and there fell their wares, and take away
the Relief of the inhabitants of the faid Cities &c.
to the great decay and utter undoing of the inhabitants of the fame, if fpeedy reformation therein be
not had in time convenient. (4) For remedy
whereof and for the better amendment of the faid
Cities &c. to the end that the fame Cities &c. may
be better able to pay the faid Fee-farms, and alfo
to bear the other ordinary charges within the fame
Cities &c. and to furniſh the King and Queen's
majeſties with numbers of able perfons, like as they
have heretofore done in times paſt, in times of War.

It was enacted, That any perſon or perſons which do now inhabit and dwell, or hereafter ſhall inhabit and dwell in the Country anywhere, or County within this Realm of *England,* out of any of the ſaid Cities, Boroughs, Towns Corporate or Market Towns, from and after the Feaſt of St. *Michael* the archangel next coming, *ſhall not ſell or cauſe to be ſold by retail,* any woollen cloth, Linen Cloth, Haberdaſhery wares, Grocery wares, Mercery wares, at or within any of the ſaid Cities &c., or within the Suburbs or Liberties of the ſaid Cities, &c., within the ſaid Realm of England (*except it be in open Fairs*) upon pain of forfeiting 6s. 8d. and the whole Wares ſo ſold, proffered and offered to be ſold contrary to the form and intent of this act as above is ſaid. But all ſuch perſons might ſell their products wholeſale; and perſons dwelling in the Country, but afterwards becoming free of any City &c. would be thus placed outſide the operation of this act. And perſons might ſell by retail all manner of Cloth, Linen or Woollen of our making anywhere notwithſtanding this act. " Provided alway that this act or anything therein contained ſhall not be prejudicial or hurtful to the Liberties and Privileges of the Univerſities of *Cambridge* and *Oxford,* or either of them."

Horſe Fairs.—1555. The 2 and 3 Philip and Mary, c. 7 related to the facilities for dealing in ſtolen horſes, which it was attempted to check by having duly appointed fairs for ſuch dealings. This Act gave riſe to the holding of "Horſe Fairs" ſeparately from other fairs. The Act 31 of Elizabeth c. 12 (1589) required a record to be kept of all horſes ſold at fairs.

Plague.—1625. The importance rightly attached from a ſanitary point of view to the gathering of large multitudes together at fairs is manifeſted in a very ample degree in a Royal Proclamation iſſued by Charles I. from his Palace at Woodſtock on the 4th Auguſt:

The Kings moſt excellent majeſty, out of his Princely and Chriſtian care of his loving ſubjects, that no good means of Providence may be neglected to ſtay the further ſpreading of the great infection of the Plague, doth find it neceſſary to prevent all occaſions of public concourſe of his people for the preſent, till it ſhall pleaſe Almighty God of His goodnèſs, to ceaſe the violence of the Contagion which is very diſperſed into many parts of the Kingdom already ; *And therefore remembering that there are at hand two Fairs of ſpecial note and unto which there is uſually extraordinary reſort out of all parts of the Kingdom,* the one kept in Smithfield, near the City of London, called Bartholomew Fair, and the other near Cambridge called Stourbridge Fair, *the holding whereof at the uſual times would in all likelihood be the occaſion of further danger and infection in other parts of the land,* which yet in Gods mercy ſtand clear and free, hath, with the advice of his Majeſty's Privy Council, thought good, by this open declaration of his pleaſure and neceſſary commandment, not only to admoniſh and require all his loving ſubjects to forbear to reſort for this time to either of the ſaid two fairs, or *to any other fairs within* 50 *miles of the ſaid City of London,* but alſo to enjoin the Lords of the ſaid Fairs, and others intereſted in them, or any of them, that they all forbear to hold the ſaid Fairs, or any-thing appertaining ſo them, at all times accuſtomed or at any time, till by God's goodneſs and mercy the infection of the Plague ſhall ceaſe, or be ſo much diminiſhed, that his majeſty ſhall give order for holding them ; upon pain of ſuch puniſhment as, for a contempt ſo much concerning the univerſal ſafety of his people, they ſhall be adjudged to de-ſerve, which they muſt expect to be inflicted with all ſeverity : His Majeſty deſire being ſo intentive for preventing the general Infection threatened, as he is reſolved to ſpare no man that ſhall be the cauſe of diſperſing the ſame. And to that purpoſe doth hereby further charge and enjoin, under like penalty, all citizens and inhabitants of the ſaid City of London, *that none of them ſhall repair to any fair held within any part of his kingdom,* until it ſhall pleaſe God to ceaſe the infection now reigning amongſt them : His Majeſty's intention being, and ſo hereby declaring himſelf, that no Lord of any Fairs, or others intereſted in the profits thereof, ſhall by this neceſſary and temporary reſtraint, re-ceive any prejudice in the right of his or their Fairs, or liberties thereunto belonging, anything before mentioned notwithſtanding.

Earlier proclamations and orders had prevented the holding or had curtailed the period of St. Bar-tholomew fairs on ſeveral occaſions viz. 1348, 1593, and 1603 ; and other fairs had likewiſe been ſtayed or poſtponed.   Theſe will be noticed in dealing with ſuch fairs ſpecifically.

1630. The Plague was prevailing in Cambridge, and a Royal Proclamation was iſſued, dated Aug. 1, prohibiting the holding of the " three great Fairs of ſpecial note, unto which there is an extraordinary reſort from all parts of the Kingdom " viz. thoſe of Bartholomew, Sturbridge, and Southwark.

Coinage.—1662. The preceding year was that of the Reſtoration, and it was by Proclamation ordered that the coinage of the Commonwealth ſhould be no longer current than the laſt day of November. The " Kingdom's Intelligencer " for Aug. 22-25 this year contained the following : " Whitehall Aug. 23.   There hath been a diſcovery of divers perſons who have coined both gold and ſilver, and of other perſons who have vended the ſame in great quantities &c. intending to utter the ſame to Clothiers and at Fairs ; which is publiſhed to an end that honeſt perſons may not be deceived by receiving ſuch monies."

Sale of Printed Matter, &c.—1698. In the 9 and 10 William III. c. 27—*An Act for Licenſing Hawkers and Pedlars* &c. ſection 9 is as follows: Provided always . . . That this Act or anything contained ſhall not Extend to Prohibit any perſons from ſelling of any Acts of Parliament, Forms of Prayer, Proclamations, Gazettes, licenſed Almanacks or other Printed Papers, licenſed by authority, or any Fiſh, Fruits or Victuals; nor to hinder any perſon or perſons, who are the real workers or makers of any Goods or Wares within the Kingdom of *England*, Dominion of *Wales*, and Town of *Berwick* upon *Tweed*, or his her or their Children, Apprentices, Agents or Servants, to ſuch real Workers and makers of ſuch Goods or Wares only, from carrying abroad, expoſing to Sale, or ſelling any of the ſaid Goods and Wares of his, her, or their, own making in any Public Mart, Fairs, Markets, or Elſewhere ; nor any Tinkers, Coopers, Glaziers, Plummers, Harneſs-menders, or other perſons actually trading in mending kettles, Tubs, Houſehold Goods or Harneſs whatſoever, from going about and carrying with them proper materials for mending the ſame.

And by Section 12 it is further enacted : That nothing herein contained ſhall extend or be conſtrued to extend to hinder any perſon or perſons from Selling or expoſing to ſale any ſorts of Goods or Merchandiſes, in any public mart, Market, or Fair within the Kingdom of *England*, Dominion of *Wales* and Town of *Berwick* upon *Tweed*, but that ſuch perſon or perſons may do therein as they lawfully might have done before the making of this act ; anything herein contained to the contrary notwithſtanding.

Altering the Calendar.—1751. Under 24 Geo. II. c. 23—*An Act for Regulating the Commencement of the Year ; and for correcting the Calendar now in uſe*, it was provided Section 4 (*inter alia*) that the terms for holding and keeping of all markets, fairs and marts, " whether for the ſale of Goods or Cattle, or for the hiring of Servants, or for any other purpoſe, w^h are either fixed to certain nominal

days of the month, or depending upon the beginning, or any certain day of any month, & all
Courts incident & belonging to, or uſually holden
or kept with any ſuch Fairs or Marts, ſhould be
holden & kept upon or according to the ſame
natural days upon or according to w^h the ſame ſh^d
have been ſo kept or holden in caſe this act had not
been made."

This act was amended by 25 Geo. II. c. 30,
which enacted that all ſuch events as before enume-
rated were to take place " according to the new
Calendar."

CHAPTER VI.

MODERN LEGISLATION.

1839—1874.

N the 2nd and 3rd Vict. c. 47—*An Act for the Further Improving the Police in and near the Metropolis*—it is provided that Inquiries may be made regarding Fairs within the Metropolitan Police Diſtrict, alike as to the authority to hold ſuch Fair, and alſo as to the time during which it may be holden. If the authority for holding the Fair be doubtful the owner or occupier of the ground may be ſummoned to ſhow his right and title to hold ſuch Fair: and if the Fair be declared unlawful, then Booths &c. may be removed. But the owner or occnpier by entering into recognizances, may reſerve the queſtion of the right or title to hold ſuch Fair, to be tried in the Court of Queen's Bench—ſee 1868.

1843. The 6 and 7 Vict. c. 68—*An Act for Regulating Theatres*—recites "Whereas it is expedient "that the Laws now in force for regulating "Theatres and Theatrical Performances be repealed,

" and other Proviſions be enacted in their ſtead."
And ſection 23 is as follows : And be it enacted
that in this act the word "Stage-play" ſhall be
taken to include every Tragedy, Comedy, Farce,
Opera, Burletta, Interlude, Melodrama, Pantomime,
or other entertainment of the Stage, or any part
thereof : Provided always, that nothing herein contained ſhall be conſtrued to apply to any Theatrical
Repreſentation in any Booth or Show which by the
Juſtices of the Peace, or other Perſons having
authority in that behalf, ſhall be allowed in any
lawful Fair, Feaſt, or cuſtomary meeting of the like
kind. This act was only to extend to Great
Britain.

1844. The 7 and 8 Vict. c. 24—*An Act for
Aboliſhing the Offences of Foreſtalling, Regrating,
and Engroſſing, and for repealing certain Statutes
paſſed in Reſtraint of Trade*—enacts (ſection 4)
" That nothing in this act ſhall be conſtrued to
" apply to the offence of knowingly and fraudulently
" ſpreading or conſpiring to ſpread any falſe rumour,
" with intent to enhance or decry the Price of any
" goods or merchandiſe, or to the offence of pre-
" venting or endeavouring to prevent by Force or
" threats any goods, wares, or merchandiſe being
" brought to any Fair or Market, but that every
" ſuch offence ſhall be inquired of, tried, and
" puniſhed as if this act had not been made."

1847. There was enacted 10 and 11 Vict. c. 14—
*An Act for conſolidating in One Act certain Proviſions
uſually contained in Acts for Conſtructing or Regulating Markets and Fairs*—which however was only

to extend to ſuch markets or fairs as ſhould be authoriſed by any Act of Parliament hereafter to be paſſed, which ſhould declare this Act to be incorporated therewith; and then all clauſes of this Act, except ſo far as they might be varied or excepted from ſuch Act were to apply. The details of this meaſure will fall to be reviewed more in detail under MARKETS.

1868. There was enacted 31 and 32 Vict. c. 51— *An Act to amend the Laws relating to Fairs in England and Wales*—under which "in caſe it ſhould appear to the Secretary of State for the Home Department, upon repreſentation duly made to him by the magiſtrates of any Petty Seſſional Diſtrict, within which any Fair is held, or by the owner of any Fair in England and Wales, that it would be for the convenience and advantage of the Public that any ſuch Fair ſhall be held in each year on ſome day or days other than thoſe on which ſuch Fair is uſed to be held, it ſhall be lawful for the Secretary of State for the Home Department to order that ſuch Fair ſhall be held on ſuch other day or days as he ſhall think fit." Provided notice of ſuch repreſentation be duly advertiſed, and alſo notice of order as therein provided. (See 1873.)

A act of the ſame ſeſſion (c. 12) gave powers to facilitate the alteration of days upon which and of places at which fairs might be held in *Ireland.* It was upon the ſame lines as the preceding.

Another meaſure of the ſame ſeſſion (c. 106)— *An Act for the Prevention of the holding of unlawful Fairs within the Limits of the Metropolitan Police*

Diſtrict—provides that where any Fair is holden or notice given of any Fair propoſed to be holden on any ground within the Metropolitan Police Diſtrict, other than that on which a Fair has been holden during each of the ſeven years immediately preceding, it ſhould be competent for the Commiſſioner of Police to cauſe inquiry to be made as to right and title to hold ſuch Fair, after the manner provided by the act of 1839. This is deſignated " The Metropolitan Fairs Act 1868."

1871. There was enacted 34 Vict. c. 12—*An Act to further Amend the Law relating to Fairs in England and Wales*—which recites: " Whereas cer- " tain of the Fairs held in England & Wales are " unneceſſary, are the cauſe of grievous immorality, " and are very injurious to the inhabitants of the " Towns in which ſuch Fairs are held, and it is there- " fore expedient to make proviſion to facilitate the " abolition of ſuch Fairs." It is then provided that the Secretary of State may on repreſentation of magiſ- trates with conſent of owner, order fairs to be aboliſhed. The machinery being the ſame as under the Act of 1839 applying to the Metropolitan Police Diſtrict. This Act is known as " The Fairs Act, 1871."

1872. The Local Government Board (Ireland) Act 1872 gave (35 and 36 Vict. c. 69, ſection 10) powers to the governing body of any town, being the owners of any fair held therein (under the Local Government (Ireland) Act 1871) with the conſent of two thirds of the members of ſuch governing body, and with the conſent of the Local Government Board—and of any perſon being the owner of any fair, with the conſent of the laſt named body—to alter and fix the days for holding fairs.   Notices being given as therein preſcribed.

1873. The Act of 1868 was repealed, but almoſt preciſely ſimilar proviſions were re-enacted by 36 and 37 Vict. c. 37. The term " owner " (uſed as in the previous act and in this) was defined to mean any perſon or perſons, or body of companies, or body corporate, entitled to hold any fair, whether in reſpect of the ownerſhip of any lands or tenements, or under any charter, letters patent, or otherwiſe howſoever.

This meaſure was not to apply to *Scotland* or *Ireland*.

1874. There are a great number of acts relating to the ſale of Intoxicating Liquors at Fairs and Races. The lateſt 37 and 38 Vict. c. 49 (1874) by ſection 18, enacts that " occaſional Licences " are required in all ſuch caſes, except where the ordinary licenſed premiſes fall within the boundaries of ſuch fair or race ground.

STURBRIDGE FAIR.

CHAPTER VII.

HE origin of this Fair—like that of moſt of the great fairs of the world— is involved in obſcurity. The firſt trace of it is found in a charter granted about 1211 by King John to the Lepers of the Hoſpital of St. Mary Magdalen at Sturbridge, by Cambridge—a fair to be held in the Cloſe of the Hoſpital on the Vigil and Feaſt of the Holy Crofs.

The Commiſſioners appointed by Edward I. to make inquiry into the rights and revenue of the Crown, viſited Cambridge; and concerning its ſeveral markets and fairs reported (*inter alia*) the exiſtence of this fair to which faƈt I ſhall make further reference, under date 1278.

Whatever its origin, it became in a comparatively ſhort time after the period of which I am now ſpeaking the moſt important fair held in Great

Britain, and fome writers have declared—without much apparent information to guide them—in the world. The incidents in its hiftory are fo remarkable, and throw fo much light upon the cuftoms of our forefathers, that I propofe to give them in confiderable detail. They have been brought together from various fources—the chief being Cooper's "Annals of Cambridge," compiled by Charles Henry Cooper, F.S.A., who held the office of Town Clerk, and who confequently had unreftricted accefs to the records. The "Hiftory and Antiquities of Barnwell Abbey," 1786, has been largely confulted. While the ample notes appended to the "Life of Ambrofe Bonwicke," as edited by Prof. John E. B. Mayor, M.A., 1870, have been made available. I have followed as beft fuited to the circumftances, a ftrictly chronological arrangement.

As queftions continually arife in the progrefs of our record regarding the rights of the town of Cambridge over the fair, it will be well here briefly to indicate how thefe may have arifen. In the inquifition of the Commiffioners already referred to, it is recorded that " the keepers of this Hofpital hold twenty four acres and a half of land in Cambridge field, for the fupport of the Lepers therein dwelling according to ancient right and cuftom." From other fources it appears that the Hofpital was at the difpofal of the burgeffes of Cambridge previous to 1245 ; but that about this time Hugh de Northwold, the then Bifhop of Ely "unjuftly got the patronage of it." The burgeffes ftill claimed that the advowfon of the Hofpital " be-

longed by right to them." The fact probably
being that the hospital was established by the town,
before it was converted into a religious foundation;
that upon such conversion the Church claimed sole
jurisdiction; but as the original grant of land was
not relinquished the townsmen still asserted their interest; and it will be seen, in the end—and after
centuries of conflict—obtained it. See 1544.

There is a further element of conflict, of a far
more pertinacious character than the preceding,
running almost entirely through our six centuries of
record—and this is with the University, as distin-
guished from the Town, of Cambridge. It was the
custom to grant to University towns very large
powers regarding the food supplies, *i.e.* the control
of the markets; as also, and necessarily, the control
of the morals, and therefore the amusements, of the
scholars. Such a fair as that of Sturbridge affected
alike the food supplies, and the moral discipline of
the students; and hence the whole machinery of
the University was put in force to secure and maintain control. It is in this view that many of the
details of the University Proclamation of the Fair
(see 1548) can alone be explained. On the other
hand the Town authorities always had in view their
rights over the Lepers Hospital; and hence their
reversion in the tolls of the fair. Other points
will make themselves apparent; but these are the
broad views from which many of the following
incidents have to be regarded.

Name of the Fair.—The first point of interest is
the name of the Fair. It is occasionally spelled in

fuch a manner as to be entirely mifleading as to its locality; and hence many have come to regard it as being in the weftern, inftead of the eaftern part of the kingdom. The fpelling indeed has varied much at different periods. The original defignation was Sterefbrigg, fo called from the little river of *Stere*, or *Sture* flowing into the *Cam*, near Cambridge. There have been feveral fanciful origins affigned by thofe who were too indolent to inveftigate proper fources: fuch as (by Bloomfield) that it was derived from the toll paid for all young cattle, or *fteers* paffing over the bridge! I have throughout this record followed the fpelling of the authorities under quotation.

CHAPTER VIII.

CHRONOLOGY, THIRTEENTH TO FIFTEENTH CENTURIES—STURBRIDGE.

1278.

THE Commiffioners of Edward I. (already referred to) returned upon inqueft that King John had granted this Fair for the benefit of the Hofpital for Lepers which ftood there. " To the faid Hofpital belongs a certain Fair, held at the Feaft of the raifing and exaltation of the Crofs, which continues to this eve of Holy Crofs, within the meadow belonging to the faid Hofpital, which Fair our fovereign Lord King John, the predeceffor of our prefent Lord the King, granted to the faid Hofpital, for the ufe and fubfiftence of the Lepers dwelling therein."

1351. A writ was on 3rd Oct. directed to the Sheriff of Cambridgefhire requiring him to convey to the Keeper of the King's Wardrobe in the Tower of London, thirty-feven ftrait cloths, and one cloth of colour, lately feized in the Fair of Sterefbrigge to the King's ufe, by his deputy

Alnager, as not being of the affize and which were then in the cuftody of the Mayor of Cambridge.

1376. This year the Corporation of Cambridge made an Ordinance, prohibiting any burgefs to take Sturbridge Chapel to farm, except to the ufe of the mayor and bailiffs, or to keep market there, under the penalty of 10 marks, or to make any booth there, or let any place for the building of a booth, under the penalty of 10*s.* ; and any burgeffes con-victed of a breach of this Ordinance before the twenty-four [members of the Common Council] was to be deprived of his freedom at their difcretion.

1382. The King being informed that many falfe weights and meafures had been theretofore ufed in Sterefbrigge Fair, to the deception of his fubjects reforting thereto, iffued a Writ on 3rd Sept. re-quiring the Chancellor of the Univerfity to be vigilant in exercifing in that fair the powers con-ferred on him by the late Charter [1381] refpecting weights and meafures.

Two years later a difpute arofe between the Cor-poration and the Univerfity regarding the exercife of this right. The King confirmed the privilege of the Univerfity.

1395. Richard II. made order that the Sheriff was to apprehend all perfons who broke the peace in Bernwell Fair, whether fcholars or townfmen.

1397. On Hoch Tuefday the commonalty of Cambridge made Ordinances to the following effect: . . .

ii. That all burgeffes having any booths at the Fair of Sterebrigge, and who fhould let them to farm to any outcomers or foreigners for certain fum agreed upon between them, fhould pay to the mayor and bailiffs the third part of the fum for which the fame fhould be fo let.

iii. That no freeman fhould occupy two booths of one art.

1403. The Corporate Ordinances made by Cambridge this year contain (*inter alia*) the following :

Item . . . Every man burgefs of the town of Cambridge, may freely have one booth in the fair of Stirbridge, without rendering any thing therefore to the mayor and bailiffs for the time being, whether he occupy it or let it to farm. And that no burgefs have in the fair aforefaid more than one booth, unlefs he render therefore to the mayor and bailiffs for the time being, toll and cuftom as others do who are not burgeffes.

Item. It is ordained on the fame day, that if any bailiff or other burgefs of the town aforefaid, in future, leafe or lend to any Citizens of London, the place for the booth called the Tolbooth, in the fair aforefaid, that the bailiffs pay to the commonalty of the Town of Cambridge £10, and the burgeffes 100s. for every default, namely *tociens quociens*, to lofe their freedom.

Item. The fame day it is ordained that no burgefs of the town aforefaid profecute againft any one by writ or plaint, before the Chancellor nor elfewhere, for any contract which can be determined before the mayor and bailiffs [in the Piepowder Court?] nor fummon a defendant to the Chancellor, &c., under the pain of every one &c. 40s. to be paid to the commonalty of the town aforefaid, and the lofs of his freedom (fee 1427-8).

Item. The fame day it is ordained, that no ferjeant of the town aforefaid for the future fhall be attorney or of counfel, *with any foreigner, againft any burgefs of the fame town,* in the Court of the Town aforefaid, under the pain of 40*d.*, to be paid to the commonalty of the town aforefaid, *tociens quociens.* See 1575.

1405. The Corporation of Cambridge enacted the following Ordinances :

Be it remembered, that on the day of election of mayor and bailiffs for the town of Cambridge in the 6th year of the reign of Henry IV., it is ordained that every burgefs within the town aforefaid having a booth or booths in the fair of Sterbrige, may well and lawfully give, fell and furrender the faid booth to the ufe of any other burgefs of the fame town, before the Mayor and one of the Aldermen of the fame town, in the Court there holden on every Tuefday in the year, and on every Monday in the Court of the Liberty : Provided always that the faid booth or booths be furrendered freely, quietly and wholly, without condition, annexed or exprefled, for him and his, according to the cuftom of the borough. And this under the pain or forfeiture of the fame booths to the burgeffes of the town aforefaid.

1411. On 15 Nov. John Arondell, cuftos of the free chapel of St. Mary Magdalene, otherwife called Sturbridge chapel near Barnwell, exhibited his bill in the Exchequer againft John Effex,

fadler, John Warwyk, fkinner, John Chaucer and
William Bufh, late bailiffs, then prefent in Court on
their account.   In this bill plaintiff averred that he
and his predeceffors, had immemorially had ftallage
of all perfons merchandifing upon the Chapel-
yard, parcel of his chapel, where part of the fair of
Sturbridge was accuftomed to be held, and where
merchants were accuftomed to erect their fhops
during the fair-time.   That one Thomas Spryggy
merchant and Clothier, and other merchants to the
number of 20, would have made their fhops there
at the fair holden at Sturbridge on Monday the
feaft of the Exaltation of the Holy Crofs then preceding, and would have paid the ftallage 6s. 8d. each
but that the late bailiffs unjuftly and by colour of
their office would not permit the merchants to build
their fhops in the Chapel-yard by which he loft his
ftallage amounting to 10 marks, to the difherfion of
the chapel, and to his damage of £10.   The defendants by their plea, after protefting that the chapel
was founded within the time of memory and that
the bailiffs of Cambridge were feized of ftallage of
merchandize brought to the fair, denied that the
cuftos or his predeceffors were feized of fuch ftallage.   On this plea iffue was joined, and a verdict
returned in favor of the cuftos whofe damages were
affeffed at 5 marks with £10 cofts.   The proceedings in this caufe were exemplified by letters under
the Exchequer feal, tefted by John Cokayn Chief
Baron, on the 4th March 1412-13.

1419. At this time there was a fuit pending before the King's Council between the Chancellor and

Scholars of the Univerſity, and the mayor, aldermen and citizens of London, each of whom claimed
the Cuſtody of Aſſize and aſſay of Bread, wine and
beer, and the ſupervifion of the meaſures and
weights of the citizens of London coming to Sturbridge fair. On the 14th July the King (Henry V.)
directed letters patent to Sir Wm. Aſenhull, knt.
ſheriff of the County, commanding him to exerciſe
the before-mentioned cuſtody and ſupervifion over
the citizens of London in the fair of Sturbridge,
till the matter was decided, and requiring the liti-
gating parties to aſſiſt the Sheriff.

From the accounts of the Priories of Maxtoke
(Warwickſhire) and of Biceſter (Oxon) during the
reign of Henry VI. it is ſeen that the monks laid in
yearly ſtores of various common neceſſaries, at this
fair—diſtant at leaſt one hundred miles from either
monaſtery. Wharton (" Hiſt. of Engliſh Poetry ")
commenting on this fact ſays: " It may ſeem ſurpriſing
that their own neighbourhood, including the Cities
of Oxford and Coventry could not ſupply them
with commodities neither rare nor coſtly, which
they thus fetched at a confiderable expenſe of carriage." But he remembers that it was a rubric in
ſome of the monaſtic rules *De Euntibus ad Nundinas.*

1423. In the parliament of Henry VI., this year,
the following petition was preſented:

Prien the wife and worthi Communes, that for
as muchell as in the Citee of London, and in the
Suburbes ther of, diverſes perſones occupying the
craft of Brauderie, maken divers werkes of Brauderie
of unſuffiſaunt ſtuff, and unduely wrought, as well

upon Velowet, and Cloth of Gold, as upon all other Clothes of Silk wrought with Gold or Silver of Cipre, and Gold of Luk, or Spaynyfsh laton togedre, and fwich warkes, fo untrewely made by fwiche perfones aforefaid, dredyng the ferche of the wardens of Brauderie in the faid Citee of London, kepen and fenden unto the fayres of Sterefbrugg, Ely, Oxenford and Salefbury, and ther thei outre hem, to greet defeit of our foverain Lord the Kyng, and al his peple. That it like oure foverain Lord the Kyng, wyth his Lordes Spirituell and Temporell, in this prefent Parlement, to ordeyne by ftatute, that all the werk of Brauderie fo undwely made as above is declared, be forfait to oure foverain Lord the Kyng. And that the Wardeins of Brauderes of the faid Citee of London, for that tyme beyng may, by auctorite of this prefent parlement, have warant by patent to make ferche of all werk of Braderie put to felle at the faid faires of Sterefbrugg, Ely, Oxenford and Salefbury, and thoo werkes of Brouderie there founden unfuffifant, to forfaite and arrefte to the ufe of our Soverain Lord the Kyng, as ofte tymes as fuch werk be founde.

To which anfwer was made :

Be it enacted that all works and ftuff with gold and filver broidery of Cyprus or Gold of Luke, or with laton of Spain, and fold to the deceit of the fubjects of the King, be forfeited to the King, or to the Lords and to others having franchifes of fuch forfeitures, in which franchife fuch works be found. And that this enactment endure only until the next parliament.

The valuable commodities fold at this fair are here in part indicated.

Same year the commonalty of Cambridge, on the Thurfday after the Nativity of the Virgin made an Ordinance to this effect :

That the bailiff of the Bridge fhould not take toll for carriage, nor ftall-pence nor cuftom, from the bridge, nor elfewhere (except in the fair) for merchandife coming to the fair of Sterbrigg, from the vigil of the nativity of the bleffed Mary until the fair was ended.

1425. The accounts of Richard Parentyn prior of Burchefter, in Oxfordfhire, and Richard Albon canon and burfar of that houfe, for the year ending Michaelmas, contain feveral items which fhew the varied and extenfive trade of Sturbridge fair about this time: For the expenfe of Albon in going to and from Sterifbrugge fair for five days with three horfes to buy victuals &c. 12s. 6d. is charged. The following articles are alfo ftated to have been purchafed here : " Three collars, one baffe [a rufh collar for cart-horfes] and three headftalls 5s 10½d;" " a bolt [long narrow piece] of red fay [filk] for making a cope 4s 8d " " Six eftregbords [Eaftern boards] viz Waynfcots 2s 3d "; " 100 halfwax-fyche [dried fifh?] 21s.; " "324 lbs of Spanifh iron, with the portage of the fame 18s 5d "

1459. Richard Andrewe, *alias* Spycer, burgefs of Cambridge by his will dated 30 Aug. bequeathed to the mayor and bailiffs of that town 80 marks to be kept in a cheft there provided, and portions thereof lent on loans from time to time in

fums not exceeding 26*s*. 8*d*. To the keepers of this
Cheft he gave, three booths and certain booth-
ground in Sturbridge Fair, and a houfe in St. Andrew's parifh abutting on Preachers' lane, the profits
to be applied to the celebration of his anniverfary
in Great St. Mary's Church, to be diftributed in
various fmall charities there fpecified. See Cooper's
" Annals," i., p. 210.

1464. By 4th Edward IV. c. 8 power is given
to the Wardens of the Company of Horners to
fearch for defective wares in London and twenty-four
miles round, alfo in the fairs of Sturbridge and Ely,
and to feize defective manufactures and bring the
fame before the Mayor of London or the Mayors
or Bailiffs of the aforefaid fairs, for the time being.
In 1609 this act was revived by 7 James I. c. 14,
fec. 2.   The act was repealed in 1856.

1487. The Corporation of London made an Ordinance prohibiting the freemen of that City to go
to any fair out of the City with any manner of
merchandife to fell or barter.   This Ordinance was
repealed by act of parliament in the preamble of
which it is recited that there " be many fairs for the
common Weal of your faid liege people, as at Salifbury, Briftol, Oxenford, Cambridge &c."   If this
order of enumeration had any reference to the relative importance of the fairs (which I fufpect it had
not) it puts this fair only fourth.   This act has
already been fet out in detail in Chapter V.

This year Sir Wm. Littlebury alias Horn,
citizen and falter, and alfo Lord Mayor of London,
gave 500 marks towards repairing the highways be-

tween London and Cambridge. This was probably in view of benefiting thofe attending the fairs.

1496. On 20th July Katherine Cooke widow of John Cooke fome time mayor, granted to the mayor, bailiffs, treafurers, and burgeffes and their fucceffors, to the ufe of the Treafury of the Town of Cambridge, three booths fituate in the Soper's lane, the Chepe, and the Petimercerye, in Ster-brigge fair. To the intent that the Treafurers fhould perpetually uphold yearly on the 25 Feby., a fpecial dirge and mafs in the parifh Church of St. Mary the Virgin next the market for the fouls of John Cooke and William Colles, and Katherine, Joan, and Lucy their wives, and pay to the bell-man for going about the town for the faid fouls 3*d*; with other fmall bequefts to the poor &c. Cooper's "Annals," i., p. 246.

CHAPTER IX.

1501.

THE accounts of the Treafurers of Cambridge for this year contained the following item :

Paid John Fynne, Clerk to make up the farm of the land called the Chapel ground lying in Sturbridge Fair leafted to the Mayor, bailiffs and burgeffes, beyond the money received for the farm of the fame this year, *becaufe a great part of the fame was not levied this year, by reafon that the merchants of London withdrew themfelves from the Fair*, 100s.

This leafe had been taken on 7th Aug. 1497 for a term of 99 years at a rent of £12, and five tapers of wax for the chapel of equal weight, and weighing in the whole 3 lbs.

1503. William Kentte the younger, Clerk, by his will devifed two booths in Sturbridge fair, and the reverfion of a tenement called the Crown in the parifh of St. Andrew in Cambridge, the mayor and burgeffes entered into covenants with his executors

to obſerve and keep a yearly dirge in the Church
of St. Benedict, on the firſt Wedneſday of the
kalends of May, and other ſpecified obſervances of
a religious character.

1510. There was a ſuit between Kings Lynn
and Cambridge regarding Toll at this fair. How
the matter was then diſpoſed of does not appear.
See 1541.

1517. Miſunderſtandings having ariſen between
the Town of Cambridge and the Prior and Convent of Barnwell the matter was referred to arbi-
tration, and the Award determined that the town
for evermore ſhould have hold and enjoy, keep and
maintain the fair as well within the ſaid town of
Barnwell &c, as in all other lands and fields of the
ſaid prior and convent, lying on the eaſt between
the ſaid monaſtery and town of Barnwell, and a
bridge called Sturbridge, from the feaſt of St. Bartholomew unto the feaſt of St. Michael in Sept. ,
and that they and their farmers might, without let
or moleſtation of the ſaid prior and convent, build
ſtalls, ſhops, &c, the mayor &c throwing down
all banks, chimneys, &c within four days after
Michaelmas, and provided that all ſuch farmers
of any houſe or ſhop letten by the Prior and
Convent ſhould pay but one ſhilling by the year
to the mayor &c for his and their houſe and
ſhop. " Hiſt. and Antiq. of Sturbridge Fair,"
p. 77.

1519. A diſpute which had ariſen between the
mayor, bailiffs, and burgeſſes of Cambridge and
the mayor, burgeſſes, and comburgeſſes of *North-*

ampton, as to the claim of the freemen of the latter town to *exemption from toll in Sturbridge Fair,* was referred to the arbitrament of Sir Richard Elliot, and Sir Lewis Pollard, Juſtices of the Common Pleas, who on the 4th June awarded that the Corporation of Northampton ſhould pay 10*s.* yearly to the Corporation of Cambridge in full ſatisfaction of all toll and cuſtom due from the freemen of Northampton, for all manner of ſtuff, barrelled ware, and other merchandiſe, brought by them to Sturbridge fair, and all other paſſages and carriages through and by the town of Cambridge, at all times of the year, or and beſides twopence for every cart laden with their ſtuff going out of the fair. A deed of Covenant founded on this award was entered into by the two Corporations on the 10th of July. "Corp. Crofs. Book."

1521. About this time there were proceedings in the Court of the Duchy of Lancaſter by the tenants of *Hertford,* againſt Richard Clark mayor of Cambridge, who was complained againſt for ſeizing for toll in this fair.

A little later there was a like ſuit pending between the tenants of the Duchy in Walden, and the bailiffs of Cambridge. *A decree in favour of* the Exemption was made in Eaſter term 1524.

1533-4. The Heads of the Univerſity claimed the following rights in the Fair:

1. The Proctor's Commiſſary and other officers of the univerſity keep a court in the fair, becauſe it is within the ſuburbs of Cambridge, and the univerſity are clerks of the market, and have the over-

fight and correction of weights and meafures, and victuals in the fair.

2. They hold plea in the faid court of contracts and trefpaffes made within the faid fair as without, which was one of the things agreed upon in a compofition with the town, viz. that the univerfity fhould have the like privileges there as the mayor.

3. They hear and determine pleas perfonall as well between fcholars, fervants, as all foreigners and others of the kings fubjects, if a fcholar or fcholars fervant be one party by the commiffary in the fair court by the order of the civil law by witnefs or otherwife, excepting in caufes relating to victuals, wherein they determine according to the common or ftatute law.

4. They make proclamation in the faid fair before the proclamation of the mayor of Cambridge, by virtue of the King's letter patent as confervators of the peace, and as having the overfeer of victuals which is the firft thing fold in the fair.

5. The Proctors fearch all manner of fifh as well falt-fifh as other, pewter, brafs, &c, haires, girthwebb, filks, furs, beds, and all upholftery wares, fpices and grocery, rape-feed, muftard-feed, fuftians, worfteds, fago, honey, foap, oil, tallow, wax &c. brought to be fold in the faid fair, and take the forfeitures of the fame when faulty &c. This they do by virtue of royal charters.

6. The Proctors by virtue of the King's writt directed to the univerfity, and as clerks of the market are the proper gaugers in the fair to gauge all manner of barrelled wares brought to be fold,

and take the ufual fees allowed by the law for the fame, as alfo for weighing, viz. of every one that bringeth falmon or any thing of like nature to be fold, 12*d.* for every laft gauging. For every laft of oil gauged 12*d.* Item, for every laft of foap weighing and guaging 12*d.* For every laft of honey weighing and gauging 4*s.* &c. and the fines and forfeitures for want of weight and meafure.

7. The Taxers take of all victuallers in the fair a greater or leffer fum according as they can agree for breach of the affize of bread and beer which they fell in the fair. N.B. This taken in lieu of heavier penalties which the offending victualler incurrs, and the taxers may lawfully inflict, for fuch offence.

8. For every cart load of oats to be fold in the fair they take 4*d.* &c.

This declaration of rights and privileges was in reply to charges made by the town againft the Univerfity—twenty-three in all, amongft which was (15) of that of holding within the town a Civil Court weekly whereat they held plea of all manner of contracts ' and actions perfonal, as well between foreigners as burgeffes, and hold proceedings in the Civil law in derogation of the King's Crown. All this the Univerfity replied they did by the King's Charter. That (16) they had excommunicated two of the mayors of the town. To which anfwer was, they did this for perjury! They had punifhed a foreftaller of honey from Banbury. They had punifhed a burgefs for felling tallow to a merchant at Lynn (20). Admitted—" There was muche talow conveyed owte of Cambridge fo as the Kyngs people myght have no candle fufficient." The anfwers to the charges had been given verbally in St. Mary's Church, and record taken. There was much commotion on the occafion, but afterwards " all dranke together at the Pompe Taverne, and the Unyverfyte payd for all." See 1534.

Same year, 7th Sept. Princefs Elizabeth (afterwards the famous Queen) was born at Greenwich. Intelligence was brought to the mayor by the Queen's minftrels, during the time of the fair, and was there celebrated by bonfires and rejoicings. In the accounts of the treafurer of the borough for that year are thefe items:

Item, payed to the Qwenys mynftrells that brought letters to Mr. Mayer of the birthe of the Pryncefle v*s*.

Item, paid for ij loads woode for gaudes at the bone fyer in Stirrebygge fayer made in certain places within the faid fayer iij*s* x*d*.

Item, for iiij galonns wyne fpent at the faid Gaudes ij*s* viij*d*.

1534. There was enacted the 25 Henry VIII. c. 4—*An Acte agaynft Forftllyng and regraytyng of Fyfshe*—which recited previous acts againft forftalling victuals and other merchandife in the markets and fairs of the kingdom, " which former Statutes not only for lake of due exeucion of the fame but alfo for lake of condigne punyfshement in the feid Statutes conteyned be lytill feared or regarded ; for dyverfe and many of the Kinges fubjectes contrary to the meanyng of the faid Eftatutes nothing re-

gardyng the difpleafure of Allmyghty God and of
the Kynges Highnes, ne yet the love and charitie
that they ought to have to theire neyghbours and
commen welthe of this .Realme, for theire pryvate
lucre and finguler avayle commenly in every markett and fayre within this Realme doo forftall and
regrate all maner of victuall as corne wynes fyfshe
and flefhe, and efpecially in *Sturbruge* fayre, *Seynte
Ives* faire, and *Elye* fayre, *being the moft notable faires
within this Realme for provyfions of fyfshe,* and
mooft to the releff of the Kynges fubjectes yf fuch
forftallyng and regratyng myght be fett on fyde,"
&c. &c.

After ten years experience of its mifchievous
tendency this act was repealed (1544).

The difputes between the Univerfity and the
town ftill continuing, a grace was this year paffed
empowering fuch parties as were therein named to
anfwer determine and conclude all fuch controverfies as fhould be propounded by the mayor and
burgeffes before the Lord Chancellor and the Duke
of Norfolk ; and by another Grace, proctors were
appointed on the part of the Univerfity to anfwer
in all caufes before the King's Council. On the
24th July the parties on both fides met at Lambeth
Palace, "where it was decreed by the faid Lordes
" that Styrbridge Faire was in the Subarbes of
" Cambridge, and that the Vice-chancellor or his
" commyfary might kepe courte cyvyll ther for plees
" wheare a fcolar was the one party. *Item*, that in
" the fame faire the univerfity lead the overfight,
" correction and punyfhemente of all weightes and

" mefures, of all maner of victayll, of all Regreators
" and Foreftallers. *Item*, It was determyned that
" fpyces be vytaill." The expences of the Univerfity this year for journies to London &c, in confequence of the difputes with the townfmen
amounted to nearly £80.

There was ftill fome further controverfy on the
point, in which Thomas Crumwell, Secretary of
State, took part. See Cooper's " Annals of Cambridge," i. 373.

1639. In Hilary term John Baker the King's
Attorney General filed an information in the Court
of King's Bench againft the mayor, bailiffs, and
burgeffes, charging that they for four years, and
more then laft paft, had ufed to have a mart or
fair at Barnwell and Sturbridge, on the morrow of
St. Bartholomew the Apoftle, and continuing from
that time till the fourteenth day after the exaltation of
the Holy Crofs, with all liberties and free cuftoms
to the faid mart or fair belonging and appertaining;
alfo to have and hold by their fteward and other
minifters a Court of Piepowder, and by colour of the
fame to attach difquiet and aggrieve the fubjects of
the King reforting to the faid fair, as well by their
bodies as by their goods and chattels, and take from
the King's fubjects divers fines and amerciaments,
and to apply the fame to their own ufe; and alfo
to have all forfeitures and royalties whatfoever
within the precincts of the faid mart or fair during
its continuance; all which liberties and franchifes
they ufurped upon the King and his prerogative
royal, to his great prejudice and damage and in

contempt of his crown. Procefs was thereupon awarded, requiring the mayor, bailiffs, and burgeffes to anfwer this information, and to fhow by what warrant they claimed thefe liberties and franchifes. They fuffered judgment againft them by default, and the liberties and franchifes in the information fpecified, were feized into the King's hands.

This proceeding was confequent upon the diffolution of monafteries ordered in the preceding year —the original grant of the fair having been made as we have feen to a religious houfe. The Corporation prayed for a new charter, and agreed to pay 1,000 marks for the fame. The Charter was granted, but the money, on the authority of Cooper (" Annals," i., 393), was not paid for many years afterwards. The fair however was regularly held. The Charter is a very lengthy document; and as the grant was confirmed half a century later by the charter of Elizabeth (1589), which I fhall have occafion to notice in fome details for reafons then appearing, I fhall not dwell upon the prefent one.

1541. By 33 Henry VIII. c. 39—*The Bill for Town of Lynne towching the revoking of two Fairs*— it is recited For fo much that as well the burgeffes and inhabitants of the faid borough of King's Lynn, as many and divers other perfons dwelling near the faid borough have made regrated and gotten into their hands and poffeffion great numbers of falt fifh as ling, lob, falt falmon, fhellfifh and herring, " to the gret hindraunce and lofs of many of the King's ſubjects that yerely have repayred and com to *Styr-bige fair* Ely faire, & other Fayres & marketts in the Countie of Cambryge & Huntyngton and other ſhyres for the provyſion of ſalt fyſhe, & Heryng for theire houſeholdes, & for the proviſion of dyverſe other ſhires within this Realme of Englande, whiche regratyng is contrary to a comen welth and to dyverſe ſtatutes in that caſe providede, and contrari to the good entente and meanyng of the graunt of the ſaid Fayres and marte " It is enacted that the grant of the ſaid Fairs to King's Lynn be and was thereby repealed.

1542. Leland in his famous " Itinerary " at this date records : " The brothers of Sturbridge poſſeſs an antient houſe in that part where is the Fair for the ſale of woollens, commonly called the Duddery."

1544. On 27 Sept. Thomas Biſhop of Ely, the Dean and Chapter of the Cathedral Church òf the Holy and Undivided Trinity of Ely, and Chriſtopher Fulneby, incumbent of the Free Chapel of St. Mary Magdalene called Styrrebrige in the County of Cambridge, demiſed to the mayor, bailiffs, bur-geſſes, and commonalty of the town of Cambridge, the aforeſaid free Chapel, with all glebe lands, tene-ments, meadows, paſtures, booths, and booth grounds, ſtandings, liberty of building booths, rents, hereditaments, oblations, commodities and profits (except the advowſon, patronage, and donation of the ſaid free chapel) for 60 years at the rent of £9 per annum.

By means of this the entire temporal control of

the fair merged into the Corporation of Cambridge.

1546. There appears to have been fome fuit pending at this time regarding the Fair, for at a meeting of the Corporation of Cambridge Robert Chapman and feven others were appointed to commune and determine what they thought beſt to be done for Sturbridge Fair, and how the charges of the fuit therof ſhould be borne, and all other things concerning the fame. *Vide* "Corporation Common Day Book."

1547. At the Common Day held on Friday after the Aſſumption it was ordered that the Bailiffs ſhould enter their wards at this Fair on the 6th Sept. yearly, at 5 o'clock in the morning, and ſhould pay as follows: for the Bridge ward £18, for the Market ward £12, and for the High ward £13.

The proctors of the Univerſity upon freſh complaints made going their rounds one night " had taken certain evil perſons in houſes of fin," and had brought them to the Tollboth, in order to commit them there. But having fent to the mayor for the keys, he abſolutely refuſed to part with them. So they were fain to carry their priſoners to the caſtle, where they left them in cuſtody. But the mayor's fon, after an hour or two let them all out, " to return if they pleaſed to their former lewdneſs; to the breach of the law; and the affront of the magiſtrate." This led to further diſagreements.

By an Order of the Privy Council dated 3rd Oct. this year the mayor and underſheriff of the County were required not only to acknowledge before the

Vice-chancellor, heads of colleges and proctors, that they had interfered with the privileges of the Univerſity in this fair, but alſo "that the mayor in common hall ſhall openly, among his bretheren, acknowledge his wilfull proceeding." The breach conſiſted of John Fletcher, the mayor, having re-fuſed to receive into the tolbooth [priſon] certain perſons of "naughty and corrupt behaviour," who were priſoners taken by the proctors of the Univer-ſity, in the laſt Sturbridge Fair; wherefore he was called before the Lords and others of the Council, and his fault therein "ſo plainly and juſtly opened" that he could not deny it, but did "ſincerly and willingly confeſs the ſaid fault." Dyer's "Privileges of Cambridge," i. p. 111.

About this time Nicholas Elton, burgeſs of Cam-bridge by his will deviſed a booth in Sturbridge fair to the mayor, bailiffs and burgeſſes, after the death of his wife—It is ſuppoſed for charitable purpoſes.

There had been ſome ſuggeſtion that the Univer-ſity ſhould ſell their privileges in the Fair to the Corporation—ſee 1858.

1548. The following is the *Proclamation* uſed by the Univerſity of Cambridge about this date in "Crying the Fair":

The Crye in Sturbridge Fayer.

Wee charge & ſtraightlie comaund in yᵉ name of yᵉ Kinge of England oʳ Soveraigne Lord, and in yᵉ name of my Lord Chauncellʳ of yᵉ Univerſitie of Cambridge, yᵗ all manner of ſchollers, Schollers Ser-

vants, and all other perfons in this Fayer, and the
precinct of yᵉ fame, keepe the Kings peace, & make
no fraye, cry, owtaffe, ["out alas!", old exclama-
tion(?)] fhrekinge, or any other noyfe, by yᵉ which
Infurations, Conventicles, or gatheringe of people
may be made in this Fayer, to yᵉ trouble vexinge
and difquietinge of yᵉ Kings leage people or lettinge
of the officers of yᵉ Univerfity to exercife there
offices, under the payne of Imprifonment & further
punifhment as the offence fhall require.

Alfo wee charge & comaund, that all manner of
Schollers, and Schollers fervants weare no weapon,
to make any fraye upon any of yᵉ Kings people,
neither in cominge nor in goinge from this Fayer,
under yᵉ payne of banifhment.

Alfo wee charge & comaund, yᵗ all manner of
ftraungers, that come to this Fayer, that they leave
theire weapons at theire Innes, that yᵉ Kings peace
may be the better kept and for yᵉ occafion enfue-
inge of the fame, under the payne of forfettinge of
their weapons, and further punifhment, as the
offence fhall require.

Alfo wee charge & comaund, in yᵉ Kings name
of England, & in yᵉ name of my Lord Chauncellor
of yᵉ Univerfity, fhall all manner of Bakers, yᵗ bake
to fell, that they make 2 loofes for a penny, and 4
for another, good paft, good bowltell, & lawfull
fyfe, after as grayne goethe in yᵉ markett, & every
baker yᵗ baketh to fell, have a marke upon his bread,
whereby it may be knowne who did bake it, under
yᵉ payne of forfeiture of his bread.

Alfo wee charge & comaund, that all common

women, and miſbehavinge people, avoyde and with-drawe themſelves owte of this fayer, and precincts of yᵉ ſame, ymediatelie after this crye yᵗ yᵉ Kings ſubjects may be the more quiet, and good rule may be the better mayntayned, under yᵉ payn of im-priſonment.

Alſo that all Bakers ſhall obſerve and keepe ſuche ſyzes of bread as ſhall be given them by the officers of yᵉ Univerſity, under yᵉ payne of forfeiture of theire bread, if it happen any Baker to be founde fawtie in any article apperteyninge to unlawfull bread accordinge to yᵉ Kings lawes, that then ſuch bakers, after 3 monitions, ſhall be impriſoned & puniſhed on yᵉ pillory, accordinge to yᵉ lawes of oʳ Sovereigne Lord yᵉ Kinge.

Alſo that no Brewer ſell into the Fayer nowe here within yᵉ precinct of yᵉ Univerſitie, a Barrell of good Ale above 2 s.; And a Barrell of Hoſtell Ale above xij d.; no longe Ale, no red Ale, no ropye Ale, but good and holſome for mans body, under yᵉ payne of forfeyture. *And* yᵗ every Brewer have a mark upon his Barrell, whereby it may be known who owneth it, under yᵉ payne of impriſonment and fyne at yᵉ diſcretion of yᵉ officers of yᵉ Uni-verſitie.

Alſo yᵗ every Barrell of good Ale hold and con-teyne xiiij gallons, xiij gallons of cleere Ale, and one gallon for the reſt : and the Hoggett vij gallons, that is to ſay, ſixe gallons, and one pottel of cleare Ale, and the reſidew of reſt, under the payn of for-feit, and further puniſhment after the diſcretion of the officers of the Univerſitie.

Alſo wee comaund that yᵉ bearebrewer ſhall ſell a kylderkyn of double beare in this fayer for ij s. and a kylderkyn of ſingle beare for xij d.

Alſo yᵗ no Tipler no gauger ſell in the ſayd fayre nor within the precinꞔts of the Univerſitie, A gallon of good Ale above iiij d: nor a gallon of the Hoſtill ale above ij d. and the beare brewers a gallon of double beare above iiij d. and a gallon of ſingle beare above ij d, under the payn of xij d. for every tyme.

Alſo that no Tipler or gauger ſell by other mea-ſure than by gallon, pottle, quart, pint, and halfe pint, under the payne of xij d. for every tyme.

Alſo where great detriments, hurts, and deceites have beene to the Kings ſubjeꞔtes in tymes paſt, by reaſon of falſe and unlawfull meaſure, brought by Potters and other perſons to bee ſould in this fayre and the precinꞔt of the ſame; for avoydinge there-fore the ſayd hurts and untrew meaſures, wee ſtraightlie charge and comaund that every Potter, and all other perſons as bring ſuch pots to bee ſould in this fayre, or the precinꞔt of the ſame, that ye and all other from hensforth ſell and buy trew goods and laweful meaſures, as gallons, pottles, quartes, pintes and halfe pints, under the payne of impriſonment, and that to remain till they have made fyne at the will of the ſayd officers.

Alſo if any Bruer be found fauty in any of the premiſſes after that hee hath bene iij times Amerced, then yᵉ ſaid brewer ſhal bee comited to priſon, there to remayne till hee have fined at the will of the officers of the Univerſitye.

Also that every Tipler or Guager, that felleth ale in this fayer that they have theire meafures well and lawfullie fealed and affyzed according to the ftanderd of the Univerfitie; and y^t every Gauger, and bere-brewer y^t hath Ale or bere to fell, have a figne at theire booth, whereby they may ye better be knowne, under ye payne of imprifonment.

Also that every Vintener, that hath wyne to fell in this fayre, as white wyne, redd wyne, Clarett wyne, Gafkyn wyne, mamfey, or any other wyne, that they fell no dearer than they doe at London, except a ob. in a gallon towards ye carriage; and y^t every vintener have theire potts and theire meafures fyfed and enfealed after the ftandard of the Univer-fitie, under ye payne of forfeiture, and theire bodyes to prifon.

Also that all perfons that bringeth linge fyfhe falt fyfhe, ftocke fyfhe, or any other falt fyfhe, to fell in this fayre, or within ye precinct of ye fame, that they fell no rott fyfhe, no burnt fyfhe, no ruftie fyfhe, but good, lawfull, and holefome for man's body, under ye payne of forfeiture of ye fyfhe and theire bodyes to pryfon.

Also all manner of perfons which have famon herringe or eels to fell in this fayer, that ye veffels called Butts, Barrells, half Barrells, and firkins, you fell none of them before they be fene and fearched, & y^t ye butt hold and conteyne 84 Gallons, well and trulie packed upon payne for every butt, barrell, half barrell fo lackinge theire faid meafure vj s. iiij d. *And* y^t ye great falmon be well and trulie packed by itfelf, without meddlinge of any grills, or

broken-bellied famon with the fame : and that all
fmall fyfhe called Grilles be packed by themfelves,
and without any meddlinge upon payne of forfeiture & loofing of vj s. viij d. for every butt, barrell,
and halfe barrell fo found faltye, contrary to the
ftatute of yᵉ parliament ; on the which ftatute thefe
poynts and other more bee more playnly xpreffed.

Alfo that every Pikemonger that bringeth frefh
fifh to this fayre to fell, as Pike, Tench, Roche,
perche, eele, or any other frefh fifhes, that the fifhe
be quicke and lymifhe, and of the fize and bigneffe
according to the ftatute thereof made, under the
payne of forfeiture, and their bodyes to prifon.

Alfo that every butcher, that bringeth flefh to fell
in this faire that he bring no rotten flefhe, no
muireynes, no fuffiners, [foul or unwholefome
meat (?)] but lawfull and holefome for man's bodye,
and that every butcher bringe the fide [hide ?] and
the tallowe of all fuch flefh as hee fhall kill, to fell in
the faire, and that every butcher bring with him the
liver and the longes of all fuch beaftes under the
payne of forfeiture.

Alfo that every Baker that baketh horfe Bread to
fell that hee fell iij loaves for A penny, after good
and lawful fize, and after fuch fize as fhall be given
them, and that it be made of good peafe beanes
and other lawful ftuffe, upon the payn aforefayd.

Alfo fhall all browne bakers, as well Inholders and
others, obferve and keepe fuch fyfe of horfe bread
as fhall be given them by yᵉ faid officers, under yᵉ
payne and punifhment as of other Bakers is re-
herfed.

Alſo that every perſon yᵗ ſelleth by meaſures, as
by ell or by yard, woollen clothe, or Lynnen clothe
Sylke, worſteds, fyſed and unſealed, that they have
theire ells and theire yards fyſed and enſealed after
yᵉ ſtandard of yᵉ Univerſitie, under the payne of
forfeiture, and their bodyes impriſonment.

Alſo that every perſon that ſelleth any meaſure,
as by Buſhell, half Buſhell, Pecke, or half Pecke, as
Coales, Salt, Muſter Seede, or any other thing, that
theire Buſhells half Buſhells and pecks be fyſed and
ſealed after yᵉ ſtandard of the Univerſitie, under the
payne of impriſonment, and more puniſhment as the
offence ſhall require.

Alſo that all perſons that waigh have good and
lawful waights fyſed and enſealed, and to agree with
yᵉ ſtandard waight of yᵉ Univerſitie.

Alſo that no man ſhall regrate none of yᵉ fore-
ſayd things, as Lynge fiſhe, Salt fyſhe, Stocke fyſhe,
herringe, Salmon, Pike, tench, waxe, flax, oſiern,
[for oſmunds, a preparation for ſtiffening linen (?)]
roſyn, yarne, pitch tarr, cloth, nor none other things
of Grocery ware, or any other marchandiſe in this
Fayer, under payne of forfeiture, and theire bodyes
to priſon, and to make fyne as it ſhall pleaſe yᵉ
officers of yᵉ Univerſitie, and the regrater is he that
byeth any of the ſayd things afore reherſed, or any
other manner of marchandiſes of any man in this
Fayre, and ſelleth again the ſayde things in the ſayd
Fayre, inhawnſeing yᵉ price of any of the ſayd things
more than it was before.

Alſo if theire be any perſon that will ſue for any
perſonal action either for debt, victualles, injuri and

trefpas, or thinke themfelves wronged in any of the premiffes or otherwife, let him complayne to my Lord Chauncellors Comefarye and other officers of the Univerfitie, which fhall hould and keep Courts daylie and howerlie in this fayer duringe ye fame to the intent y^t he fhall be hard with lawful favour in right and confcience and after the liberties of the fame. *Alfo* that every butcher y^t bringeth flefhe to fell in this markett, that he fell none of ye Tallowe of all fuch beaftes as he fhall bringe to fell in this markett, but to fuch Rafement and Tallowe chaundelers, as are dwellers within ye Univerfitie, and precinĉt of the fame; and they to make ye faid Tallowe in good and lawfull candell, fo y^t ye faid Univerfitie, and Town of Cambridge, be in no wyfe difappointed, but the better ferved, & y^t you fell not a pound of candles above 1d. and y^t ye fayd Butcher fell not a fton of Tallowe above viij d.

Alfo y^t every Innekeeper y^t keepeth Inne, y^t he have his bottels of hey well and lawfullie made and fyfed and y^t every bottle way vij^{li}, And that ye fell not lefs than three horfe loves, good and lawful, for a penny, under ye payne of punifhment after the difcretion of ye officers of ye Univerfity.

Alfo that every Carryer, y^t bringeth woode to fell in this markett, that they bringe good wood, and yf it be faggott, let ye faggot therof be well filled and fized, and that everye faggott be full vij feet longe, and every faggott to have two bonds and xli faggotts in a load, well filled after ye faid lenght, under ye payne of forfeiture.

Alfo that every Collier y^t bringeth charecool to

fell, that every ſack called a quarter ſacke, hold viij buſhells, ſavinge yᵗ they be allowed for Culme breaking by the way, after yᵉ diſcretion of yᵉ officers of the Univerſitie, under yᵉ payne of forfeiture.

Alſo that every perſon yᵗ bringeth grayne to ſell in this markett, yᵗ they open not before Tenne of yᵉ clocke, nor to ſtand after one of yᵉ clock, under ye payne of forfeiture.

How long this form of Proclamation remained in force does not appear, but probably for ſeveral centuries later. See 1855. It is ſeen that regulations againſt adulteration and other wrongdoings of traders, are not ſo modern as is ſometimes ſuppoſed.

About this period, and probably earlier, a piece of ſtuff for a gown was bought for every fellow of St. John's College at this fair. See " Early Stat. of St. John's Col. Cambr." 1859.

CHAPTER X.

SECOND HALF OF THE SIXTEENTH CENTURY.

1550.

OR the better prefervation of peace during the fair the Lieutenants and Commiffioners of the Univerfity ordered a "night watch" to be kept by the fcholars and townfmen. The colleges were to fupply the watchmen to the number of twenty in the aggregate "to be thir in redynes, harnefhed and weponed, befor the bell of St Johns at vii of the clock be ceafed; in defawt whereof every college in whom fuch defawt fhal be, to paye to the Proctours xii d, wherewith to find other in their roms" *Item*, that over and beyond the faid number the faid Colleges have in redynes other xxiiii according to the rate aforefaid.

The town paid £2 4s. 4d. to the bailiffs and others "for monye fpent at the watche in Stirbridge fayer." Thefe watchmen wore red coats and went the round of the fair every half hour, calling out luftily " Look about you there."

Pewterers Company of London.—On the 10th Sept. in this fair the Wardens of the Pewterers Company of London feized certain falt-fellers, pots and covers of pewter, which were of infufficient metal, and which they therefore alleged to be forfeited. The fearchers of the Univerfity and Town, however, claimed exclufive jurifdiction of the Fair, and took the pewter from the Wardens, who exhibited an information in the Exchequer againft one of the Efquire Bedels and one of the Searchers; but on the 21ft Nov. the Privy Council fent the following letter to the Wardens :

Whereas the Univerfitie of Cambridge have bi the kings majeftie, and other his noble projenitours, charters, among other things the viewe, ferche, correction, and forfeture, of all pewter that comyth to Sturbrige fayr unmerchantable, and youe John Daye and Stephan Rowlandfon intermedled with the ferche therof clayming the moytie of all fuch pewter as ther was found forfeted, and being therof denyed have put in to the kings majefties court of the efchekyr for the recovery of the fayde moytie, an information agaynft John Mere one of the bedels for the faid univerfitie, and the officer appointed with other for the ferche therof aforefayd. The kings majefties pleafure is, for faving of the fayd privileges, that youe procede no further therin, but fuffer the fame to ftaye and hang untyl his majefties wyll be further knowen, and this fhall be your fufficient warrant for the fame. Fare ye wel,

From the Kings palace of Weſtminſter, yᵉ xxi
November, 1550.

> Your lovyng Friends
> EDW. SOMERSET, T. CANT. J. WARWICKE.
> J. BEDFORD W. NORTH[AMPTON], ED.
> CLYNTON. W. PAGET, T. ELY,

There is a letter of the King's (Edward VI.)
extant which ſhows preciſely why the Council took
this courſe :

Aftre our hartie comendacions ; wheras contrary
to certain privileges graunted by the kings majeſtie
and his noble progenitours unto his univerſitie of
Cambridge oone John Daye and Stephan Roland-
ſon wardens of the crafte and miſtery of the pewterers within the citie of London, have put in a
certaine information with you in the King's courte
of Thexcheker agaiſt John Meare oone of the kings
bedells for the univerſitie of Cambridge for certaine pewter ſeaſed unto the king's uſe at the laſt
Sturbridge feare, his highneſs' pleaſure is that you
proceade no further to judgement therein, but ſuffre
the ſame to ſtay and hange untill his majeſtie's will
be further knowne, and theſe ſhall be your ſufficient warrant for the ſame.   Fare you well, from
the kings majiſtie's palace of Weſtminſter the 22
of November 1550

> Your loving frend.

This ſent to the barons of th' Exchequer from the
counſayl.

Item another to the promoters ut infra by the
ſame counſaylors.

In the accounts of the Fair of this year are the
following items—the result probably of causes heard
by the Court of Piepowder—recorded thus : "receyved bi the Bedel and the Townsmen & partly
found by promoters":

Rychard Lylye of Stow of Thold
  [Stow-in-the-Wold] in Glosseter-
  shere hathe put to sale contrary to
  the Statute vii peces of welshe frese
  and hathe paid for his fyne to
  Draper the partye that sued xx *s*,
  and for the quenes parte . . vi *s.*

Receyved of Mr Caree of Bryftow for
  xv peces of karsey put to sale contrarye to the statute . . . iii l.

And of Maye for felts forfeited . v s. iiii d.

Receyved of Tho. Mate for 11 kar-
  seys and 1 frese . . . . xxx s.

Receyved of Mr. Ryngfted for ex-
  chaunge old sylver and from John
  Holls xxv s. whereof Tho. Gar-
  dener the promoter had xx s. and
  v s. for the quene.

Receyved of Thomas Daye for iii
  peces of karsaye put to sale contrarye to the act and seafed for
  the quene . . . . . xxx s.

Receyved of the 11 Streaches and
  Bowldry of Walden for clothes
  forfeyted . . . . . x s.

Receyved of the Wardens of the Pewterers for pewter forfeited . . viii s. iiii d.

Receyved of Smythe Twyffyn and
Hadſtack for . . . . ii s. viii d.

Receyved of Mr Coxe of Bryſtow for
viii peces . . . . . xl s.

Receyved of Mr. Chambers Habber-
daſher for a . . . cappe ſold .

Receyved of Mr. Kytchyn Goldſmith
for byeinge of . . . . x s.

Receyved of Mr. Hamlett for mat-
treſſes forfeyted . . . . v s.

Receyved of Geo. Alys for the lyke. v s.

At the bottom of the page, in a different hand-
writing are the three following items of diſburſe-
ment:

Item, for the women for the ſewing . ii *s.*
Item, paid Wyllm Grange for a cappe ii *s.* iiii *d.*
Item, for our chargys at the fayre . x *s.*

New Charter.—1553. On the Feaſt of St. Mark
the Evangeliſt, it was agreed by the Mayor, Alderman and Twenty-four, that the Town for their
poſſeſſions and the other poſſeſſioners [owners of
ſtalls and booths] in Sturbridge fair, ſhould pay the
King (Edward VI.) 1000 marks for the fine for
Sturbridge Fair; that the body of the town ſhould
pay one half of all charges of obtaining the new
charter, and the town for their poſſeſſions and the
other poſſeſſioners to pay the other half. It was
alſo agreed that the Recorder and others ſhould
have authority under the Common Seal to ſue to
the King's majeſty and his honourable Council for

a new Charter for the fair; and further that Mr.
Robert Chapman and Mr. John Ruft fhould pay
no money towards the charges of the charter, in
confideration of their pains in obtaining thereof,
and £90 1s. od. was paid then towards the firft
inftalment of 200 marks for the King's fine.

The Charter was not however obtained in this
reign, though the 200 marks were actually paid.
" Annals," ii. p. 70. See 1555, 1561, 1574, 1576,
1577, 1584, 1589—when new Charter was obtained
by the town.

1555. 30 Jany. The Mayor, Aldermen,
Twenty-four and Bailiffs gave authority to Mr.
Robt. Chapman and Mr. John Ruft to go to
London to make fuit to the Council touching the
fupplication made to them for the payment of the
800 marks; and for the fetting forth and making
the patent for the confirmation of Sturbridge fair.

1556. The queftion of Lynn Fair—apparently
as to its revival—came on again this year, and on
2nd Aug. the Corporation ordered that the Mayor,
Mr. Chapman, and Mr. Ruft fhould frame an
anfwer to a letter from the Bifhop of Ely concerning Lynn Fair, and make objections in fhewing
why the fame ought not to be had; and that the
Town Clerk fhould carry the anfwer to his Lord-
fhip.

1557. On 23 June the King and Queen (Philip
and Mary) by letters patent, granted to the Mayor,
bailiffs and burgeffes, a certain annual rent of
£8 15s. 2d. iffuing out of fhops and booths in
Sturbridge, which had been granted for the main-

tenance of *obiits* and anniverfaries (fee 1459, 1496, 1503, 1547), and alms to the poor of the town. The letters patent ftate, that this Rent had been feized into the hands of the Crown, under the ftatute of Chantries (1547) and that £6 10s. 6d. part thereof had been paid to the mayor, bailiffs and burgeffes for diftribution amongft the poor. This is expreffed to be made from the King and Queen, that the rites and ceremonies of the Catholic Church fhould be maintained, and the wills of the donors performed! And alfo becaufe the fhops and booths in Sturbridge Fair, *being of cuftomary tenure, were not within the Statute of Chantries.*

The fame King and Queen granted the following tolls payable for the merchandife brought to the fair. This is important as fhowing the nature of the goods brought at this period:

Cuftom and Toll due in the time of Sturbridge Fair for divers wares brought thither:

For every cade of red herrings at the bying .	1 d.
For 100 of ling	6
For every 100 of wabboks ling . . .	4
For every 100 of codds	4
For every 100 of wabboks codds . .	2
For every heap of fifh to be retailed laid upon a mat of the old affize . . .	2
Of every jule of cured fifh for groundage .	2
Of grinftones every foot	$\frac{1}{2}$
Of every perfon that retaileth foap, for his ftanding in the fair	2

Of every hundred wainſcot . . .	8 d.
Of every dicker of leather	2
Of every 100 calf-ſkins	4
Of every 100 ſheep-ſkins	2
For groundage of every load of pales, ſhovels, pack-ſaddles, cart-saddles, and goddends .	4
Of every great ſalt-ſtone	2
Of every buſhel of muſtard ſeed . . .	$\frac{1}{2}$
Of every load of baſkets, farms ſkepps leeper and ſuch other	4
Of every ſtranger ſelling freſhwater fiſh in kemblin	1
Of every cart load of oiſters for cart and ſtanding	4
Item a barrel of oſmonds	2
Item a barrel of pitch	2
Item a barrel of tar	2
Item a barrell of herrings	2
Item a barrell of cork for dying . . .	2
Item for every barrel of cured fiſh . .	2
Item a barrel of ſalmon	4
Item a barrel of oil	4
Item a barrel of honey	4
Item of ſturgeon a barrel	4
Item a barrel of ſope	4
Item a barrel of eels	4
Item a barrel of birdlime	4
Item cart laden with poles	1
Of every cart loaden with heboldines . .	1
Of every horſe with a wombtye loaden .	$\frac{1}{2}$
Of every cart loaden with beyondſea claſs-hold	2

Item 100 of beyondſea claſshold for groundage   1 d.

Of every cart loaden with Engliſh claſshold
   and lying down   2

Of every horſe ſold   1

Of every load of hobboldynes for groundage   1

Of every cart loaden with faggots, beſides the
   fall penny .   .   .   .   .   . $\frac{1}{2}$

Of every cart loaden with ſmiths coals.   .   2

Of every cart loaden with timber   .   .   2

Of every cart loaden with lathes   .   .   2

Of every cart loaden with boards   .   .   2

Of every cart loaden with cheeſe   .   .   2

Of every load of boards, hurdles, ſpokes, and
   lathes, for groundage   2

Of every load of hewn timber for groundage   2

Of every ſodder of lead, for groundage   .   2

Of every cart or wayne loaden with lead, for
   groundage   2

Of every load of iron, for groundage if he
   have no booth   2

Of every cart loaden with iron, for laying
   down   2

Of every cart loaden with hayres   .   .   2

Of every cart loaden with ſackcloath .   .   2

Of every cart loaden with any manner of
   merchandize then aforeſaid, at lying down,
   beſides the groundage   2

Of every cart or wayne loaden with nails, at
   lying down   2

Of every perſon ſelling nails, for groundage .   6

Of every keel or boat that beareth a helm, as
   oft as he cometh   2

Of every keel or boat that beareth no helm,
as oft as he cometh . . . . 1 d.
Of every heap of coals, ... 4
Of every cart loaden with merchandize difcharged at Barnwell, ... 2
Of every cart charged with merchandize at
Barnwell, other than the inhabitants' goods
of Cambridge, coming from the Barnwell
to the fair and there difcharge, . . 1
Of every cart charged with the inhabitants'
goods at Cambridge or at Barnwell and
difcharged at the fair . . . . $\frac{1}{2}$
Of every cart loaden with merchandize or
wayne goying out of the fair, . . 2

1558. The Univerfity of Cambridge being in
want of money the queftion was again raifed (fee
1547) of felling to the Corporation of Cambridge
all privileges in this fair. The propofal met with
ftrong and fuccefsful oppofition from the Provoft of
King's College (*vide* Fuller's " Hift. of Univ. of
Camb."). In the " Hiftory and Antiquities of
Barnwell Abbey," 1786 (p. 78, part ii.) there is
the following: "Robert Braffil . . . who being
Vice chancellor, in 1558, was much commended for
his wifdome in withftanding the heads & mafters
of Colleges in this univerfitie; when, as they had
all except him, confented & concluded to fell all their
wrightes and jurifdictions in Sturbridge Faire to the
mayor, bayliffes & burgeffes of the towne of Cambridge."

Drapers, Merchant Taylors, and Clothworkers of

London.—On 3rd Sept. 1557, a letter was addreſſed to the Vice-chancellor and Proctors of the Univer-ſity by Nicholas Hethe Archbiſhop of York, Lord High Chancellor of England, and Thomas Thirleby, Biſhop of Ely, ſtating that complaint had been made unto them by the Drapers, Merchant Tailors, and Clothworkers of the City of London, that they repairing theretofore with their cloths to Sturbridge fair, had been troubled in the ſale thereof, through unlawful ſearches pretended by divers light perſons more for their own private gain and the vexation of the merchants than for any good intent to have the Statutes duly executed. Their Lordſhips there-fore required, that in future no ſuch unlawful ſearches ſhould be made by any ſuch light perſons, and that merchants ſhould not be otherwiſe diſquieted or ordered than was ordained and provided by the Statutes of the realm. " Annals of Camb." ii. p. 135.

1559. There were again diſputes between the Univerſity and Town of Cambridge reſpecting the watch at time of the fair. The following me-morandum drawn up by the mayor embodies the the views of Lord North and the Lord Chief Juſtice of the Common Pleas thereon :

After our verye harty commendacions, Where we of late with the adviſe and conſent of the reſt of the Juſtices of peace of this Shire take order for the better & more quyet governement of this ſhire, That duringe this Stirbridge fayre tyme the watches for the Univerſitie & Towne of Cambridge ſholde lovinglie joyne togither & be dubled, whereof our

verye frende Mr Baron Frevyll dyd take upon him
to advertyfe you of the fame, by occafion wherof
we dyd forbear to wryte unto you therein. We
now ar enformed that ye ar not as yet fully agreed
to joyne togither in the execucion of the fame for
certaine refpects that ye have to the prefervation of
your liberties, Wherefore we do feare great inconve-
niens and perill may growe, onles ye do fpedelye
conforme yourfelves thereunto. Thefe are therefore to advertyfe you & requyre you for the more
quietnes of this cuntrye & Towne, and for the
Queenes Majefties better fervyfe that ye forthewith
conjoin yourfelves togithers accordinglie, notwith-
ftandinge any perfuafion to either of you to the
contrarye.

And furthermore underftandinge that there ar
allredie a nombre of Sturdye Vacabonds & mafterles
men come unto Cambridg for fome yll purpofe as
it is fuppofed; We therefore do likewyfe defyer &
requyre you in hir majefties behalfe, that ye do take
a great refpect unto the apprehendinge of them,
and to the fafe keepinge of them untill the faire be
paft. We meane fuch as come not to the intent to
labor, or otherwife lawfullie to get their livinge
prayenge you that if upon eny examinacion of anye
of them ye fhall fynde eny matter worthye to be
further examined & tryed out, to advertyfe us im-
mediatelie therof fo that we maye ye better ayed
& affift you for your better fervice & procedinge
in the fame, nothinge doubtinge but ye will
lovinglye & effectually confider the premiffes in
fuche wyfe as both you and me maye avoide dif-

pleafure and blame. And thus we byd you hartelye farewell. From Carleton this Mondaye, the iiij of Septembre, A° 1559.

1561. The Corporation appear to have renewed their application for a grant of the fair. It was ordered that the expenfe of the inquifition for the new charter fhould be borne by the town.

1562. There was a great flood, fo that the portion of Sturbridge called the "Waterfair" could not be occupied by the booths accuftomably built there. Whereupon the Corporation directed Robert Chapman and others to affign another place for fuch booths for this year's fair only.

1567. This year George Aylfton, merchant, on behalf of the Corporation of *Sudbury* inftituted proceedings in the Duchy Court of Lancafter againft Chriftopher Fletcher alderman of Cambridge, for taking his goods at this fair. Fletcher alleged that he took the goods as a diftrefs damage feafant, and it feems had a decree in his favour.

1568. *Citizens of London.*—On 4th Nov. the the Corporation of Cambridge deputed Roger Lord North the mayor, Francis Hinde Efq., and the Counfel-at-law of the town to deliberate in what way it could be contrived that the citizens of London might return to Sturbridge fair, as of old they were accuftomed. "Annals," ii. p. 235.

1571. As early as 1545 there had been paffed by the Corporation of Cambridge "an Ordinance for the fetting of Willows." This ordinance "for planting willows on the commons, drains, moors, marfhes and fens of the town" was renewed this year. Every alderman might fet fix fcore of poles and every burgefs four fcore up the banks of any furface, drains, ditches, &c. They to lop and top for their own ufe and advantage, cleanfing from time to time the drains &c. on which the fame were planted. The faid willows to be held on the fame terms as the booths at Sturbridge fair were held by the burgeffes, &c. See 1575.

1574. On the 21ft Nov. Dr. Perne, Vice-chancellor, wrote to Lord Burleigh on the fubject of the Plague vifitation in Cambridge, and in the poft-fcript to the letter made the fuggeftion of a new charter being granted to the Univerfity as follows :

I am enformed that there is fute made to ye Queen's majeftie by fome of her highneffe privie chamber for Sturbridg faire, for that it hath ftand feafed unto her highnes hand fithence ye tyme of the raign of her highnes father, the w^h if it might pleafe her highnes to beftowe to the Univerfity, there might be fuch a worthie and perpetual monement made by the rent thereof, as her majeftie did moft gratioufly promife at her laft beinge at Cambridg in her highnes Oration made there, & the Townefmen that be nowe occupiers thereof, yeldinge a reafonable rent to ye univerfity for their feverall boothes. Thus I am bold to put your honor in mynd of this, referringe the whole matter to your honors beft confideracion to do herein as yow fhall thinke good.

1575. At a Common Day held in the Round Church (probably on account of the Plague being near the Guildhall) on the 25th March the Corpora-

tion made a Declaration as to the tenure of booths at
Sturbridge fair of which the following are the principal portions :

Forafmuch as fome queftion hath bene made of
the maner of tenure of booths in Sturbridge Fayer,
fome houlding one opinion, & fome another, everie
man fpeakinge his fantafie therein, affirminge his
owne opinion to be the true cuftome, and that it
ought to ftande for truethe ; for that it hath not
bene generally knowne to all men whether any
Cuftome hath remained written in any records of
this towne concerninge the fame fayre, yea or no :

Commandment therefore had been given to the
Town Clerk to fearch the records of the town.
This had been done and " it is founde in the oulde
and ancient record called the Crofs Booke of the
fayde Towne, that remaineth there written." This
I have already given, under date 1403. The fame
was reaffirmed ; and it was now ordered that every
burgefs claiming a booth muft have his title thereto
entered in a book to be kept by the Corporation for
that purpofe ; and thereafter he might alienate the
fame to any other free burgefs by due entry in the
faid book in manner and form provided.

1576. 8th Dec. The Corporation fealed a power
of attorney (dated 30th Nov.) authorizing the
Recorder and others named to act in all matters
before the Queen and her Council, and in all caufes
and bufineffes touching the town, particularly the
redemption and confirmation of Sturbridge Fair.
To this end the Corporation empowered the Mayor
and others to rate the poffeffioners of booths in the

fair towards the payment of 1000 marks for the fine for the fair.

On 13th of fame month Lord Burleigh the Chancellor, and the Earl of Leicefter High Steward of the Univerfity wrote to Dr. Goad the Vice-chancellor, defiring that there might be a conference between the heads of the Univerfity and Town relative to the contemplated grant of the fair. Lord Burleigh it feems had obtained from the Queen a declaration that no petition of the townfmen refpecting their fair fhould be received to the prejudice of the Univerfity.

A meeting took place early in the following year but no friendly underftanding could be arrived at.

1577. The matter of renewing the charter of the fair was again before the Queen. On a petition being prefented on behalf of the Corporation the Royal reply was " that fhe would not take away any privileges that fhe had granted the Univerfity, but would rather add to them "; and for this declaration the Univerfity returned her a letter of thanks. " Annals," ii. 358.

At the fair this year the Mayor, Recorder, and Aldermen of the Corporation ordered a haberdafhery booth to be pulled down. Reafon not ftated. The Corporation fuftained the order.

The following articles were purchafed at the fair for the houfehold of Lord North. The record of prices is particularly important :

A C. Salt Fifh, Lix^s ; whight falt, iij ftone, 1 qt. iij lb. xiij^s; bay falt, iij qt. Lvj^s; 2 kettles, xiij^s vj^d ; ix duft bafkets, iiij^s ; vj pailes, ij^s vj^d ; 2 firkins of foape, xxix^s; Feather bed tike, xix^s; a Jacke ij^s ij^d; a frieng panne, ij^s ij^d hors meat xvj^d; 20 lb. of raiffins, v^s; 20 lb. Corants, vij^s vj^d; 10 lb. prewens, xx^s; Liiij lb. gon Powder, Lviij^s vjd.; 14 lb. of matches, iij^s ix^d; dogg cowples xx^d; 10 lb. Sugar, xij^s vj^d.

1578. The "provifion bought at Sturbridge Fayer" for the houfehold of Lord North this year, comprifed : Codds bought ccccli. vij^{li} xv^s; Soape bought 2 firkins xxviij^s; Salte bought iij^{li} xiij^s iiij^d; Lynen clothe pd. for xxxvij^s.

1584. An unfuccefsful attempt at accommodation between the Univerfity and the Town was made in 1580. The former fought for additional privileges which the latter would not grant. This year a more fuccefsful attempt was made, and except upon three points, the parties had agreed to " both books" (*i.e.* draft charters). The points were thefe :

1. As to an interpretation of "common minifters."

2. The demand of the Univerfity is unreafonable to have all graduates in England go toll free. " That the towne affentith as they ment it at the firft, That all graduates for lernings fake abydyng in the Univerfety or Towne fhall goe toll free."

3. The town had already affented that the Univerfity fhould have more retained fervants than they had before. " But fquyre beadalles fhould eche of them have one reteyned fervaunt priviledged (being themfelves but fervauntes), The Towne thinkith it inconvenient, and neither did, nor yet doth affent therunto : for all other matters concerning both bookes, both parties are agreed. So as that be

perfourmed which hath bene concluded in former conferences."

1586. The negociations between the Univerfity and the Town were renewed this year. The following document fhows the pofition of the negociation, as alfo that the town were to have the new charter; it alfo fhows the extreme jealoufy with which each body viewed the acts and proceedings of the other —it was a genteel manifeftation of "Town and Gown" divergencies, which have become hiftorical:

Sturbridge. The towne hath obtained of her majeftie a graunt of Sturbridge feyre, to the booke of that graunt the univerfitie addith a provifo to this effect viz that neither that graunt nor anything therein conteyned fhould any ways prejudice the univerfitie of Cambridge, or any member thereof, in fuch thinges as the univerfitie enjoyed before the fayd graunt! The towne fayth that that provifo is to large, forafmuch as it may be extended to all thinges which the univerfitie befor enjoyed, as well within the feyr as els whear, we confeffe it is fo; and we fay it is great reafon it fhould be fo, leaft under the colour and pretenfe of Sturbridge feyre, they might carry away fome other of our commodities w^h her highnefs never meant. So fhortly we fay thus muche; feing our provifo is nothing but a reftreint of their book: How farre fo ever their book reachith, fo farre reachith our provifo and no further.

This is the brief our prefent difference, &c. &c.

This year was fimplified the form of proceffion

made in proceeding to read the Proclamation of the
Univerfity.

New Charters.—1589. The proceedings already
recorded (with fome others in 1587 not fpecifically
referred to) ended in the grant of new charters of
the fair to the Town and alfo to the Univerfity of
Cambridge refpectively. The charter to the town
paffed the Great Seal at Drayton on 15th Aug.;
that to the Univerfity on 30th Aug.

The charter to the *Town* commences with a re-
cital that previoufly to the 30 Henry VIII. the
mayor, bailiffs, and burgeffes had from time immemorial had and ufed a fair called Sturbridge Fair
held at Barnwell and Sturbridge, in the county of
Cambridge and within the liberty of the town, beginning on the Feaft of St. Bartholomew the
Apoftle, and continuing from thence till the fourteenth day next after the Feaft of the Exaltation of
the Holy Crofs; which fair, from the advantages
of the place, its contiguity to the Univerfity, and
the fitnefs of the feafon, *far furpaffed the greateft and
moft celebrated fairs of all England; whence great
benefits had refulted to the merchants of the whole
kingdom, who reforted thereto, and there quickly fold
their wares and merchandifes to purchafers coming from
all parts of the Realm* to buy and provide falt-fifh,
butter, cheefe, honey, falt, flax, hemp, pitch, tar,
and all other wares and merchandifes, and from the
profits of which fair the mayor, bailiffs and burgeffes levied the greateft part of their fee farm, and
fupported and maintained the town in its ways,
ftreets, ditches [fewers] and other burthens.

Of the Quo Warrant in the 30th Henry VIII. and the fubfequent proceedings thereon. The Queen had been requefted to grant a charter and had af- fented " moved thereto by royal pity, by a fenfe of the utility of the fair to the town and to the mer- chants of the kingdom, and that the town fhould be lightened in its burthens, and increafed and honoured under her profperous and peaceful government." The Queen therefore delivered out of her hands and conferred to the mayor, bailiffs, and burgeffes and their fucceffors, the fair in queftion, with all profits, commodities, courts, profits of courts, autho- rities and jurifdictions, booths and power of build- ing booths in the accuftomed places in the fair.

All rights had or enjoyed by the *Univerfity*, or its officers under any gift, grant, or confirmation from the crown, or any act of parliament, or " ufed for the greater part of 20 years then laft paft " were referved to it.

Power given to Corporation to make rules and ftatutes for the peaceful and quiet government of the fair; and with refpect to the building and re- moving of booths, and the difpofition and affurance thereof by will, gift, furrender or otherwife; and alfo for placing the feveral arts, occupations, myf- teries, merchants, workmen, and others holding booths in the fair in the places affigned and accuf- tomed to the fame arts &c and efpecially in that part of the fair called Cheapfide. Such Ordinances &c. not to prejudice the right, title, or intereft of burgeffes holding or poffeffing booths according to the cuftoms and ordinances of the town, or to derogate from the privileges of the Chancellor, mafters, and fcholars ufed during the greater part of twenty years then laft paft. New rules might be altered and revoked as circumftances fhould require.

The fellers of mercery or grocery ware were forbidden to be ftationed or to occupy any booth in the fair for felling fuch wares except in Cheapfide. Woollen cloths were to be expofed for fale only in the "Duddery." Goldfmiths were not to be ftationed, or expofe their goods to fale any where except in Soper Lane, otherwife Goldfmith's Row; and pewterers and braziers were in like manner to be confined to Pewtry Row and Brazier Row.

The burgeffes who held any booth for life or years, or who fhould afterwards acquire any, were to hold the fame as theretofore.

The charter to the *Univerfity*, expreffed to have been granted by the authority of parliament, contains provifions relating to the town as well as to the fair. I fhall confine my abftract to the latter. It was granted out of love of the Univerfity, to confirm and eftablifh the privileges, liberties, immunities, pre-eminences, authorities, powers, jurifdictions, profits and commodities of that body in Sturbridge Fair, as granted by the charter fhe had given in the 3rd year of her reign. She granted to the Chancellor mafters and fcholars and their fucceffors folely and wholly for ever the office of " Clerk of the Market," and the affay of bread, wine, and ale or beer, and the keeping and governance of the fame and the correction and punifhment of offenders, with the fines, forfeitures and amerciaments thence arifing in the fair and the precincts of the fame. Also the fupervifion of meafures and weights, and the jurif-diction to inquire of all foreftallings, regratings, and ingroffing of victuals and other things and wares within the fair or its bounds and precincts, and to banifh, chaftife, and correct according to the laws of the realm and the cuftoms of the Univerfity. Also right of fearch in the fair for harlots and vaga-bonds.

The proclamation of the fair was to be made by the Univerfity and Town in alternate years. All goods carried to or by the fair, or to the town, or in the river to the ufe of the Chancellors, mafters, fcholars, or colleges, or to or for any of the graduates refiding within the town or Univerfity, or within five miles thereof to be *free of toll*.

The Univerfity to have exclufive jurifdiction in fuits wherein fcholars, fcholars fervants " or com-mon minifter of the Univerfity " were one of the parties. Also to hear and determine plaints con-cerning victuals or contract for victuals arifing in the fair, except in cafes between a burgefs and a foreigner not privileged of the Univerfity, which fhould be heard before the Mayor, &c. The court of the Chancellor &c within the fair to be a court of record with all powers according to the ftatutes of the realm, or the laws and cuftoms of the Uni-verfity. The laft named court to be held within the fair or its precincts, and the Queen granted a fufficient piece of ground for the purpofe. But if by flood or other chance the accuftomed place fhould be unfit another place was to be provided.

The Univerfity to have exclufive authority to infpeⅽt, fearch, try, affay and gauge all viⅽtuals in the fair. The daily infpection and fearch of all other wares (except leather and fackcloth) to be made by four fuitable men, appointed by the Chancellor and Mayor refpeⅽtively. And the court for adjudication upon the fame to be held by the Chancellor and Mayor in alternate years, each aiding the other in the performance of the duties. The remaining numerous provifions are not neceffary to be cited in view of our prefent purpofes.

It was the belief of the townfpeople that this charter to the Univerfity had been obtained by reafon of a betrayal of the rights of the town by the then Mayor. And the following was recorded at the foot of a tranfcript of this charter. " One Gawnt was Mayor of Cambridge, who att London affented to thefe new jurifdictions of the Univerfitie, and therein betrayed the towne, who fhortlie after was putt [out!] of his Aldermanfhipp & lived the remaynder of his life in great want and miferie, and hatefull to all the townfmen."

1591. On 30th Aug. the Corporation made orders that all the provifoes, conditions and articles contained in the new charter touching booths in Sturbridge Fair, fhould be inviolably kept and obferved in all points, according to the tenor, true intent and meaning of fuch charter: that it fhould not be lawful to any tenant or owner of any booth to admit or fuffer any merchants or artificers of fundry wares to ftand and fell wares in one booth: and that it fhould not be lawful to any merchants or others bringing wares to Sturbridge Fair to fell any wares, except falt, out of any veffels upon the water there, until the fifh booths were let to farm.

On 15th Sept. Richard Parifh of Chefterton " a very violent and turbulent perfon, attacked and wounded with a dagger fome fcholars who were with him in the ferry-boat between Chefterton and Sturbridge Fair. He was arrefted by a mafter of arts of Trinity College and others, but was refcoued from them by the prentifes in the faire." A new manifeftation of the " town and gown " troubles.

1592. On 28th Aug. the Corporation of Cambridge made orders that none but freemen fhould, in time of Sturbridge Fair, fell and deliver fifh in any hut or veffel on the water, until the fifh booths in the water-fair were let, and then to make compofition with the bailiff of the ward. And that all except freemen, who brought pitch and tar to the fair to be fold, fhould pay 2*s.* per laft for grinding to the bailiff of the ward ; and that if any fuit or controverfy at law fhould arife about executing the premifes, the charges fhould be borne by a levy to be affeffed upon the burgeffes.

1595. Memorandum, that this daye and yeare by a common confente, it is agreed, that the order made . . Feby anno Regni Hen. Octavi 13° concerninge enjoyers of booths to dwell within the towne ; and fhewinge in what time he fhall fell them yf he go out of the towne, fhall ftand, remaine and be in full force and effecte ; and that no maior of the towne of Cambridge from henceforthe fhall propounde any grace, or do any acte or actes,

devife or devifes whatfoever, to the breache or
violating thereof; and that the maior of this towne,
yearly to be chofen, on the daie of his election, or
on the daye that he taketh the oathe againft vintinge,
fhall make folemn oathe to the obfervation hereof.
" Hift. and Antiq. of Barnwell Abbey " (p. 96,
part ii.).

1596. 16th Aug. The Corporation made an
order that every burgefs who fhould thereafter buy
any booth or booth-ground in this fair fhould at the
time of his admiffion thereto, make folemn oath
before the mayor, that he had bought the fame
fimply to the ufe of himfelf and his heirs, and not
to the ufe of any foreigner or foreigners, without
fraud, collufion, or deceit.

CHAPTER XI.

THE SEVENTEENTH CENTURY.

1600.

N 16th Aug. the Corporation of Cambridge made ordinances that no bailiff
fhould " by any wayes, meanes, or
culler whatfoever demife or lett to
ferme his bayliwich within this Town or Fayers,
or eny profitts belonging to the fame, to eny per-
fone or perfones whatfoever, uppon payne of dis-
frannchifinge."

1601. New caufes of difpute arofe between the
Univerfity and the Town, this time about the
" King's beam " (*Pondus Regis*) or the right of the
former to a beam for weighing articles fold at the
Fair. The Queen (Elizabeth) wrote to the parties :

To our loving friends the Vicechancellor and
Proctors of the Univerfity of Cambridge and the
Mayor Bailiffs and Burgeffes of the Town :

Whereas there were at the laft Sturbridge fair
fome contentions about a pair of fcales ufed by you
of the Univerfity : We require you of the Town
in all peaceable fort, to fuffer the Univerfity to

exercife and ufe the fame in the accuftomed place
as they have ufually done for the moft of thefe ten
years laft paft ; and what contention foever fhall
feem to arife about the fame fcales, either for the
intereft of the ground whereon they are fettled, or
for the payment of any rent for the fame : We
think it fit and fo we require of you, that it be
peaceably reconciled hereafter in a lawful courfe,
without giving any occafion of diforders. And fo
we heartily bid you farewell. Aug. 27, 1601.

1603. The kingdom was threatened with another
vifitation of the plague. The new King (James I.)
iffued a Proclamation, dated from Hampton Court
8 Aug., whereby it was ordained that for " defire
of preventing an univerfal contagion among our
people " (*inter alia*) Stourbridge Fair fhould not
be held nor anything appertaining to it at the time
accuftomed, " nor any time till they [it] fhall have
been licenfed by us."

1604. On 23rd July this year the King iffued
the following mandate, prohibiting all idle games,
plays, or fhows in or within five miles of Cambridge;
and under its authority the regulations of the Fair
were confiderably modified :

James by the grace of God King of England
Scotland France and Ireland defender of the faith,
&c :

To our chancellor and vice-chancellor of our
univerfity of Cambridge in the County of Cambridge, and to all and fingular our juftices of peace
mayors fheriffs bailiffs conftables gaolers and all
other our minifters and officers within the faid

univerſity and the town of Cambridge and county aforeſaid and to every of them greeting,

For the better maintenance ſafety and quietneſs of that our ſaid univerſity and all and every the ſtudents there, and to remove take away and prevent all occaſions that may tend either to the infecting of their bodies or minds, or to the withdrawing or alienating the younger ſort from the courſes of their ſtudies there intended, we do by theſe preſents authorize will and command you our ſaid chancellor and vice-chancellor of our ſaid univerſity, and either of you and your ſucceſſors, that you do from time to time for ever hereafter by virtue hereof, wholly and altogether reſtraine inhibit and forbid as well all and all manner of unprofitable or idle games plays or exerciſes to be uſed or made within our ſaid univerſity and the town there, and within five miles compaſs of and from the ſaid univerſity and the town there, and within five miles compaſs of and from the ſaid univerſity and town, eſpecially bull-baiting, bear-baiting, common plays, publick ſhews, interludes, comedies and tragedies in the Engliſh tongue, games at loggets, nine-holes, and all other ſports and games whereby throngs concourſe or multitudes are drawn together, or whereby the younger ſort are or may be drawn or provoked to vain expence loſs of time or corruption of manners; as alſo all and all manner of perſons that ſhall go about to publiſh act ſet out or make any ſuch unprofitable or idle games publick plays or exerciſes within the ſaid univerſity or town or within five miles compafs of or from our faid univerfity or town, any indulgence, privilege, liberty or authority, by us granted or to be granted to any our officers or fervants, or to any other perfon or perfons whomfoever, to the contrary in any wife notwithftanding.

Provided that it is not our pleafure and meaning hereby to abridge the ftudents of their accuftomed exercifes in any kind whatfoever within their feveral colleges.

And if any perfon or perfons under colour pretence or virtue of any licence or authority by us or any other whomfoever granted or to be granted, or by any other means colour or pretence, fhall refift or refufe peaceably to obey your commands herein, then our will and pleafure is and we do hereby authorize you our faid chancellor and vice-chancellor of our faid univerfity, and either of you, and your fucceffors and deputy or deputies of you and either of you and your fucceffors, from time to time to apprehend all and every fuch offenders, and them to commit to prifon either in the caftle of Cambridge or any other goal within the town of Cambridge, there to remain without bail or mainprize until they fhall willingly fubmit themfelves to your faid commands and abide fuch further order as to you in your difcretions fhall be thought meet ; willing and by thefe prefents commanding all you our faid juftices of peace, mayors, fheriffs, bailiffs, conftables and gaolers, and all other our faid minifters and officers, that upon intimation and fhew of this our will and command herein, you and every of you being required thereto, fhall be aiding and affifting to our faid chancellor and vice-chancellor of our faid univerfity, and their fucceffors and their and either of their deputy or deputies from time to time in the due execution of the premifes according to the purport and true intent hereof, as you will anfwer to the contrary at your peril.

Given under our fignet at our palace of Weft-minfter, the three and twentieth day of July, in the fecond year of our reign of England France and Ireland and of Scotland the feven and thirtieth.

1606. In the records of the Skinners Company there is an item under this date " To the wardens for their allowance in riding to Stourbridge Fair £3 : 6 : 8 ; and 13*s.* 4*d.* to me the Recter Warden for my pains." But very foon after this period there are figns of a falling-off in the importance of the fair in this particular : In 1616 it is the accountant who receives " in allowance towards his charges in riding to Stourbridge Fair £6." The wardens had ceafed to attend perfonally.

1612. In the " Letters of Archbifhop Williams" (1866) is one dated from the Proctors' booth in the fair this year.

1613. In Dr. Nathan Drake's "Shakefpeare and his Times" it is recounted that at this date the fair had acquired fo great a celebrity that Hackney coaches attended it from London. Subfequently not lefs than fixty of thofe coaches plied the fair (fee 1688, &c.). He adds that vaft quantities of butter and cheefe found there a ready market; that it ſtocked the people in the counties of Norfolk, Suffolk, and Eſſex with clothes and all other neceſſaries; and that the ſhopkeepers ſupplied themſelves from hence with the commodities wherein they dealt.

1615. On the 22nd June the Corporation ordered that Mr. French the mayor ſhould have an irrevokable power of attorney under the Town Seal to proſecute with effeᴄt all the ſuits already begun againſt thoſe who *kept any fair or market to the prejudice of the town*, and to commence and proſecute ſuits againſt all who had done or ſhould do the like; and it was ordered that all charges ſhould be paid by the treaſurers on demand.

1620. On 17th Sept., there was held a ſeſſion of Goal Delivery in Sturbridge Fair, in the place where the courts there were uſually kept ("Annals of Camb." iii. p. 136). No explanation of the circumſtance is given.

1622. The ſuit concerning the right to ereᴄt booths in the yard of Sturbridge Chapel which had been pending for ſome time was this year terminated. The Corporation obtained a grant of the Chapel from the Queen.

1625. In conſequence of the Plague again being prevalent in the kingdom Charles I. by Royal Proclamation forbids the holding of this, as alſo Bartholomew's Fair, by reaſon of the uſual "extraordinary reſort out of all parts of the kingdom" of perſons to attend this fair, which would if held lead to the common danger. This proclamation is given *in extenſo* in our chapter on "Legiſlation."

1630. The plague exifting in Cambridge the holding of this, and alfo Bartholomew and Southwark Fairs, was prohibited by Royal Proclamation.

1633. A queftion arofe as to Dower, or the right to dower of the widows of booth-holders in this fair; and the Corporation on the 14th May enacted the following declaration :

The cuftom in fuch cafe is (and fo hath ever time out of mind been ufed) that the relict and widow of her hufband (who in his life was feifed of booths in Sturbridge fair) fhall have her dower of fuch booths only whereof her hufband was feifed and died inteftate. But where the hufband in his life time made fale of his booths or devifed them by his laft will and teftament, the wife and relict in fuch cafe fhall have no dower of any booths.

1636. The King (Charles I.) addreffed a letter to the Vice-chancellor of the Univerfity and the mayor of Cambridge (dated Hampton Court, June 14), fetting forth that the town had been often infected with the plague by means of perfons repairing to the fairs, with goods brought from infectious places, whereby the fcholars had been forced to forfake their ftudies and fcatter themfelves for fafety unto remote parts of the kingdom : to avoid the like mifchief from the contagion then raging in London and other places H. M. required the Vice-chancellor and Mayor to take order that Midfummer fair fhould not be kept this year, nor the goods of Londoners or others be fold within the town or three miles of the fame. Refractory perfons were to be bound to appear before the King or the Privy Council to anfwer the contempt, or on their refufal might be committed to prifon. All juftices of the peace of the county and town were commanded to be aiding and affifting.

In confequence of this letter it was feared that a fimilar order might be made as to Sturbridge Fair; and accordingly on Common Day, held 2nd Aug. fteps were taken by the townfmen in view of procuring this fair to be held. But the refult was the following letter dated 21 Aug.

To our truftie and wel beloved The maior & Aldermen of our Towne of Cambridge.

Charles R. Truftie and wel beloved we greete you well, whereas out of our royal care of our Univerfitie and Towne of Cambridge, and to prevent the encreafe and further fpreading of the plague within our Kingdome by fuch a publique concourfe of people as doth ufually refort to Sturbridge faire from all parts thereof, wee have thought fitt to forbid the keepinge of the faid faire for this yeare, and have accordingly given order for fignifyeing our royall pleafure therein by a Proclamacion, which requireing fome time for the folemne publicacion thereof; to ye end ye may not in the meane while proceede to proclaime and fett forth the precincts of the faid faire, as wee are informed that your cuftome is to doe on the 24th of this prefente moneth, Wee doe by thefe our Letters declare our faid purpofe to you of putting off the faid faire for this yeare. And in confequence thereof, Our will and pleafure is, That you now forbeare to make any fuch preparacion to the faid Faire or to doe any act whatfoever apperteyning thereunto, under paine of our royal difpleafure.

Given under our Signett at our Courte at the Caftle of Warwicke, the 21th day of Auguft, in the Twelfe yeare of our raigne 1636.

The Town Clerk, the Attorneys of the Town Court and other of the Corporation were ordered to attend at the fair-field to publifh his majefty's pleafure and command. This was accordingly done on 24th Aug., the letter being read at the ufual place of proclaiming the fair.

A proclamation prohibiting the fair was iffued; and although it bore date prior to the Royal letter was only received after it. The proclamation contained this paffage:

. . . And his majefty doth hereby further charge and command, under the like penalty, all Citizens and Inhabitants of his City of London, that none of them for this prefent year, fhall bring or fend any of their Goods or merchandize to *Ely, Newmarket,* or any other place near to the Univerfity of Cambridge, at or about the ufual time appointed for Sturbridge fair, which were but to transfer that fair to other places, with no lefs Danger of difperfing the Sicknefs throughout the Kingdom. Given at our Court at Warwick Caftle, the 20 day of Aug.

1637. The fair was alfo again prohibited on account of the prevalence of plague.

1638. Although the Plague prevailed this year alfo, it feems that the fair was held. On the 24th Aug. the Corporation impofed a rate of 1*s.* in the £ on the booth-holders for defraying the

charges of procuring the fair to be kept again—
" being otherwife in danger of being put by "; and
for endeavour of a like nature in the two preceding
years.

1644. A writer in the parliamentary intereſt referred to the " Goodly and full Fair " held at Sturbridge this year " with free trade and comforable commerce as was formerly accuſtomed in our former
moſt peaceable times."

1647. The Univerſity complained to the Houfe
of Lords againſt the bailiffs of the Corporation for
contempt of the order of the Houſe in favour of
the Univerſity in the matter of the " Stourbridge
fayer privileges."   The matter appears fomewhat
obſcure.

1649. This year an event occurred which had a
conſiderable though indirect bearing upon this fair.
The " Act for the Draining of the Great Level of
the Fens " was paſſed.   This led to conſiderable
alterations in the navigation between Lynn and
Cambridge.   The tide, which formerly flowed up
as far as Ely—bringing merchandiſe at eaſy charge
up to that point—did not, on the completion of
theſe works, come within twenty miles of that
place.   In 1653 the Univerſity and Corporation of
Cambridge juſtly petitioned Parliament on the ſubject (" Annals of Camb." iii. p. 455).   I believe no
redreſs was obtained.   There were obviouſly fome
counterbalancing advantages in leſſening the fre-
quency of floods, and in rendering better roads
poſſible.

1650. At a Common Day, held 24th Aug., the

Corporation, taking notice that of late years there had been controverſies about a preaching miniſter for Sturbridge Fair, agreed that the power of election being in the mayor and aldermen, ſuch preacher ſhould be elected yearly on the day of the election of mayor, bailiffs, and other officers. See 1710.

1654. About this time the Corporation of Cambridge erected a banqueting-room and court-houſe at Sturbridge fair. It was commonly called the Mayor's Houſe. At a later period (1670) ſome diſputes aroſe regarding this building being erected upon grounds ſubject to the right of commonage.

1655. When the office of " Lord of the Taps " was founded does not appear, but on the 20th Aug. this year the Corporation made the following order :—" It is agreed that xxˢ ſhall be given out of the moneys in the cheſt to Michael Wolfe towards the buyinge of a Coate againſt Sturbridge fayer now next enſuinge, he being Lord of the Taps this preſent yeare." The coat in queſtion was a crimſon one, gaily decorated with taps. The office of the Lord of the Taps was to taſte the ale in any or all the booths in the fair, and aſcertain if it were in ſuitable vendible condition. " Ned Ward " ſpeaks of this functionary (1700) as going " arm'd all over with ſpiggots and foſſets, like a porcupine with his quills, or looking rather like a fowl wrapped up in a pound of ſauſages."

1658. In " Worthington's Diary " there is an entry made at the Vice-chancellor's court at the fair. In Brathwaite's " Honeſt Ghoſt," publiſhed this year (p. 189), there occurs the following :—

> " When th' fair is done, I to the colledg come,
> Or elfe I drink with them at Trompington,
> Craving their more acquaintance with my heart,
> Till our next *Sturbridg faire ;* and fo we part."

Local events were affociated with the fair, as the moft prominent recurring incident in the diftrict, and dated by reference to it.

1660. Worthington fpeaks of this fair as " the Carpenter's harveft."

1665. The fair was again prohibited this year on account of the prevalence of the plague.

1666. The like by an order in Council " to prevent the fpread of the infection."

1668. Pepys received fo earneft an invitation from his kinfman, Roger Pepys, that he refolved to let his wife go to this fair. His entry, under date 15th Sept., is:—" Up by times . . . took wife and Mercer and Deb. and W. Horner (who are all to fet out this day for Cambridge, to cofen Roger Pepys to fee Sturbridge Fayre) . . . faw them gone, there being only one man in the coach befide them." He probably followed fome days after, or about the 29th; but unfortunately the diary is a blank up to 11th October. It would have been matter of fome intereft to know his views of this great gathering.

Edward Kemp preached a fermon at St. Mary's Church, Cambridge, on the Sunday before the fair, which was publifhed.

1673. In the Vice-chancellor's " Little Black Book " is given a copy of the following letter from Charles II. reftoring to the Univerfity the right of

weighing hops, which had been affumed by the
Town during the Civil War troubles :—

Charles R.   Trufty and well beloved we greet
you well.   Whereas wee are informed from our
Univerfity of Cambridge that feverall of their rights
and priviledges (which they have heretofore injoyed
by charter and cuftome) have in thefe late yeares of
publick diftraction been intrenched upon by our
towne of Cambridge, and fome of the officers thereto
belonging, particularly the right of fetting up the
fole publick beame for the weighing of hops and
other things of great bulk in Sturbridge faire, which
did anciently belong to the faid Univerfity and
their officers, and which as we are informed (befides
other evidences) appears by the acts of your courts
regiftred in the mayoralty of Mr Foxton.   Now
wee being defirous to keepe a good correfpondence
between our faid Univerfity and towne, and that
either body fhould enjoy their juft rights, have
thought fitt to requeft you to permitt our Univerfity and their officers (till you fhall fhew fufficient
caufe to the contrary) to enjoy without difturbance
the aforefaid right of fole weighing fuch hops as
fhall be fould at Sturbridge faire, together with all
other their antient priviledges.   And upon notice fhall
be carefull, that no intrenchment bee made upon
any of thofe rights which you may juftly claime.
Given under our fignet manuell at our court of
Whitehall the thirtieth day of Auguft in the twelfth
yeare of our reigne.   (Signed) William Morrice.

To our trufty and well beloved the mayor and
aldermen of the towne of Cambridge.

The original was delivered to Mr John Ewen, mayor, by me Matth. Whenn.

1677. The Corporation of Cambridge ordered the common feal to be affixed to a petition to the King for the prevention of a new fair at Maidftone, which might be prejudicial to Sturbridge Fair. This oppofition I affume had reference to the large trade in hops here tranfacted. (See hereon De Foe's account of this fair under date 1723.) There is this curious entry in the Corporation Common Day Book :—" It is agreed that Mr. Langley who took great paines in keeping of the Patent for the intended Faire at Maidftone fhall have two gynneys given him, to be paid by the Treafurers."

1683. Dixon, in his " Canidia, or the Witches," publifhed this year, fays :—

> " A fire licking a Child's hair
> Was to be feen at *Sturbridge fair*,
> With a lambent flame, all over a fweating mare."

And again :—

> " Women-dancers, Puppet-players,
> At Bartholomew and Sturbridge-Fairs."

1686. Mr. Millington, book auctioneer of London, fold in Cooks' Row in the fair this year (8th Sept.) the library of James Chamberlain, fellow of St. John's College (1700).

1688. On 10th September the Corporation made an order that the prices of hackney coachmen who drive from Cambridge to Sturbridge fair, or from that fair to Cambridge, from fun rifing to funfet, fhould be 12*d.* for one, two, three, or four perfons,

and after funfet 18*d*. for the like number of perfons.

1696. Mr. Morley in his " Memoir of Bartholomew Fair " (1859), writing of this period fays,
" The great fair near Cambridge—Stourbridge Fair
—was in the days of which we are now fpeaking, a
place of large commerce " (p. 351).

CHAPTER XII.

THE EIGHTEENTH CENTURY.

1700.

HERE was publifhed " A Step to Stir-bitch-fair, with remarks upon the Uni-verfity of Cambridge," by Edward Ward. Like all " Ned Ward's " books, it is written in a coarfe flangy ftyle; and I do not find anything throwing much light upon the fair, except in the matter of book auctions, of which his account is very amufing.

1701. The mayor and corporation having given a company of actors leave to perform at the fair without the fanction of the Vice-chancellor, and in defiance of his authority, the fenate, on the 4th Sept. paffed a grace enacting that the privileges of the Univerfity fhould be defended and vindicated at the public charge ; and in the meantime, to pre-vent a breach of difcipline the authority of proctors during the time of the fair was conferred on fixty-two Mafters of Arts, and it was decreed that whoever difobeyed them fhould *ipfo facto* incur the penalty of expulfion.

It feems that the Vice-chancellor (Dr. Bentley) committed Dogget the actor to gaol, and ordered the booth built for the theatre to be demolifhed.

1705. The London newfpapers of this year announced " That the fair would be proclaimed on the 7th Sept. with great folemnity by the Vice-chancellor of the Univerfity, the Mayor of the Town, accompanied by Lord Duplin and Mr. Cadogan, the reprefentatives in Parliament, the Recorder, Aldermen, &c., preceded by red-coats and other officers on horfeback, with mufic playing before them ; that it was expected there would be greater concourfe of people and a more flourifhing trade than had been known for feveral years paft, owing to the conduct of a fet of gentlemen who were endeavouring to revive the reputation of a fair not many years ago the moft confiderable in Europe." This announcement, which in great part contained nothing out of the common, it turned out was inferted at the inftance of a Londoner who was going to fee the fair for the firft time; and it had the effect of drawing together more people than had been feen there for ten years. The vifitor in queftion records in the " Gentleman's Magazine " that he regularly took coach every afternoon at the Market-hill (Cambridge) with other gownfmen, drinking tea at the Coffee-booth, " where now and then we had the company of fome very agreeable ladies of Cambridge town and education, and a fortnight was thus fpent."

1709. There was publifhed in London: " Nundinæ Sturbrigienfes," a poem in Latin hexameters, of some five hundred lines, by Th. Hill, Coll. Trin. Cant. Soc. It is included in vol. ii. " Musæ Anglicanæ," editio quinta. Londini, ex officina J. S. R. Tonfon and J. Watts, 1741. An * indicates that the poem in question was added to this edition, and not found in former ones. The poem gives a description of the fair as it existed in the reign of Queen Anne.

1710. The question of the preacherfhip of the fair referred to under date 1650, came up this year in ftrong force. The corporation had ufually appointed the minifter of Barnwell, but this year they appointed another, a fellow of King's College. Their right to the nomination was now difputed by the improprietor and minifter of Barnwell. The corporation refolved to maintain their nominee, and the oppofing parties advertifed their intention of ftanding on what they regarded as their rights. Proceedings were accordingly commenced in the Bifhop of Ely's court. The following year (Sept. 1711) the Vicar of Barnwell publifhed the following:—

Whereas 'tis the refolution of the corporation of Cambridge, againft the prefent incumbent of Barnwell, to fet up a preacher in Sturbridge Fair; being led thereinto by artificially perfuading fome of his predeceffors into an illegal note, againft the patron, his clerks and fucceffors in the faid living: and Sturbridge Fair being in the parifh of Little St. Andrew's, Barnwell, and the minifters thereof have (when right and law prevail) time out of mind, without any difturbance (the faid corporation of

Cambridge finding alwaies a pulpit) performed the
fervice of the two Lord's-days during the faid fair,
with their congregation, fervice-books, veftments,
pulpit ornaments, and parifh-clerk, in gratitude for
the collection that hath been there alwaies made,
for the better fupport of themfelves under their
fmall parochial income, till the laft year 1710; for
which intrufion, then, the unwary ufurper was cen-
fured in the Bifhop's ecclefiaftical court: Thefe do
humbly give notice to the gentlemen of the fair,
that the pulpit not being allowed this year as ufual,
and it not being known foon enough to provide
one, the fervice of the Lord's day, during this prefent fair, will be performed in the parifh-church,
morning and evening, by the minifter of Barnwell.

Will. Piers.

Mr. Piers appears to have carried his point, as
no mention of a Sturbridge fair preacher fubfequently to 1711 occurs in the Corporation books.
Dr. Hurd, Bifhop of Worcefter, was, whilft fellow
of Emmanuel, preacher at Sturbridge fair.

Preaching in the Fair.—The fervices were performed during the two Sundays occurring in the
principal period of the fair, both morning and afternoon. The fermon was preached from a pulpit
placed in the open air, in the centre of the large
fquare, fome 300 by 240 feet, called the *Duddery*,
where the woollen-drapers, wholefale tailors, and
fellers of fecond hand clothes took up their refidence, in fpacious booths. In the centre of this
fquare was formerly a tall maypole, with a vane

at the top. It was the moft orderly part of the
fair.

Ned Ward, in his book already referred to
(1700), mentions this part of the fair, and fays there
ftands "an old weather-beaten pulpit, where on Sunday a fermon is delivered for the edification of the
ftrolling finners, who give open attention, as in a
field-conventicle" (p. 242).

1718. On the 21ft Sept. died, aged 89, Samuel
Newton, one of the Aldermen of Cambridge. By
his will he gave to the town four booths in the
fair, and a fermon in his commemoration was for
many years preached at St. Edward's before the
mayor and corporation on the Sunday next preceding
the 22nd Sept.

1727. I do not know if there was any fpeciality
in the proceffion to proclaim the fair this year.
The following details are given in Cooper's "Annals
of Cambridge," under this date. The order was
thus: The Crier in fcarlet on horfeback; twenty-
eight petty Conftables on foot; three drums;
banners and ftreamers; the Grand Marfhal; two
trumpeters; the Town mufic (twelve in number),
two French horns; the Bellman in ftate with a
ftand, on horfeback; four Serjeants at Mace on
horfeback; the Town Clerk on horfeback. The
Mayor in his robes mounted on a horfe richly cap-
rifoned, led by two footmen called red coats with
white wands. The two reprefentatives in Parliament on horfeback. Twelve Aldermen according
to feniority on horfeback (three and three) in their
proper robes, the fix feniors having their horfes at-

tended by as many henchmen or red coats with wands. The twenty-four Common Councilmen, three and three according to feniority. Eight Difpenfers in their gowns, two and two; four Bailiffs in their habits (two and two). The Treafurers in their gowns. The Gentlemen and Tradefmen of the town.

The proceffion was followed by a great number of the boys of the town on horfeback, who as foon as the ceremony of proclaiming was over, rode races about the place; and on returning to Cambridge each boy had a cake and fome ale at the Townhall.

This proceffion was maintained until about 1758, when it began "to be abridged," owing as it is faid to the trouble and charge of keeping it in fuitable condition.

De Foe's Defcription of the Fair.—1723. This year the fair was vifited by Daniel De Foe, and he gives an account of it which I regard as of great value. He underftood how to grapple with what he faw, and how to record the refults of his inquiry. I give his defcription with very fmall curtailment. The account was not publifhed until 1724:

I now draw near to Cambridge, to which I fanfy I look as if I was afraid to come, having made fo many Circumlocutions beforehand; but I muft yet make another Digreffion before I enter the Town; (for in my way, and as I came in from Newmarket, about the beginning of September;) I cannot omit, that I came neceffarily through Sturbridge Fair, which was then in its height.

If it is a Diverſion worthy of a Book to treat of
Trifles, ſuch as the Gayety of Bury Fair, it cannot
be very unpleaſant, eſpecially to the Trading part
of the World, to ſay ſomething of this Fair, which
is not only the greateſt in the whole Nation, but in
the World; nor, if I may believe thoſe who have
ſeen them all, is the Fair at Leipſick in Saxony, the
Mart at Frankfort on the Main, or the Fairs at
Nuremberg or Auſburg, any way to compare to
this Fair at Sturbridge.

It is kept in a large Corn-field, near Caſterton,
extending from the ſide of the River Cam, towards
the Road, for about half a Mile Square.

If the Huſbandmen who rent the Land, do not
get their Corn off before a certain Day in Auguſt,
the Fair-Keepers may trample it under foot, and
ſpoil it, to build their Booths : On the other Hand,
to ballance that Severity, if the Fair-Keepers have
not done their Buſineſs of the Fair, and remov'd
and clear'd the field by another certain Day in September, the Plowmen may come in again, with Plow
and Cart, and overthrow all and trample it into the
Dirt ; and as for the Filth, Dung, Straw, &c, necef-
ſarily left by the Fair-Keepers, the Quantity of
which is very great, it is the Farmers Fees, and
makes them full amends for the trampling, riding,
and carting upon, and hardening the Ground.

It is impoſſible to deſcribe all the Parts and Cir-
cumſtances of this Fair exactly ; the Shops are
placed in Rows like Streets, whereof one is call'd
Cheapſide ; and here, as in ſeveral other Streets, are
all ſorts of Trades, who ſell by Retale, and who

come principally from London with their Goods; fcarce any trades are omitted, Goldfmiths, Toy-fhops, Braziers, Turners, Milleners, Haberdafhers, Hatters, Mercers, Drapers, Pewterers, China-Ware-houfes, Taverns, Brandy-Shops, and Eating-Houfes, innumerable, and all in Tents, and Booths, as above.

This great Street reaches from the Road, which as I faid goes from Cambridge to Newmarket, turn-ing fhort out of it to the Right towards the River, and holds in a Line near half a Mile quite down to the River-fide : In another Street parallel with the Road are like Rows of Booths, but larger, and more intermingled with Wholefale Dealers, and on one fide, paffing out of this laft Street to the Left Hand, is a formal great Square, form'd by the largeft Booths, built in that Form, and which they called the Duddery; whence the name is deriv'd, and what its Signification is, I could never yet learn, tho' I made all poffible fearch into it. [Duddery is evidently derived from the old word Dudde, fig-nifying cloth (" Promptorium Parvulorum," ed. Way, i. 134). Duds for clothes is ftill ufed as a cant word, and by the Scotch (Bailey's " Dic-tionary;" Gloffaries to Burns and Walter Scott).] The area of this Square is about 80 to 100 yards, where the Dealers have room before every Booth to take down, and open their Packs, and to bring in Waggons to load and unload.

This place is feparated, and Peculiar to the Whole-fale Dealers in the Woollen Manufacture. Here the Booths, or Tents are of a vaft Extent, have different apartments, and the Quantities of Goods they bring are fo Great, that the Infides of them look like another Blackwell Hall, being as vaft Ware-Houfes pil'd up with Goods to the Top.   In this Duddery, as I have been inform'd, there have been fold £100,000 worth of Woollen Manufactures in lefs than a Week's time, befides the prodigious Trade carry'd on here, by Wholefale Men, from London, and all Parts of England, who tranfact their Bufi-nefs wholly in their Pocket-Books, and meeting their Chapmen from all Parts, make up their Accounts, receive money chiefly in Bills, and take Orders :   Thefe they fay exceed by far the Sales of Goods actually brought to the Fair, and deliver'd in Kind; it being frequent for the London Wholefale Men to carry back orders from their Dealers for £10,000 worth of Goods a Man, and fome much more.   This efpecially refpects thofe People, who deal in heavy Goods, as Wholefale Grocers, Salters, Brafiers, Iron-Merchants, Wine-Merchants, and the like ; but does not exclude the Dealers in Woollen Manufactures, and efpecially in Mercery Goods of all forts, the Dealers in which generally manage their Bufinefs in this manner.

Here are Clothiers from Hallifax, Leeds, Wake-field and Huthersfield in Yorkfhire, and from Roch-dale, Bury, &c, in Lancafhire, with vaft Quantities of Yorkfhire Cloths, Kerfeyes, Penniftons, Cottons, &c., with all forts of Manchefter Ware, Fuftians, and things made of Cotton Wool; of which the Quantity is fo great, that they told me there were near a thoufand Horfe-Packs of fuch Goods from that

fide of the Country, and thefe took up a fide and a
half of the Duddery at leaft; alfo a part of a ftreet
of Booths were taken up with Upholfterer's Ware,
fuch as Tickings, Sackings, Kidderminfter Stuffs,
Blankets, Rugs, Quilts, &c.

In the Duddery I faw one Ware-houfe or Booth
with fix Apartments in it, all belonging to a Dealer
in Norwich Stuffs only, and who they faid had
there above £20,000 value in thofe Goods, and no
other.

Weftern Goods had their Share here alfo, and
feveral Booths were fill'd as full with Serges, Du-
Roys, Druggets, Shalloons, Cantaloons, Devonfhire
Kerfies, &c, from Exeter, Taunton, Briftol, and
other Parts Weft, and fome from London alfo.

But all this is ftill out done, at leaft in fhow, by
two Articles, which are the peculiars of this Fair,
and do not begin till the other part of the Fair,
that is to fay for the Woolen Manufacture begins
to draw to a Clofe; thefe are Wooll, and the Hops,
as for the Hops there is fcarce any Price fix'd for
Hops in England, till they know how they fell at
Sturbridge Fair; the Quantity that appears in the
Fair is indeed prodigious, and they, as it were,
poffefs a large Part of the Field on which the Fair
is kept, to themfelves; they are brought directly
from Chelmsford in Effex, from Canterbury and
Maidftone in Kent, and from Farnham in Surrey,
befides what are brought from London, the growth
of thofe, and other places.

Enquiring why this Fair fhould be thus, of all
other Places in England, the Center of that Trade;

and fo great a Quantity of fo Bulky a Commodity be carry'd thither fo far: I was anfwer'd by one thoroughly acquainted with that matter, thus: The Hops, faid he, for this part of England, grow principally in the two counties of Surrey and Kent, with an exception only of the town of Chelmsford in Effex, and there are very few planted anywhere elfe.

. . . . . I muft not omit here alfo to mention, that the River Grant, or Cam, which runs clofe by the N.W. fide of the Fair in its way from Cambridge to Ely, is Navigable, and that by this means, all heavy Goods are brought even to the Fair-Field, by Water Carriage from London, and other Parts, firft to the Port of Lynn, and then in Barges up the Oufe, from the Oufe into the Cam, and fo, as I fay to the very Edge of the Fair.

In like manner great Quantities of heavy Goods, and the Hops among the reft, are fent from the Fair to Lynn by Water, and fhipped there for the Humber, to Hull, York, &c, and for New Caftle upon Tyne, and by New Caftle, even to Scotland itfelf. Now as there is ftill no planting of Hops in the North, tho' a great Confumption, and the Confumption increafing Daily, this, fays my Friend, is one reafon why at Sturbridge Fair there is fo great a Demand for the Hops: He added, that befides this, there were very few Hops, if any worth naming, growing in all the Counties even on this fide Trent, which were above forty miles from London; thefe Counties depending on Sturbridge Fair for their fupply, fo the Counties of Suffolk,

Norfolk, Cambridge, Huntingdon, Northampton, Lincoln, Leicefter, Rutland, and even to Stafford, Warwick, and Worcefterfhire, bought moft if not all their Hops at Sturbridge Fair.

Thefe are the Reafons why fo great a Quantity of Hops are feen at this Fair, as that it is incredible, confidering too, how remote from this Fair the Growth of them is, as above.

This is likewife a teftimony of the prodigious Refort of the Trading people of all Parts of England to this Fair; the Quantity of Hops that have been fold at one of thefe Fairs is diverfley reported, and fome affirm it to be fo great, that I dare not copy after them; but without doubt it is a furprifing Account, efpecially in a cheap Year.

The next Article brought hither, is Wool, and this of feveral forts, but principally Fleece Wool, out of Lincolnfhire, where the longeft Staple is found; the fheep of thofe Countries being of the largeft Breed.

The Buyers of this Wool, are chiefly indeed the Manufacturers of Norfolk and Suffolk and Effex, and it is a prodigious Quantity they buy.

Here I faw what I have not obferv'd in any other county of England, namely, a Pocket of Wool.

This feems to be firft call'd fo in Mockery, this Pocket being fo big, that it loads a whole Waggon, and reaches beyond the moft extream Parts of it, hanging over both before and behind, and thefe ordinarily weigh a Ton or 25 Hundred weight of Wool, all in one Bag.

The Quantity of Wool only, which has been fold at this Place at one Fair, has been faid to amount to £50,000 or £60,000 in value, fome fay a great deal more.

By thefe Articles a Stranger may make fome guefs at the immenfe Trade carry'd on at this Place; what prodigious Quantities of Goods are bought and fold here, and what a confluence of People are feen here from all Parts of England.

I might go on here to fpeak of feveral other forts of Englifh Manufactures, which are brought hither to be fold; as all forts of wrought Iron, and Brafs-Ware from Birmingham; Edg'd Tools, Knives, &c, from Sheffield; Glafs-Wares and Stockings from Nottingham, and Leicefter; and an infinite Throng of other things of fmaller value, every Morning.

To attend this Fair, and the prodigious conflux of People which come to it, there are fometimes not lefs than fifty Hackney Coaches, which come from London, and ply Night and Morning to carry the People to and from Cambridge; for there the grofs of the People lodge; nay, which is ftill more ftrange, there are Wherries brought from London on Waggons to plye upon the little River Cam, and to row People up and down from the Town, and from the Fair as Occafion prefents.

It is not to be wondered at, if the Town of Cambridge cannot Receive or Entertain the Numbers of People that come to this Fair; not Cambridge only, but all the Towns round are full; nay, the very Barns, and Stables are turn'd into Inns, and made as fit as they can to Lodge the meaner Sort of People.

As for the People in the Fair, they all univerfally Eat Drink and Sleep in their Booths and Tents; and the faid Booths are fo intermingled with Taverns, Coffee-Houfes, Drinking-Houfes, Eating-Houfes, Cook-Shops, &c, and all in Tents too; and fo many Butchers, and Hagglers from all the Neighboring Counties come into the Fair every Morning with Beef, Mutton, Fowls, Butter, Bread, Cheefe, Eggs, and fuch things; and go with them from Tent to Tent, from Door to Door, that there's no want of any Provifions of any kind, either dref'd or undref'd.

In a Word, the Fair is like a well Fortify'd City, and there is the leaft Diforder and Confufion (I believe) that can be feen anywhere, with fo great a Concourfe of People.

Towards the latter End of the Fair, and when the great Hurry of Wholefale Bufinefs begins to be over, the Gentry come in, from all parts of the County round; and tho' they come for their diverfion; yet 'tis not a little Money, they lay out; which generally falls to the fhare of the Retailers, fuch as Toy-fhops, Goldfmiths, Brafiers, Ironmongers, Turners, Milleners, Mercers, &c, and fome loofe Coins, they referve for the Puppet Shows, Drolls, Rope-Dancers, and fuch-like, of which there is no want, though not confiderable like the reft : The laft Day of the Fair is the Horfe-Fair, where the whole is clofed with both Horfe and Foot-Races, to divert the meaner Sort of

People only, for nothing confiderable is offered of that Kind : Thus Ends the whole Fair, and in lefs than a week more, there is fcarce any fign left that there has been fuch a thing there. . . . . .

I fhould have mention'd, that here is a Court of Juftice always open, and held every Day in a Shed built on purpofe in the Fair ; this is for keeping the Peace, and deciding Controverfies in matters Deriving from the Bufinefs of the Fair : The Magiftrates of the Town of Cambridge are Judges in this Court, as being in their Jurifdiction, or they are holding it by Special Priviledge : Here they determine Matters in a Summary way, as is practif'd in thofe we call Pye-Powder Courts in other Places, or as a Court of Confcience ; and they have a final Authority without Appeal.

1729. This year was paffed " An Order for the Regiftering and Regulating the Prices of Hackney Coaches at Sturbridge Fair," which was quite a formidable document.   I give one paragraph only : . . . And whereas in purfuance and by virtue of fuch immemorial prefcription ufage and Charters the faid mayor bailiffs and burgeffes have from time to time taken on themfelves the regulation of Hackney Coaches coming to the faid fair ; and did heretofore take a toll of 5*s.* from each coach coming to the faid fair, which of late years they have omitted to receive in confideration of the great expenfes of fuch hackney coachmen coming to the faid fair ; and did order appoint and eftablifh the prices to be taken by all coachmen coming to the faid fair and there tendering themfelves to carry paſſengers and perſons from the town of Cambridge to the ſaid fair, and from the ſaid fair to the town of Cambridge, at the price or ſum of 3*d*. . .

The price (after many more recitals) was fixed at 6*d*.

1733. There was a diſpute between the Univerſity and the Corporation as to the right to weigh hops in the fair, as indeed there had been for ſeveral previous years. The matter was referred to the Commiſſary of the Univerſity and the Recorder of the Town, who decided in favour of the Univerſity. A paper on the ſubject was drawn up and publiſhed by Thomas Johnſon of Magdalen College, one of the taxors.

1738. The Univerſity publiſhed a ſevere edict againſt ſchiſmatical congregations at Stourbridge fair, and appointed Pro-proctors to ſee it executed. Theſe meaſures were occaſioned by the fear that the famous John Henley would erect an oratory in the fair. He had applied to the Vice-chancellor for leave to hold an oratory there and had been refuſed.

1741. A great gale this year blew down many of the booths at the fair, and cauſed great inconvenience and ſome damage.

1747. On 29th June the Court of Common Pleas gave judgment in an action of treſpaſs brought by James Auſtin againſt King Whittred for ſeizing his cheeſe, &c., at this fair in 1745; which treſpaſs the defendant juſtified by way of diſtreſs damage feaſant made by him as ſervant to the Cor-

poration, the owners of the fair. The court held
the plea bad in fubftance, as *every perfon had of
common right a liberty of carrying his goods to a
public fair for fale.*—" Willes Reports," 623.

1748. A company of players from the theatres
in London performed a pantomime called "Harle-
quin's Frolics or Jack Spaniard caught in a Trap," in
Huffey's Great Theatrical Booth. There were alfo
fome entertainments of finging and dancing. It
was believed thefe were permitted in honour of the
approaching peace. But in the following year there
were alfo companies of players prefent.—" Annals,"
iv. p. 262, note.

1749. The Land Tax affeffed on the fair this
year amounted to £112 7s. 10d.

Carter the Hiftorian of Cambridge publifhed an
account of the fair this year. I fhall only quote
from it fuch points as have not been mentioned by
De Foe and others. He refers to the name of the
fair being obvioufly derived from the rivulet called
the Stour, which has a bridge over it near the fite
of the fair.

" During the fair Colchefter oyfters (natives) and
white herrings, juft coming into feafon are in great
requeft, at leaft by fuch as live in the inland part of
the kingdom." . . . "The fair is like a well governed
city. . . . If any difpute arife between buyer and
feller &c, on calling out ' Red-coat' you have in-
ftantly one or more come running to you; and if
the difpute is not quickly decided, the offender is
carried to the faid Court [of the fair] where the cafe
is determined in a fummary way. . . ."

1757. Poſtlethwayt in his "Dictionary of Trade and Commerce," 2nd edition, ſpeaks of the fair as "beyond all compariſon the greateſt in Britain, and perhaps in the world"—as it certainly was at this time.

1759. The Corporation ordered the collector of the tolls to provide weights and ſcales for weighing hops and other goods at the fair, and agreed to indemnify him againſt any ſuit in relation to the weighing of ſuch goods.

Peculiar cuſtom of the Fair.—1762. At this fair about this date, there was in practice the cuſtom of "Initiation" or "Chriſtening." It took place uſually on the evening of the horſe-fair day—perhaps becauſe there was a ſpecies of horſe-play about the performance, at the "Robin Hood" inn, famous in the annals of the fair. The formula was as follows :—The freſhman was introduced to the elder members in the parlour of the inn, and two ſponſors being previouſly choſen for him, he was placed in an armchair, his head uncovered, and his ſhoes off. Two vergers, holding ſtaves and lighted candles, aſſiſted the officiator, who was robed in a Cantab's gown and cap, with a bell in one hand and a book in the other. He commenced the ceremony by aſking "Is this an Infidel?" Anſwer, "Yes." "What does he require?" Anſwer, "Inſtruction (or to be inſtructed)." "Where are the ſponſors? let them ſtand forward!" A bowl of punch or a bottle of wine was placed on the table handy for the officiator, who then chaunted the following doggrel :—

> Over thy head I ring this bell,
> Becaufe thou art an infidel,
> And I know thee by thy fmell— [1]
> > *Chorus.* With a hoccius proxius mandamus,
> > Let no vengeance light on him,
> > And fo call upon him.

With feveral verfes more of the fame fort.

Then the officiator turned round and inquired " Who names this child ? " The fponfors replied " We do," and then they called the novitiate by fome flang name, as " Nimble-heels," " Stupid Stephen," " Tommy Simper," or other ludicrous defignation. The officiator then drank and gave the novice a full bumper, continuing the chaunt :—

> " Nimble-heels " henceforward fhall be his name,
> Which to confefs let him not feel fhame
> Whether 'fore mafter, mifs, or dame—

And then the chorus as before. Then,—

> This child firft having paid his dues,
> Is welcome then to put on his fhoes,
> And fing a fong, or tell a merry tale—
> > As he may choofe.

Chorus and conviviality ending up by a formal fupper. If feveral novices were offered together, one ceremony fufficed, with a few neceffary verbal alterations.

1771. In a letter of the Rev. Michael Tyfon,

---

[1] In the days of flavery in the United States of America, there was in frequent ufe the following couplet :

> " The Lord him knows the nigger well,
> He knows the nigger by *the fmell,*" &c.

dated *Corpus Chriſti College, Cambridge,* Sept. 12th, this year, occurs the following paſſage :—" There is an old and curious plan of Sturbridge Fair in the mayor's booth, taken when it was in its ſplendour, when its ſtreet and ſquare extended all over thoſe fields by Barmwell. I mean to make a copy of this, and to draw up an *Hiſtoriola* of the Fair; but this is too local to be of any entertainment but to thoſe connected with Cambridge. Thank Heaven my Deanſhip ends on Michaelmas day. . ." —Nichols' " Literary Anecdotes," viii. 569.

1778. Violent ſtorm during the fair ; Bailey's large muſic booth blown down and many others injured.

1783. At the Quarter Seſſions of Cambridge held July this year the following order was made :

" Whereas ſome diſputes have ariſen, touching the Intercommon of Stirbridge Fair Green, between the Commoners of Cambridge, and thoſe of Barnwell within the ſaid Town, and a ſuit hath been inſtituted in order to try the right of the ſaid Common : It is this day agreed and ordered, that the Coſts of ſuch ſuit on the part of the ſaid town of Cambridge, touching the ſaid intercommon, be paid and borne by the ſaid town ; and that the Town Clerk be deſired to proſecute the ſaid ſuit, to aſſert the right of the inhabitants of the ſaid town to the ſaid Common.

It is recorded that ſome of the ſcenes at the fair about this date were of a reprehenſible character, and tradition eſpecially points to a booth raiſed by Charles Day, the character of one of whoſe patrons is sketched with a free hand in "Nichols' Literary Anecdotes," viii. p. 540.

1786. There was published "The History and Antiquities of Barnwell Abbey, and of Sturbridge Fair" (being a reprint of "Bibliotheca Topographica Britannica," No. xxxviii.), from which I have drawn some of the preceding details.

1789. An interesting and amusing account of the fair as it appeared in 1789—reign of George III.—is given in "Reminiscences of Cambridge," by Henry Gunning, formerly an Esquire Bedell, vol. i., pp. 149-158, second edition, London, 1855.

CHAPTER XIII.

THE NINETEENTH CENTURY.

1802.

URING the performance at the theatre in the fair, 27th Sept., a cry of "fire" arofe in different parts of the houfe, which was greatly crowded. Although the manager and performers affured the audience that the alarm was without foundation, and tried every perfuafion to obtain order, a general rufh took place. Some threw themfelves over from the upper boxes into the pit; others were trampled upon and bruifed on the ftairs. In the end three girls and a boy were taken up dead, and many others were more or lefs ferioufly injured. It was fuppofed the cry was got up for the purpofes of robbery; one hundred guineas reward was offered for the offenders, but they efcaped detection.

1827. In Hone's "Year Book" is given a graphic account of this fair as it had exifted within the memory of the writer, whofe "perfonal recollections of more than fixty years ago," are embodied therein; from which I condenſe the following, as giving a view of its later, but not laſt ſtage:

The firſt booths, on the north ſide of the road were occupied by the cuſtomary ſhows of wild beaſts and wild men, conjurors, tumblers and rope-dancers. Mr. Baker's company of "comedians" was reſpectable; and Lewy Owen the clown, a young man of good family, who had abandoned himſelf to this way of life, full of eccentric wit and grimace, continually excited broad grins. The late Mrs. Inchbald was a performer at this fair. There was a large theatrical booth, occupied by a reſpect-able company of comedians from Norwich, under the management of Mr. Bailey, formerly a merchant of London. He was a portly good-looking man, of gentlemanly manners and addreſs, the compiler of the Directory bearing his name—a work of much merit, containing beſides the names of reſidents in the ſeveral towns, conciſe yet correct topogra-phical deſcription of the places : the book has now become very ſcarce. Other ſhow booths, occupied by giants and dwarfs, ſavage beaſts and other ſavages, extended with ſtunning din along this noiſy line. In front of theſe were the fruit and ginger-bread ſtalls. . . . On the ſouth ſide of the road oppoſite to theſe booths was the cheeſe fair. Dealers from various parts took their ſtands there, and many tons weight were diſpoſed of. Such as were fit for the London market were bought by the cheeſe factors from thence; and cheeſe from Cheſhire, Wilts, and Gloſter by the gentry and farmers and dealers from Suffolk, Norfolk, and adjoining counties; large quantities of Cottenham and cream cheefes being brought by farmers from thofe counties for fale. Oppofite to the eaft end of the cheefe fair, on the north fide of the road ftands an ancient chapel or oratory, no doubt erected for the devout dealers and others reforting to this fair, and for fuch pious travellers as paffed or repaffed the ferry to Chefterton [various references have been made to it; ftill ftanding, 1882]. At and nigh to this fpot were the wool-fair and the hop-fair. Large ftores of fack-cloths, waggon-tilts, and fuch like were near the fkin, leather fellers' and glovers' row, where the finer articles of leather and leather gloves were fold. Little edifices of general convenience were numerous.

At the end of the fhow-booths and facing the row began the principal range of booths, called Garlick-row. This range of fhops was well conftructed. Each booth confifted of two rooms; the back room feparated from the fhop by a boarded partition served for a bed chamber and other domeftic purpofes, from which a door opened into a field. A range of booths was generally appropriated to furniture fellers, ironmongers, filverfmiths, jewellers, japanners and fine cutlery dealers. Another range to filk-mercers, dealers in muflin, toys and millinery. Yet another to dealers in Norwich and Yorkfhire manufactures, mercery, lace, hofe, fine made fhoes, boots, clogs and patterns (*fic*). While dealers in fafhionable wares from London, as furs, fans, toys, &c. occupied a diftinct group. A further group was devoted to oilmen, dealers in pickles, and preferves,

one of whom—Mr. Green from Limehoufe—kept a
moft important ftore here.   His returns were from
£1,500 to £2,000 during the fair.   The father of
the writer from whom I am quoting " kept the
fair " for forty years and upwards, "and ufually
brought home £1,000 or more for goods fold and
paid for, befides felling to half that amount on
credit to reputable dealers and farmers.   At the
end of this row ftood the dealers in glafs-ware, look-
ing-glaffes and fmall articles of mahogany furniture.
The Inn—the King's Arms, I believe—was the
common refort of the horfe-dealers.   Here fat the
Pied-poudre court, having a pair of ftocks and a
whipping-poft in front, and a ftrong room under-
neath.   Clofe adjoining northward was the oyfter
fair.   The oyfters brought from Lynn were very
large, about the fize of a horfe's hoof, and were
opened with pincers ; the more delicate from Colchefter and Whitftable were very fmall.   In the
meadow adjoining were the coal fair, pottery fair
and Staffordfhire dealers.   The greater part of thefe
articles were delivered from on board veffels which
drew up clofe to the bank of the river.

Oppofite to the oyfter fair was a clofe wherein
the horfe fair was kept.   The fhow of beautiful
animals in that place was perhaps unrivalled, unlefs in Yorkfhire.   The fineft racers and hunters
from Yorkfhire, the moft brawny and mufcular
draught horfes from Suffolk, and from every other
country famous for breeding horfes animated the
fcene.   This horfe fair drew together a great concourfe of gentry, farmers and dealers from all parts

of the neighbouring counties, and fcores of valuable animals changed mafters in the fpace of a few
hours. The horfe fair was held on the firft Friday
after the fair was proclaimed.

Higher up, and about fifty yards from the road
was Ironmongers' row, with booths occupied by
manufactures from Sheffield, Birmingham, Wolver-
hampton, and other parts; and dealers in agricultural tools, nails, hatchets, faws, and fuch like
implements. About twenty yards nearer the road
were woollen drapers; and further on, and oppofite
to Garlick-row weftward, were booths for flop fellers,
and dealers in haubergs, or waggoners' frocks,
jackets, half-boots, and fuch like habiliments for
robuft ploughmen and farm labourers. Then followed the hatters' row, clofe to which was a very
refpectable coffee-houfe and tavern, fitted up with
neat tables covered with green baize, having glazed
fafh-windows and a boarded floor, kept by the pro-
prietor of Dochrell's coffee-houfe in Cambridge,
famed for excellent milk punch. There were alfo
a number of futtling booths where plain and fub-
ftantial dinners were ferved up in a neat com-
fortable ftyle, well cooked and moderately charged,
" except on the horfe fair and Michaelmas days,
when an extra fixpence was generally tackt to the
tail of the goofe."

Shoemaker row was at the end of Garlick-row
and confifted of ten or twelve booths. The bafket
fair, Tunbridge ware fair, and broom fair, were
behind nearly at the top. In the bafket fair were
to be had all kinds of hampers, bafkets and bafket

work; hay rakes, scythe-hafts, pitchfork and spade-handles, and other implements of husbandry, waggon loads of which were piled up there. In the Tunbridge ware section were malt, shovels, churns, cheese-presses and other wooden ware.

The circuit of the fair at the period to which this account relates was estimated at three miles. A list of many of the principal London dealers who attended this fair is appended to this account. Vide Hone's "Year Book," 1841 ed. col. 1539-48. A rough plan or chart of the fair is there given.

1828. The formal opening of the fair is described in Wall-Gunning, "The ceremonies observed in the senate-house of the University of Cambridge." Camb. pp. 129-31.

1842. The practice—the origin of which I have not been able to trace—of the Proctors of the University giving entertainments at the Midsummer and Sturbridge fairs was this year discontinued by a Grace passed 2nd July.

1855. The University, for the last time, "called the fair" on 18th Sept. this year. The following form was used on the occasion—very much modified from that of 1548.

Proclamation of the Fair, by the University.—Oyez! Oyez! Oyez! All persons are desired to keep silence while Proclamation of this Fair is being made.

His Royal Highness Prince Albert, Chancellor of this University Doth in the name of our Sovereign Lady Queen Victoria strictly charge and command:

That all perſons who ſhall repair to this Fair or the precinᘐts thereof Do keep Her Majeſty's peace, and make no affrays or outcries whereby any gathering together of people be made, nor that they wear any weapons upon pain of impriſonment and loſs of their weapons and further correᘐtion as ſhall be thought fit by the Officers of the ſaid Univerſity.

That all unhoneſt women, all vagrant and unruly perſons avoid and withdraw themſelves from this Fair and the precinᘐts thereof immediately after this proclamation, that Her Majeſty's Subjeᘐts may be quieter, aad good rule the better maintained upon pain of impriſonment and further correᘐtion at the diſcretion of the Officers of this Univerſity.

That all Bakers baking bread to ſell at this Fair or the precinᘐts of the ſame Do bake and ſell good and wholeſome bread, and of ſuch goodneſs as the law doth require, upon pain of the Statute in that behalf provided. [Bale ("Declaration of Bonner's Articles," fo. 21 b, about 1550), mentions the Baker-Boyes crye, as he ſat between his Bread-Panners at the fair, "Buy and beare away; ſteal and runne awaye," &c.]

That all perſons who ſell Ale or Beer within this Fair or the precinᘐts of the ſame Do ſell by no other meaſures than by Gallon, Pottle, Quart, Pint, and half-pint, ſized and ſealed according to the Standard of this Univerſity upon pain and penalty of the Statute in that behalf provided, and that every ſuch Viᘐtualler and ſeller of Ale and Beer have a ſign at his door upon pain of Three Shillings and four pence.

That all perfons who fell by weights and meafures any kinds of Victuals, Wares, or Merchandize, that their weights and their meafures be fized and fealed, and be in all refpects according to the Standard of this Univerfity upon pain of the Statute in that behalf provided.

That all Vintners do fell good and wholefome wines without mixing or impofition, and that their wine Pots be fized and fealed according to the Standard of this Univerfity upon pain of three fhillings and four pence for every offence.

That no perfons in this Fair Do fuffer, keep or maintain any unlawful gaming in their houfes or grounds, upon pain of the Statute in that behalf provided.

That no perfon receive into his houfe or booth any perfon of ill life and converfation or fufpected of the fame, upon pain of imprifonment and further correction as fhall be thought fit by the Officers of this Univerfity.

That no perfon whatfoever fell or offer to put to fale any kind of wares upon the Sunday upon pain of imprifonment and further punifhment by law provided : And that no perfon upon the faid day, efpecially in the time of fervice or fermon, receive any perfons into their houfes or booths, and there fuffer them to remain idle or drinking upon fuch pain and penalty as fhall be inflicted upon them by the officers of this Univerfity.

If there be any that will fue for any wares, Debts, Injuries or Trefpaffes, or think themfelves wronged in any of the premifes, let them make complaint to the Chancellor's Commiffary of this Univerfity who will hold and keep Court at the Great Tiled Booth on   next, the inftant at   o'clock to the intent that Juftice may be adminftered according to the Charters and and Privileges of this Univerfity.

God fave the Queen.

[Copied from the book of Formulæ in the Univerfity Regiftry.

ALFRED ROGERS,
April 28, 1882.]

1882. The fair ftill lingers on. Its commercial greatnefs has long fince paffed away—ebbed out of exiftence by flow degrees, refulting from many focial and other changes, rather than from any one marked caufe. But, as may be expected after fix and a half centuries (at leaft) of notable exiftence, it dies hard. Three of its features ftill remain. The horfe fair, always famous, was this year greater than for fome time paft. The onion fair is ftill affociated with Garlick row, while hurdles, gates, and implements of wood are ftill prominent. Thus traditions cling. In " Æfop Dreff'd "—a rare collection of fables by J. Mandeville (4to. 1704, p. 9; fhould be 33), there appeared the following :

" An afs of ftupid memory
Confef'd, that going to *Stourbridge Fair*,
His back moft brok with wooden ware."

The old affociations are, however, rapidly crumbling away.

The fair is ftill proclaimed by the mayor at the old time of commencing; but the fair is not now held until a fortnight later and only lafts three days. There are points in the Proclamation worthy of note.

Proclamation of Sturbridge Fair by the Mayor of Cambridge.—Oyez! Oyez! Oyez! Mr. Mayor doth ftrictly charge and command all manner of perfons to keep filence whilft the Fair of Sturbridge is publicly proclaimed. God fave the Queen.

Oyez! Oyez! Oyez! Our moft Gracious Sovereign Lady Victoria by the Grace of God of the United Kingdom of Great Britain and Ireland Queen Defender of the faith by Mr. Mayor of the Borough of Cambridge Her Majefty's Lieutenant of the faid Borough one of Her Majefty's Juftices of the Peace for the Borough and County of Cambridge and chief Governor of this Fair Doth ftrictly charge and command that all Merchants and other perfons that be repaired or fhall or will repair to this Fair of Sturbridge beginning on the feaft of St. Bartholomew the Apoftle (old ftyle) and continuing until the fourteenth day next after the feaft of the exaltation of the Holy Crofs (old ftyle) do keep Her Majefty's Peace.

That all idle and evil difpofed perfons within this Fair depart the fame forthwith.

That no Merchant put to fale or offer to fell any wares or merchandize but in the ufual and accuftomed places for their feveral wares and merchandizes appointed.

That Victuallers Tiplers and other perfons buy

no goods or merchandize of any wayfaring man or other perfon who fhall bring the fame to their booths or houfes to fell but only of fuch as fhall be known unto them to be of honeft converfation whom they fhall be always able to have forthcoming upon demand.

That all Merchants and other perfons within this fair ceafe from fhewing or felling any wares or merchandizes and from all labour and travel on the Lord's day.

And laftly Mr. Mayor giveth to underftand that if any Merchant or other perfon will fue or complain touching any caufe or matter done and committed within this Fair or the liberties thereof and here determinable let him repair to the place accuftomed and there according to the law of the land the fame caufe or matter fhall be heard and determined. God fave the Queen.

CHAPTER XIV.

CONCLUSION.

HILE the prefentation of the preceding details has been effential to the
plan of this work, I defire, by way of
appropriate conclufion, to eftimate the
influence of the fair upon the development of
commerce in England, and, in fome degree, alfo in
Europe.   I find a moft comprehenfive review of
this character from the mafterly pen of Prof. James
E. Thorold Rogers, M.A., in his great work, the
" Hiftory of Agriculture and Prices in England "
(1866, vol. i. pp. 142-4).

After pointing out that the port of Lynn, with
the rivers Oufe, and Cam, were the means by which
water-carriage was made available for goods—an
important point ; indeed it may be regarded as certain that in the middle ages and later, no great fair
could be held far removed from water communication—he proceeds :

The concourfe muft have been a fingular medley.
Befides the people who poured forth from the great
towns—from London, Norwich, Colchefter, Oxford,

places in the beginning of the fourteenth century of great comparative importance, and who gave their names, or, in cafe certain branches of commerce had been planted in particular London ftreets, the names of fuch ftreets, to the rows of booths in the three-weeks' fair of Stourbridge—there were, beyond doubt, the reprefentatives of many nations collected together to this great mart of medieval commerce. The Jew, expelled from England, had given place to the Lombard exchanger. The Venetian and Genoefe merchant came with his precious ftock of Eaftern produce, his Italian filks and velvets, his ftore of delicate glafs. The Flemifh weaver was prefent with his linens of Liege and Ghent. The Spaniard came with his ftock of iron, the Norwegian with his tar and pitch. The Gafcon vine-grower was ready to trade in the produce of his vineyard ; and, more rarely, the richer growths of Spain, and, ftill more rarely, the vintages of Greece were alfo fupplied. The Hanfe towns fent furs and amber, and probably were the channel by which the precious ftones of the Eaft were fupplied through the markets of Mofcow and Novgorod. And perhaps by fome of thofe unknown courfes, the hiftory of which is loft, fave by the relics which have occafionally been difcovered, the porcelain of the fartheft Eaft might have been feen in fome of the booths.

Blakeney, and Colchefter, and Lynn, and perhaps Norwich, were filled with foreign veffels, and bufy with the tranfit of various produce ; and Eaftern England grew rich under this confluence of trade.　How keen muſt have been the intereſt with which the franklin and bailiff, the one trading on his own account, the other entruſted with his maſter's produce, witneſſed the ſcene, talked of the wonderful world about them, and diſcuſſed the politics of Europe!

To this great fair came, on the other hand, the woolpacks, which then formed the riches of England and were the envy of outer nations.　The Corniſh tin-mine ſent its produce, ſtamped with the ſign of the rich earl who bought the throne of the German Empire, or of the warlike prince who had won his ſpurs at Crecy, and captured the French king at Poitiers.　Thither came alſo ſalt from the ſprings of Worceſterſhire, as well as that which had been gathered under the ſummer ſun from the ſalterns of the eaſtern coaſt.　Here, too, might be found lead from the mines in Derbyſhire, and iron, either raw or manufactured, from the Suſſex forges. And beſides theſe, there were great ſtores of thoſe kinds of agricultural produce which, even under the imperfect cultivation of the time, were gathered in greater ſecurity, and therefore in greater plenty, than in any other part of the world, except Flanders.

To regulate the currency, to ſecure the country againſt the loſs of ſpecie, and more harmleſſly to prevent the importation of ſpurious or debaſed coin, the officers of the king's exchange examined into the mercantile tranſactions of the foreign traders. To form a ready remedy againſt fraud, the mayor ſat at his court " of the duſty feet; " a mixed multitude were engaged in sale or purchase; the nobles securing such articles of luxury as were offered them, or which law and custom assigned to their rank— their rich robes of peace, their armour from Milan, their war horses from Spain. The franklin came for materials for his farm, and furniture for his house; sometimes even to buy rams in order to improve the breed of his flock. The bailiffs of college and monastery were busy in the purchase of clothing. And on holidays and Sundays, some canon, deputed from the neighbouring priory, said mass and preached in the booth assigned for religious worship.

This is certainly a not over-coloured picture of the past of this once mighty fair. Mr. Cunningham, in his most excellent work, "The Growth of English Industry and Commerce" (1882, Cambridge University Press, p. 164), says:—"By far the greater part of the commerce of this country was carried on at such fairs; and *Sturbridge* Fair was one of the most important in the whole kingdom, rivalling it was said the great fair of Nijni Novgorod, as a gathering of world-wide fame." And he adds by way of note:—"In the eighteenth century it continued to be a most important mart for all sorts of manufactured goods, as well as for horses, wool, and hops."

BARTHOLOMEW FAIR.

CHAPTER XV.

ORIGIN.

HIS is I believe the only fair, or certainly the only one of any note, ever
held within the walls of the City of
London.   Southwark Fair became
vefted in the Corporation in the fifteenth century.
I do not propofe to write anything more than an
outline hiftory of Bartholomew Fair. Mr. Morley's
moft interefting " Memoir of Bartholomew Fair "
(1859) is available to thofe who defire more minute
details.   But as an inftitution which exifted for
feven hundred years, and more or lefs illuftrates the
focial hiftory of the metropolis, and in fome fort
its trading cuftoms, during a confiderable portion
of that period, it cannot be paffed over lightly.   I
fhall adopt a chronological mode of illuftration as,
on the whole, beft fuited to the end in view.

Founding the Priory of Bartholomew, A.D. 1102.
—In the reign of Henry I., the Priory, Hofpital and

Church of St. Bartholomew, in Smithfield, were
founded by one Rahere, a minftrel of the king, and
" a pleafant witted gentleman." It feems that
Rahere was determined to this pious work in a fit
of ficknefs, during a pilgrimage he made to Rome
agreeably to the fafhion of the times, when St. Bartholomew appeared to him, and required him td under-
take the work and perform it in Smithfield. Before
that time Smithfield, or the greater part of it, was called
" the Elms," becaufe it was covered with elm trees.
FitzStephen fays the name of Smithfield is merely a
corruption of "Smooth field," or plain, which har-
monizes with the faft that the ground was ufed at
an early period for tilting matches or tournaments,
which were provided for the amufement of the
citizens, who then confifted of moft of the noble
families of the land, and who daily took their active
exercife here. Thefe "joufts" or entertainments
were carried out with great fplendour.

This monk Rahere, the founder of the Priory,
&c., has been termed the king's jefter, or court
fool. The Cotton MS. records in its quaint language and fpelling that Rahere " ofte hawnted the
Kyng's palice, and amo'ge the noyfefull preffe of
that tumultuous courte, enforfed himfelf with jolite
and carnal fuavite: ther yn fpectaclis, yn metys, yn
playes, and other courtely mokkys, and trifyllis in-
trudying, he lede forth the befyneffe of alle the
day." There always exifted at the court in thefe
early times fome one employed as ftory-teller and
companion in the king's amufements; and it feems
not to be doubted that Rahere occupied this pofition

—turning his opportunities of patronage to good account (as others occupying a like office have done) for the benefit of his fellow citizens. His memory is ftill perpetuated by the Affociation of " Rahere Almoners," who meet at ftated periods in the famed hiftorical precincts of Smithfield.

Rahere became the firft Prior of the monaftery he had thus founded, and feems to have eftablifhed a fair almoft fimultaneoufly, as was indeed the cuftom of the age. There appears to have exifted here, even at this early period, a periodical gathering known as the " King's Market," which Mr. Morley confiders may have been held amongft the trees, while the Priory was built upon the marfh or fmooth-field, around which the fair was held. The Prior is faid—either in confequence of his zeal for the monaftery, or from the old affociations of his former profeffion—to have gone annually into the fair, and exhibited his fkill as a juggler : giving the largeffes he fo received from the fpectators to the treafury of the monaftery.—*Froft*, p. 9.

Rahere alfo became Lord of the Fair, and his reprefentative prefided as judge in the Court of Piepowder attached to the fair. This court was held within the Priory gates. This at all events was the cafe down to 1445.

CHAPTER XVI.

THE TWELFTH TO THE SIXTEENTH CENTURIES.

Firſt Charter, 1133.

HE Prior obtained from the King a Charter, wherein, after providing for an independent election of a new prior by the monks in the event of Rahere's death, and after confirming the privileges and poſſeſſions of the Priory, it was declared " I grant alſo my firm peace to all perſons coming to and returning from the fair, which is wont to be celebrated in that place at the Feaſt of St. Bartholomew ; and I forbid any of the Royal Servants to implead any of their perſons, or without the conſent of the Canons, on thoſe three days, to wit the eve of the feaſt, the feaſt itſelf, and the day following, to levy dues upon thoſe going thither. And let all people in my whole kingdom know that I will maintain and defend this Church, even as my crown ; and if any one ſhall preſume to contravene this our Royal privilege, or ſhall offend the prior, the canons, clergy or laity of that place, he, and all who are his, and everything that belongs to him, fhall come into the King's power."

In addition to the King's "firm peace," and the ufual privileges, it came to be believed that there were fpecial miracles in ftore for thofe who braved the perils of diftant travel in making pilgrimage to the Feftival and Fair of St. Bartholomew. In Mr. Morley's book will be found a long enumeration of thefe. "What wonder (he afks) if to fee the miracles worked at the celebration of the Feaft of St. Bartholomew, in the firft years after the foundation of his Priory in Smithfield, the people came from far and near, and were to be found 'fhouldering each other' as well as 'dancing and rejoicing' in a concourfe at the fair"?

1154-86. We have it on the authority of Stow that Henry II. granted to the Priory the privilege of a fair to be kept yearly at Bartholomew tide for three days, to wit the eve, the day, and next morrow; to which the clothiers of all England and drapers of London repaired, and had their booths and ftandings within the Church Yard of this Priory, clofed in with walls and gates, locked every night, and watched for fafety of men's goods and wares. A Court of Piepowder was daily during the fair holden for debts and contracts. But he adds a note in regard to the time of the fair—"that forrens [foreigners] were licenfed for three days; the freedmen fo long as they would, which was fixe or feven dayes." It is clear that the venerable hiftorian had mixed and confounded various and diftinct events. I do not find other reference to this charter of

Henry II. except by Hone, who fays this charter gave the mayor and aldermen of the City criminal jurifdiction during the fair. The chief articles of commerce at the fair about this period were cloth, ftuffs, leather, pewter, and live cattle.

1292. The firft difpute between the City of London and the Priory of St. Bartholomew regarding the fair arofe this year. It was on the fubject of *Tolls*. The fair as we have already feen had fpread beyond the Prior's bounds. The Cuftos of the City—for in 1288 Edward I. upon a quarrel with the City feized its liberties, and Ralph Sandwich was appointed Cuftos to collect the Tolls for the Sovereign—applied for half the tolls. The Prior claimed the whole on the ground of ancient cuftom, &c. The King was at Durham, and the matter coming before him on the approach of the fair, made the following order:—

Dominus Rex &c.—The Lord the King hath commanded the Cuftos and Sheriffs in thefe words: Edward by the Grace of God, to the Cuftos and Sheriffs of London, greeting. Whereas the Prior of St. Bartholomew, of Smithfield in the fuburbs of London, by the Charters of our progenitors, Kings of England, claimeth to have a certain Fair there every year, during three days viz. on the Eve, the Day, and on the morrow of St. Bartholomew the Apoftle, with all Liberties and Free Cuftoms belonging to the Fair; a contention hath arifen between the faid Prior and you the faid Cuftos, who fue for us concerning the ufe of the liberties of the faid Fair, and the free Cuftoms belonging to it. And hindrance

being made to the said Prior by you the said Custos,
as the said Prior asserteth, to wit, concerning a
Moiety of the Eve and of the whole morrow aforesaid, concerning this We Will, as well for us as
for the aforesaid Prior, that justice be done as it is
fit, before our Treasurer and Barons of the Exchequer, after Michaelmas day next within a month.
We command you that sufficient security be taken
of the said Prior for restoring to us on the said day
the proceeds of the aforesaid fair, coming from
the moiety of the foresaid Eve and from the
whole morrow, if the said Prior cannot then show
something for himself, why the said proceeds ought
not to belong to us.   We command you that ye
permit the same Prior in the meantime, to receive
the foresaid proceeds in form aforesaid ; and thereto
you may leave this Brief. Witness myself at Durham
the 9th day of Aug. in the 20th year of our reign.

While the question was thus pending the dispu-
tants grew so warm that the City authorities
arrested some of the monks, and confined them in
the Tun prison on Cornhill.   They were released
by command of the King, but thereupon nine
citizens forced the Tun and released all the other
prisoners, by way of resenting the royal inter-
ference. The rioters were imprisoned in their turn,
and a fine of twenty thousand marks was imposed
upon the City; but the civic authorities proposed a
compromise, and, for a further payment of three
thousand marks, Edward consented to pardon the
offenders, and to restore and confirm the privileges
of the City.—*Frost*, pp. 10-11.

The refult of the reference above ordered to the Barons of the Exchequer &c. was unfavourable to the claim of the City, the Charter of the Hofpital was again confirmed. The queftion of the Tolls was not indeed finally difpofed of; but as it fleeps for a century or fo, we muft not now depart from the courfe of our record—fee 1445.

1305. Another and fpecial incident arofe at the fair of this year. I will quote the eloquent defcription of Mr. Morley. On the eve of St. Bartholomew, the firft day of the fair in the year 1305, the traders and pleafure-feekers, the friars and the jefters, clothiers, tumblers, walkers upon ftilts, hurried acrofs the grafs of Smithfield from the fide on which the fair was being held, to the Gallows under the Elms, where officers of ftate and a great concourfe of men awaited a moft welcome fpectacle. The priory was indeed built on the fite of the gallows; but in that fuburban gathering-place of the people— place of executions, place of tournaments, place of markets, place of daily fport, place of the great annual fair—one gallows-tree was not enough to fatisfy a juftice that loved vengeance and had flight regard for life. Under the Elms of which already mention has been made (Cow Lane now reprefents their fite)—under the Elms we read in a clofe roll, fo early as the fourth year of Henry III., gallows were built " where they had ftood before." An execution during fair time on that ancient exhibition ground, was entertainment rarely furnifhed to the public: for the Church forbade, among other work, fulfil- ment of the fentence of the law on any holiday of

feftival; *and a fair was a Saint's Holiday.* But
on this occafion, law was eager to affure the execution of its vengeance. The redoubtable Wallace,
hero of the Scottifh people, had been taken.
The rugged patriot, ftrong of heart and ftrong of
hand, had been brought to London in his chains
the day before the fair was opened, and on the
day of the opening of the fair was arraigned and
condemned at Weftminfter as a traitor, and without
even a day's refpite, at once fent on to his death.
Under the Elms, therefore, in Smithfield, ftood all
the concourfe of Bartholomew fair, when William
Wallace was dragged thither in chains at the tails
of horfes, bruifed, bleeding, and polluted with the
filth of London. The days had not yet come when
that firft part of the barbarous fentence on high
treafon was foftened by the placing of a hurdle
between the condemned man and the mud and flint
over which he was dragged. Trade in the fair was
forgotten while the patriot was hanged, but not to
death; cut down, yet breathing, and difembowelled,
mummers and merchants faw the bowels burnt
before the dying hero's face, then faw the execu-
tioner ftrike off his head, quarter his body, and difpatch from the ground five bafket-loads of quivering
flefh, deftined for London, Berwick, Newcaftle,
Aberdeen and Perth. Then, all being over, the
ftilt-walkers ftrode back acrofs the field, the woman
again balanced herfelf head downwards on the points
of fwords; there was mirth again round the guitar
and tambourine, the clothiers went back into the
Churchyard, and the prieft perhaps went through a

laft rehearfal with the man who was to be miracu-
loufly healed in church on the fucceeding day!—
" Memorials of Bartholomew Fair," pp. 71-2.

1321. In this, the 14th Edward II. there was
iffued a writ inquiring by what warrant the Priory
held its rights over Bartholomew Fair. This writ
was part of the machinery of a general inquifition
into the rights claimed by fubjects, which had in
many cafes been alienated without licenfe from the
crown, and often gave rife to private oppreffion of
the people. The Prior pleaded the Royal Charters
of his houfe and teftified upon oath that his predeceffors had held fuch a three-day fair fince times
beyond the reach of memory. The juftification
fatisfied the King's Exchequer.

1334. In this, the 7th Edward III. a new
Charter of the fair was granted to the Hofpital of
St. Bartholomew confirming the old rights and
reaffuring the King's firm peace to all perfons travelling towards, ftaying in, or returning from the fair;
alfo forbidding any fervants of a royal or epifcopal
court to implead any of their perfons " or without
the confent of the prior and canons on thofe three
days . . . to exact tolls either without the City or
within it, whether in the paffage of roads or bridges,
but let all proceeds that arife according to the
ufage of fairs belong to the canons of the aforefaid
church." This latter provifion clearly had reference to the claims of the City. See 1376.

It was a review of thefe and fimilar facts which
induced Mr. Morley to remark that in early times,
if not from the beginning, there were practically two

fairs held in Smithfield—one within and one without
the Priory bounds. The outer fair, he adds, " was
poffibly compofed of the mere pleafure givers and
pleafure feekers, who attended on the company of
worfhippers and traders then attracted to the priory,
and whofe tents were pitched in the open market of
Smithfield, outfide the gates, not [? but] free from
toll to the Church. Within the gates, and in the
Priory churchyard, the Subftantial Fair was held "
(pp. 61-2).

1348. In the preceding century licenfe had been
given by Edward I. to the brethren of the Hofpital
of St. Bartholomew in Smithfield to cover with
ftone and wood the ftream running through the
midft of the hofpital to Holborn Bridge, " on account of the too great ftench proceeding from it."
The large influx of perfons at the Fair muft have
made matters worfe. In the year 1348 the pefti-
lence broke out in London at the time of the fair,
and ended about fair-time in the following year.
During the interval between fair and fair, fo great
had been the mortality that, in addition to the
burials in churches and other churchyards, *fifty
thoufand* bodies had been buried in the graveyard
of the Carthufians, adjoining the fair ground. Mr.
Morley may well affume that it muft have been the
great object of intereft and terror to the flender
throng of men who hardly dared affemble; and
who—miffing from the annual crowd fo many
familiar faces—fpoke to each other with a feeble
hope of the apparent lifting of the plague. " What
mirth was there in that handful of the living

camped fo near the filent congregation of the dead?"
See 1593.

New Charter.—Edward III. under date Auguft
1, 1376, granted to the Prior, &c., the following
charter, which has heretofore efcaped obfervation,
probably becaufe in the records of the City it had
been endorfed as a "Writ to proclaim the Fair of
the Prior of Saint Bartholomew in Smethefelde,"
whereas it is feen to be a moft important grant or
confirmation of previous charters. I give a full
tranflation, marking certain paffages with italics :—
Edward by the grace of God King of England and
of France, and Duke of Ireland, to the Mayor
and Sheriffs of London and Middlefex, Greeting.
Whereas among other liberties and quittances
granted to our beloved in Chrift the Prior and
Convent of the church of Saint Bartholomew of
Smethefelde, London, by charters of our progenitors, former Kings of England, which we have
confirmed, it is granted to the fame—That they may
have all manner of freedom for ever, and that the
church aforefaid fhall be as free as any church in
the whole of England that is moft free, and as free
as our demefne chapel, which church alfo our faid
progenitors granted to will, maintain and defend in
manner like as our very crown ; and, moreover,
*they gave firm peace to thofe coming to the Fair that
is much frequented at the feaft of Saint Bartholomew*
in the faid place of Smethefelde, So that in thofe
three days' fpace, namely, the eve of the feaft, or
the day itfelf, or the day following, from fuch
comers, whether without the City or within, *or in*

paſſing along the ways or over the bridges, no one ſhall require any cuſtoms, but that all things which ariſe out of the right of fairs shall be to the ſaid church and the Canons ſerving God there, and that if any one ſhall preſume in any thing to contravene this Royal privilege, or ſhall offend the Prior Canons or laymen of that place, he and his men, and all that he has, ſhall devolve into our Royal right : and alſo lord Richard, formerly King of England, our progenitor, by his letters ordered the then Sheriffs of London and Middleſex, and all their bailiffs, that they ſhould neither vex not allow to be vexed the foreſaid Canons of the church of Saint Bartholo- mew (which is our demeſne chapel) concerning their fair which they have at the feaſt of the ſame church, nor require from thoſe coming to the Fair of Saint Bartholomew for the purpoſe of ſelling or buying, whether without the City or within, or alſo in paſſ- ing along the ways or over the bridges, cuſtoms or ſervices, or anything that may diminiſh the liberty of the ſaid church of Saint Bartholomew—as in the charters, letters and our confirmation aforeſaid more fully is contained: *and now we have underſtood that ſome by ſiniſter covin and conſpiracy previouſly had between them have knaviſhly deſigned to hinder mer- chants and others who wiſh to come and have been wont to come to the ſaid fair with their merchandiſe, ſo that they cannot come thither and do their buſineſs therein,* as well to the loſs of them the Prior and Convent and overthrow and weakening of their right as to the manifeſt letting and hindrance of our common people : We, duly heeding the fervent

devotion and affection which our forefaid progenitors had towards the faid church, as by the charters
and letters aforefaid more fully doth appear, and
willing (as we are bounden) to maintain and defend the faid fair, *which for fo long time hath endured*
and was granted by our faid progenitors to the
honour of God in fubvention of Holy Church, and
all other rights and privileges, left in our time they
perifh, have taken into our fpecial protection and
defence the faid Prior and Canons, and their men
and fervants, and merchants whomfoever and others
wifhing to come with their goods and things to the
faid fair, there tarrying and therefrom returning
whither they will; and fo we command you to
maintain, protect and defend the faid Prior and
Canons, their men and fervants, merchants and
others whomfoever coming to the faid fair with
their goods and things, there tarrying and therefrom returning, and to permit the Prior and Convent to hold their faid fair in form aforefaid, and to
receive and have freely and without any hindrance,
from thofe coming to the faid fair and returning
therefrom, *the cuftoms and all other the profits which
pertain to them in right of the faid fair* according to
the form of the charters, letters and confirmation
aforefaid, and as they ought to hold the fame fair
and to have and receive the cuftoms and other
things which pertain to that fair, and as they and
their predeceffors have until now held that fair and
have been wont to have and receive the cuftoms
and other things which to that fair pertain. And,
concerning any pleas or other things to the faid fair

for the faid three days appertaining, do you in no wife intermeddle, neither requiring any thing for cuftoms and other things to that fair appertaining, nor hindering, molefting, nor in any way aggrieving the Prior and Canons of the faid place as to the receiving of the cuftoms and profits aforefaid, nor, as much in you lies, permitting them to be molefted or aggrieved. And if any fhall prefume to diminifh the cuftoms and rights of the faid fair, then be you in aid to the faid Prior and Canons, or their bailiffs of the faid fair, when hereupon you fhall be requefted by them or any one of them, by fuch ways and methods as fhall feem to you the more expedient, to compel and diftrain thofe who would diminifh the faid cuftoms and rights to yield and pay the faid cuftoms and rights to the faid Prior and Convent : and this do you in no wife omit. And, that thofe all and every the premifes may come to the knowledge of all, and that no one, of what ftate or condition foever he be, under grave forfeiture to us, and under the peril incumbent thereon, may prefume in any manner to practife any covin or any other acts calculated to difturb in any way that fair or the profit of the fair, or the merchants or others, fo that they cannot lawfully, without damage and in peace come to that fair with their merchandife, and do their bufinefs there, and return therefrom, do you caufe the fame to be publicly proclaimed, obferved and held within your bailiwick and diftricts, where it fhall feem to you moft expedient, as often as and when hereupon by the faid Prior and Convent, or any one of them,

you ſhall on our behalf be requeſted. Witneſs Our-
ſelf at Weſtminſter the firſt day of Auguſt in the
fiftieth year of our reign of England, but of our
reign of France the thirty-ſeventh.   Faryngton.

¶ This proclamation was made.

Miracle Plays.—This Fair of St. Bartholomew
was long the ſcene of " miracle plays." The Company of Pariſh Clerks—an incorporated company or
gild who had charge of the records, the burials, and
afterwards of the births in London, during a very
long period—played at Skinners' Well (near Smithfield) before Richard II. and his Queen and Court,
towards the cloſe of the fourteenth century ; and
early in the following they played before Henry IV.
at the ſame place, during eight days, " Matter from
the Creation of the world."   The early plays at this
fair are believed to have been repreſentations of
great miracles aſcribed to St. Bartholomew.   Later
came the " myſteries," and finally the " moralities,"
out of which our modern drama has been developed.
All theſe in their turns were preſented at this once
famous fair.

Slaves.—In this ſame Fair of Smithfield, as well
before as after the period upon which I am now
writing, men and women—*i.e.,* ſlaves and captives—
were ſold among the articles of merchandiſe.   And
on a part of the ſite over which the fair extended,
after the acceſſion of Henry IV., men and women
were burnt alive as heretics. The martyr fires were
uſually kindled on that ſpot of ground outſide the
Priory gates, over which the lighter portion of the
fair ſpread — ground occupied by the holiday

makers, and the tumblers, jefters, and dancers by
whom they were entertained.

Tolls.—1445. At the clofe of the thirteenth century there had arifen a difpute between the City of
London and the Prior regarding the tolls of this
Fair, which was then decided in favour of the
Priory. When the matter came up for adjudication again does not feem clear. The fair had continued to grow, and its greateft expanfion was in the
direction of the City. Indeed, at this or a later
period, it extended down the weft fide of Alderfgate
nearly as far as St. Martin's-le-Grand, or to St.
Paul's itfelf. On the other fide the jurifdiction of
the City extended only to Smithfield Bars. In
1399 Henry IV. had granted to the Citizens of
London the office of gathering tolls in Smithfield.
Probably in confequence of this arrangements were
come to between the Priory and the City. Certain
is it that forty-fix years later, or in 1445 (23rd
Henry VI.), four perfons were appointed by the
Court of Aldermen as keepers of Bartholomew
Fair and of the Court of Piepowder. In that
Court, therefore, the City then became reprefented
as joint lord of the Fair with the Priory, the lord-
fhip of the City being founded on its right over
the ground beyond the jurifdiction of the Canons.
See 1538 and 1593.

Diffolution of Monafteries.—1538. This is an
eventful year in the hiftory of the Fair—the Diffolution of the Monaftery was declared. The Fair
itfelf indeed remained—it was the Priory which
created it that had melted away.

Reviewing the fair as it had exifted during the four centuries paffed fince its origin—but many of the details of which I have neceffarily paffed over in the preceding outline—we may adopt the picture thus freely drawn by Mr. Morley : Thus we have in the moft ancient times of the Fair a church full of worfhippers, among whom were the fick and maimed, praying for health about its altar ; a grave-yard full of traders, and a place of jefting and edification, where women and men caroufed in the midft of the throng; where the minftrel and the ftory-teller and the tumbler gathered knots about them ; where the Sheriff caufed new laws to be publifhed by loud proclamation in the gathering places of the people; where the young men bowled at nine pins, while the clerks and friars peeped at the young maids; where mounted knights and ladies curvetted and ambled, pedlars loudly magnified their wares, the fcholars met for public wrangle, oxen lowed, horfes neighed, and fheep bleated among their buyers; where great fhouts of laughter anfwered to the Ho ! Ho ! of the devil on the ftage, above which flags were flying, and below which a band of pipers and guitar beaters added mufic to the din. That ftage alfo—if ever there was prefented on it the ftory of the Creation—was the firft wild-beaft fhow in the fair : for one of the dramatic effects connected with this play, as we read in an ancient ftage direction, was to reprefent the creation of beafts by unloofing and fending among the excited crowd as great a variety of ftrange animals as could be brought together; and to create

the birds by fending up a flight of pigeons. Under
foot was mud and filth, but the wall that pent the
city in fhone funlit among the trees; a frefh breeze
came over the furrounding fields and brooks, whif-
pering among the elms that overhung the moor
glittering with pools, or from the Fair's neighbour,
the gallows! Shaven heads looked down on the
fcene from the adjacent windows of the buildings
bordering the Priory enclofure; and the poor
people whom the friars cherifhed in their hofpital,
made holiday among the reft. The curfew bell of
St. Martin's-le-Grand, the religious houfe to which
William the Conqueror had given with its charter
the adjacent moorland, and within whofe walls there
was a fanctuary for loofe people, ftilled the hum of
the crowd at nightfall, and the Fair lay dark under
the ftarlight.

Change produces change; and fo other events
followed at this period. For inftance, the difputations of the fcholars in the Mulberry Garden at the
time of the Fair ceafed after the fuppreffion of the
Monaftery. John Stow had witneffed thefe when
a lad, and he furnifhes the following account of
the fame, and of fome events preceding: " As for
the meeting of the Schoolmafters on Feftival Days
at Feftival Churches, and the difputing of the
fcholars logically, &c., whereof I have before fpoken,
the fame was long fince difcontinued; but the argu-
ing of the fchoolboys about the principles of grammar hath been continued even till our time; for I
myfelf, in my youth, have yearly feen, on the eve
of St. Bartholomew the Apoftle, the fcholars of

divers Grammar fchools repair unto the Churchyard of St. Bartholomew . . . . where upon a bank boarded about under a tree, fome one fcholar hath ftepped up, and there hath oppofed and anfwered till he were by fome better fcholar overcome and put down; and then the overcomer taking the place did like as the firft. And in the end the beft oppo-fers and anfwerers had rewards, which I obferved not but it made good fchoolmafters and alfo good fcholars diligently againft fuch times to prepare themfelves for the obtaining of this garland. I re-member there repaired to thefe exercifes amongft others, the mafters and fcholars of the free fchools of St. Paul's in London, of St. Peter's at Weft-minfter, of Thomas Acon's Hofpital, and of St. Anthonie's Hofpital; whereof the laft named com-monly prefented the beft fcholars and had the prize in thofe days. This priory of St. Bartholomew being furrendered to Henry the Eighth, thofe dif-putations of fcholars in that place furceafed; and was again, only for a year or twain, revived in the Cloifter of Chrift's Hofpital, where the beft fcholars, then ftill of St. Anthonie's School, howfoever the fame be now fallen both in number and eftimation, were rewarded with bows and arrows of filver, given to them by Sir Martin Bower, goldfmith. Never-thelefs however, the encouragement failed—the fcholars of St. Paul's meeting with thofe of St. An-thonie's would call them Anthonie's Pigs, and they again would call the others Pigeons of Paul's be-caufe many pigeons were bred in St. Paul's Church, and St. Anthonie was always figured with a pig fol-

lowing him ; and mindful of the former ufage, did
for a long feafon diforderly provoke one another
in the open ftreet with ' *Salve* tu quoque, placet
mecum difputare ? '—' Placet.' And fo proceeding
from this to queftions in grammar, they ufually fell
from words to blows with their fatchels full of
books, many times in great heaps, that they troubled
the ftreets and paffengers ; fo that finally they were
reftrained with the decay of St. Anthonie's fchool."

It was during this reign of Henry VIII. that
Grotwell (or Cartwell), himfelf a common hangman—for there were then many of this occupation,
and plenty of employment—was hanged with two
others, for robbing a booth at the Fair. They were
executed in the wreftling place at Clerkenwell.

I may refume the hiftorical narration. When the
King had taken the eftates of the greater monafteries,
they were put under the management of a Royal
Commiffion, with Sir Richard Rich—under the
ftyle of Chancellor of the Court of Augmentations—
at its head. The Prior's houfe became Lord Rich's
town manfion ; and with this manfion in Great St.
Bartholomew there had been affigned to him and
his for ever, the Clofe of the faid late monaftery or
priory called Great St. Bartholomew Clofe, and all
the limits and precincts of the faid Clofe ; alfo all
thofe clofes, edifices, called the fermery, the dorter,
the frater, the cloifters, the gallery, the hall, the
kitchen, the buttery, the pantry, the old kitchen,
the woodhoufe, the garner, and the Prior's ftable, of
the faid late monaftery and priory belonging ; and
alfo all that water and the aqueduct and water-

courfe coming from the conduit-head of St. Bartholomew in the manor of Canonbury.

By the fame Letters Patent the King farther
granted to Sir Richard Rich, knight, his heirs and
affigns, " all that Our Fair and Markets, commonly
named and called Bartholomew Fair, holden and to
be holden every year within the aforefaid Clofe
called Great St. Bartholomew Clofe, and in Weft
Smithfield aforefaid to continue yearly for three
days," &c. And alfo all the ftallage, piccage, toll,
and cuftoms of the fame Fair and Markets; and
alfo all our Courts of Piepowders within the fame;
alfo the fcrutiny of weights and meafures and things
expofed to fale, and the Affize of bread, wine, and
ale, and other victuals. This grant included the
tolls of the Cloth Fair, but not, of courfe, the rights
of the City to the tolls for the fair outfide St. Bartholomew's enclofure.

Growth of London.—1590. During the reign of
Elizabeth various attempts had been made to ftop
the growth of London. Proclamations had been
iffued forbidding under heavy difpleafure the building of new houfes. But the Elizabethan era was
an important one in the development of commerce,
as it had been in the foftering of learning ; and with
the development of commerce there came a greater
influx of ftrangers into the city. Thus it came
about that more houfes in the city were imperative.
It was found that the lines of trade marked at Bartholomew Fair by the ftandings of the clothiers and
others, would yield more money as ftreets of houfes
than as ftreets of booths, and fo, before the clofe of

the century, as Stow tells us, " notwithftanding all
proclamations of the prince, and alfo the act of
parliament, in place of booths within the churchyard (only let out in the fair time and clofed up all
the year after) be many large houfes built, and the
north wall towards Long Lane taken down, and a
number of tenements are there erected for fuch as
will give great rents." This laft line of trading-
houfes was fubftituted for the profitlefs dead wall.
Parallel with it, through the ground vacant of building north of the church, which that wall had enclofed, parallel alfo with one of the church walls, a
ftreet of confiderable houfes occupied the fite and
kept the name of Cloth Fair.

Plague.—1593 (53rd of Elizabeth). The plague
being now prevailing in the city, the queen iffued a
proclamation on 6th Auguft, about three weeks
before the ufual time of the fair, in fubftance as
follows :—Whereas there was a general refort of all
kinds of people out of every part of the realm to
the faid fair; but that (on this occafion) in the
ufual place of Smithfield there fhould be no manner
of market for any wares kept, nor any ftalls or
booths for any manner of merchandife, or for
victuals, fuffered to be fet up ; but that the open
fpace of the ground called Smithfield, be only occupied with the fale of horfes and cattle, and of ftall
wares, as butter, cheefe, and fuch like in grofs, and
not by retail, the fame to continue for the fpace of
two days only.

And for the vent of woollen cloths, kerfeys, and
linen cloth, to be all fold in grofs and not by retail;

the fame fhould be brought within the clofe-yard of
St. Bartholomew (afterwards known as the Cloth
Fair) where fhops were there continued (*i.e.* not
deferted by reafon of the plague) and have gates
to fhut the fame place in the nights, and then fuch
to be offered to fale, and to be bought in grofs and
not by retail; the fame market to continue but
three days—that is to fay Even, the Day of St.
Bartholomew and the Morrow after.

And that the fale and vent of leather be kept in
the outfide of the ring of Smithfield, as had been
accuftomed, without erecting of any fhops or
booths for the fame, or for any victualler or other
occupier of any wares whatfoever.

And that notice hereof be given to fuch of H.
M.'s good fubjects as for lack of knowledge of this
H. M.'s princely ordonnance might refort to London to fell or buy fmall wares by retail, and there
receive infection, and carry the fame into their countries, H. M. commanded that the Lord Mayor of
London fhould caufe this proclamation to be prefently publifhed in all the ufual places in the City,
in the time of two or three market days, and to be
alfo Proclaimed by the Sheriffs of Middlefex, Kent,
Surrey, and Effex, in fome places of thofe Counties
near to the faid City, whereby none might refort
to the City at this Feaft of St. Bartholomew, by
pretence of any Fair, but fuch as fhould have caufe
to fell or buy the commodities in grofs.

Imprifonment, without bail, during the Queen's
pleafure, or further punifhment, was to be the
penalty for the infraction of this ordinance. Mr.

Morley, reviewing this proclamation, fays the in-
ference to be drawn from it was that the fair, as a
place of wholefale commerce, was not to be fup-
preffed without more injury to trade than the fear of
plague would force the Queen's advifers to inflict.
But this confideration muft be qualified by the fact
that the chief rifk came from the throng of pedlers,
hawkers, ftall-keepers, fhowmen, and holiday-makers
from the country round about; and that the foberer
refort of merchants to the fair, while it was certainly
in one refpect a greater good, was in the other refpect alfo a leffer evil. Alfo, there was a wealthy
nobleman at court unwilling to part with a year's
tolls from the Cloth Fair and the Clofe, and able to
urge actively, from motives of felf-intereft, con-
fiderations that were, at the fame time, not wanting
in juftice.

1596. A formal agreement was made between
Lord Rich and the Corporation of London, eftablifhing a compofition of the tolls of the fair; and,
as to jurifdiction, placing both parties nearly in the
relative pofition occupied by the Priory and the
Corporation in 1445.

A Foreigner's View of the Fair.—1598. Paul
Hentzner, a German tutor, travelled this year
through Germany, France, Italy, and England,
and kept an " Itinerarum," of which many editions
have been publifhed. I quote the following defcription of Bartholomew Fair from the Aungervyle
Society's tranflation (1881) :—" It is worthy of
obfervation that every year upon St. Bartholomew's
Day, when a fair is held, it is ufual for the Mayor,

attended by the twelve principal Aldermen, to walk in a neighbouring field dreſſed in his Scarlet Gown, and about his neck a Golden Chain, to which is hung a Golden Fleece, and beſides that particular ornament, which diſtinguiſhed the moſt noble Order of the Garter . . . himſelf and they on horſeback ; upon their arrival at a place appointed for that purpoſe, where a tent is pitched, the mob begin to wreſtle before them, two at a time ; the conquerors receive rewards from the magiſtrates. After this is over, a parcel of live rabbits are turned looſe among the crowd, which are purſued by a number of boys who endeavour to catch them, with all the noiſe they can make. While we were at this ſhow, one of our company, Tobias Salander, Doctor of Phy-ſic, had his pocket picked of his purſe, with nine crowns *du ſoleil*, which without doubt was ſo cleverly taken from him by an Engliſhman who always kept cloſe to him, that the Doctor did not the leaſt per-ceive it."

CHAPTER XVII.

THE SEVENTEENTH CENTURY.

1603.

THE plague was again threatening the City, and James I. iſſued a proclamation, dated from Hampton Court, 8th Auguſt, ordaining that for the " deſire of preventing an univerſal contagion among our people," that (*inter alia*) Bartholomew Fair ſhould not be holden, " nor anything appertaining unto them, at the times accuſtomed, *nor any time till they ſhall be licenſed by us.*" Theſe laſt words might have been held to imply more than was directly underſtood.

Proclamation by City of London.—1604. The arrangement of 1596 prepared the way for the Corporation taking the active control of the fair. Hence among the Orders of my Lord Mayor, the Aldermen, and the Sheriffs for their meetings and wearing of their apparel through this year, was the following :—

" ON SAINT BARTHOLOMEW'S EVEN FOR THE FAIR IN SMITHFIELD.—The Aldermen meet my

Lord and the Sheriffs at the Guildhall Chapel, at two of the Clock after dinner, in their violet gowns lined, and their horfes, without cloaks, and there hear Evening Prayer ; which being done, they take their horfes and ride to Newgate, and fo forth to the gate entering in at the Cloth Fair, and there make a Proclamation," which was as follows :—

PROCLAMATION.—The Right Hon. the Lord Mayor of the City of London, and his right worfhipful Bretheren the Aldermen of the faid City, ftreightly charge and command, on the behalf of our Sovereign Lord the King, that all manner of perfons, of whatfoever eftate, degree, or condition they be, having recourfe to this fair, keep the Peace of our faid Sovereign Lord the King.

That no manner of perfons make any congregation, conventicle, or affrays, by the which the fame peace may be broken or difturbed, upon pain of imprifonment and fine, to be made after the difcretion of the Lord Mayor and Aldermen.

Alfo, that all manner of Sellers of wine, ale, or beer, fell by meafures enfealed, as by gallon, pottle, quart and pint, upon pain that will fall thereof.

And that no perfon fell any bread, but if it keep the affize, and that it be good and wholefome for man's body, upon pain that will fall thereof.

And that no manner of perfon buy nor fell but with true weights and meafures, fealed according to the Statute in that behalf made, upon pain that will fall thereof.

And that no manner of perfon, or perfons take

upon him, or them, within this Fair to make any
manner of arreft, attachment, fummons, or execution, but if it be done by the officer of this City,
thereunto affigned, upon pain that will fall thereof.

And that no perfon or perfons whatfoever, within
the limits and bounds of this fair, prefume to break
the Lord's Day in felling, fhowing, or offering for
fale, or in buying or offering to buy, any commodities whatfoever, or in fitting, tippling, or drinking
in any tavern, inn, alehoufe, or cook's-houfe, or in
doing any other thing that may lead to any breach
thereof, upon the pain and penalties contained in
the feveral acts of parliament, which will be feverely
inflicted upon the breakers hereof.

And finally, that whatever perfon foever find
themfelves aggrieved, injured or wronged by any
manner of perfon in this Fair, that they come with
their plaints before the Stewards of this Fair,
affigned to hear and determine pleas, and they will
minifter to all parties juftice, according to the laws
of the Land and the Cuftoms of this City. God
fave the King!

Then, the mayor, fheriffs and aldermen, fitting
on horfeback, robed in their violet gowns, having
again made this proclamation at a point between
the City Fair and that owned by the Warwick or
Holland family (as fucceffors of Sir Richard Rich?),
ride through the Cloth Fair, and fo return back
again, through the Churchyard of Great St. Bartholomew's to Alderfgate, and thence home again
to the Lord Mayor's houfe.

Tradition declares that the mayor, when he had

read the Proclamation, drank ale from a filver flagon, and that thereupon the buftle and bufinefs of the fair began. I believe as a matter of fact the proclamation was ufually read by the Lord Mayor's attorney, and repeated after him by the fheriff's officer, in the prefence of the Lord Mayor, Aldermen, and Sheriffs. The officers of the Lord Mayor's houfehold afterwards dined at the Swordbearer's table. This may have become the cuftom at a later date. See 1688.

Merchant Taylors' right of Search.—1609. An incident occurred this year which raifed the queftion of jurifdiction concerning an important function which had heretofore been deemed of much confequence. Immediately before the fair of this year the Drapers queftioned the right of fearch, for cloth pieces of infufficient length or quality, as exercifed by the Merchant Taylors. What followed is fhown by the records of the laft-named company. Its clerk was ordered thereupon to attend Drapers' Hall on the next court day with a meffage to the following purport, viz., That the Merchant Taylors' Company had right to fearch, and that they had quietly enjoyed the fame fince the 27th of Henry VI., being above 150 years past, and ftill earlier, as by the Merchant Taylors' records appeared, wherein is mentioned a lengthened lawfuit between them and the Drapers about the fame queftion of right of fearch, when a fentence was paffed for the Merchant Taylors. There is in 1612 a note of a dinner at Merchant Taylors' Hall " for the fearch on St. Bartholomew's Eve."

The Drapers were incorporated as a Guild in
1364. In their charter was a ſpecial exemption
made againſt any prohibitions to be exerciſed by
the Company regarding the ſale of cloth by any
who were not free drapers, in favour of the King's
beloved in God, the Prior of St. Bartholomew's, in
Weſt Smithfield, and other lords who had fairs in
the ſuburbs of London. A draper meant originally
one who made the cloth he ſold. It was the
London deſignation for clothier, a very few
members of the Drapers' Company being reſident
beyond the limits of the City. Therefore, ſay the
old writers, that Bartholomew Fair was frequented
by "the clothiers of England and the drapers of
London." Mercers eſpecially frequented fairs and
markets, where their ſtandings were gay with haberdaſhery, toys, and even drugs and ſpices, the ſmall
articles of traffic on which they throve. Mercers
attending the French fairs towards the cloſe of the
thirteenth century paid only half-toll when they
were not ſtall keepers, but expoſed their wares on
the ground. They, and the claſs of pedlers to
which they were allied, may have enjoyed a like
privilege in England. But while many of the
mercers were thus of the brotherhood of Auto-
lycus, others dealt largely in ſilk and velvet, and
abandoned to the haberdaſher traffic in ſmall articles
of dreſs. Whittington, thrice Lord Mayor of
London, was a mercer.—*Vide Morley*, p. 95.

Paving the Streets.—1614. This was an important year in the annals of Smithfield. It paſſed
from its old and normal condition of mud, into a

clean and paved enclofure, fuch as was familiar to many of us before the new market buildings were erected in 1866. Other changes had preceded. It was not until 1608 that the City had obtained a grant of the ground of the late Priory of St. Bartholomew, which had been conftituted into a parifh after the diffolution. Again, while it had ceafed fome time before to be the fcene of the morning performances of the common hangman—Tyburn (itfelf afterwards abforbed in May Fair) having fucceeded to the diftinction ; it had ftill remained the *locus* of a far more favage form of perfecution. The afhes of the laft martyr fire had burned out in 1611 —the victim being Bartholomew Leggatt, a pious Unitarian, burnt for diftruft of the Athanafian and Nicene creeds, by the order of James I. at the fentence of John King, newly-made Bifhop of London !

The Drama.—As if more prominently to mark the tranfition ftate laft indicated, and perchance alfo as a memento, that in the very place had been enacted (under the patronage of and for the purpofes of the Church) the firft drama that England had ever feen ; and which had ftep by ftep progreffed from myfteries to miracle plays, thence on to moralities, and was now advancing to the ftate of taking an independent ftand as a National Drama —as if, I fay, to commemorate this circumftance with emphafis, "rare Ben Jonfon" produced his celebrated comedy of " Bartholomew Fair," one of the chief features in which is the vivid painting of the characters through whom the fatirift portrays the follies of the fair. They are many and various; each one planned to bring into prominence one of the characteriftics of the motley gathering. Competent authorities have declared this to be equal to any of the beft works of the author. I confefs not to have difcovered many points for admiration. There are a few good points in it which may be reproduced. A ftranger appears in the fair, a Puritan, defignated Zealot-of-the-land Bufy. He is ordered to be put in the ftocks, and fays " I do obey thee, the Lion may roar but he cannot bite. I am glad to be thus feparated from the *Heathen* of the Land, and put apart in the Stocks for the holy caufe." Humphrey Wafp inquires who he is. He replies "One that rejoiceth in his affliction, and fitteth here to prophecy the Deftruction of *Fairs*, and May-games, Wakes, and Whitfon-ales, and doth figh and groan for the reformation of thefe abufes." Lanthorn Leatherhead recounts fome of the "motions" (plays) in which he had taken part at this fair. "'Jerufalem' was a ftately thing, and fo was 'Nineveh,' and the 'City of Norwich' and 'Sodom and Gomorrah;' with the rifing o' the Prentices . . .; but the 'Gunpowder-plot,' there was a get-penny! I have prefented that to an eighteen or twenty-pence audience nine times in an afternoon. Your home-born projects ever prove the beft, they are fo eafy and familiar ; they put too much learning in their things now o' days." In this fpirit John Littlewit had been adapting a too claffical play to the comprehenfion of the frequenters of the fair, "as for the *Hellefpont*, I imagine our Thames

here ; and their *Leander* I make a Dyer's fon about
Puddle Wharf; and *Hero* a wench of the Bank-
fide, who going over one morning to Old Fifh
Street, *Leander* fpies her land at Trig-ftairs, and
falls in love with her; now do I introduce *Cupid*,
having metamorphoz'd himfelf to a drawer [pot-
boy] and he ftrikes *Hero* in love with a pint of
fherry. . . ."

The Plague.—1625. The Plague again appeared
in the Kingdom, and Charles I. iffued a Proclamation from his Court at Woodftock, wherein he
recites that there is ufually extraordinary refort *out
of all parts of the Kingdom* of perfons to attend this
and Stourbridge Fair; hence there is prohibition
againft attending these fairs or any others held
within fifty miles of the City of London.

1630. Another like proclamation in confequence
of Plague—this time being in Cambridge. The
King remembering that there were at hand " three
great Fairs of Special note, unto which there is extraordinary refort from all parts of the Kingdom,"
atttendance at Bartholomew, Stourbridge and Our
Lady Fair (Southwark) was prohibited.

1637. Again the Plague, and there was iffued :
By the King. A Proclamation for putting off this
next Bartholomew Faire in Smithfield, and our
Lady Faire in Southwarke. Giuen at our Court
at Oatelands, the three and twentieth day of Iuly
in the thirteenth yeare of our Reigne. God faue
the King. Imprinted at London by Robert
Barker, Printer to the King's moft excellent Ma-
ieftie: And by the Affigns of Iohn Bill. 1637.

A fheet in Black Letter. Copy in Mr. Huth's Library.

New Grant to the City.—1638. Charles I. this year granted a Charter to London which contained the following :

We will alfo, and by thefe prefents for us our heirs and fucceffors declare and grant that the faid Mayor and Commonalty and Citizens and their fucceffors for ever may have hold and enjoy all thofe fields called or known by the name of . . . and alfo all that field called Weft-Smithfield in the Parifh of St. Sepulchre's, St. Bartholomew the Great, St. Bartholomew the Lefs in the fuburbs of London, or in fome of them, to the ufes, intents and purpofes after expreffed ; and that the fame Mayor and Commonalty and Citizens, and their fucceffors may be able to hold in the faid field called Smith-field, *Fairs* and *Markets* there to be and ufed to be held, and to take receive and have pickage, ftallage, tolls and profits appertaining, happening, belonging or arifing out of the fairs and markets there, to fuch ufes as the fame mayor and commonalty and citizens, or their predeceffors had, held or enjoyed, and now have, hold and enjoy, or ought to have, hold or enjoy the faid premifes laft mentioned, and to no other ufes, intents and purpofes what-foever.

Wreftling Matches.—It had been the time-honoured cuftom of this fair to have contefts in wreftling. And during the reign of James I. (ap-parently) the Corporation of the City laid down the following regulation to be obferved on the

attendance of the Mayor and members of the Corporation to witnefs the fport:

"ON BARTHOLOMEW DAY FOR WRESTLING.—
So many Aldermen as dine with my Lord Mayor
and the Sheriffs, be apparelled in their fcarlet gowns,
lined, and after dinner their horfes be brought to
them where they dine, and thofe aldermen which
dine with the fheriffs, ride with them to my lord's
houfe to accompany him to wreftling. Then when
the wreftling is done, they take their horfes, and
ride back again thro' the Fair, and fo in at Alderfgate, and fo home again to the faid Lord Mayor's
houfe."

Then there was a regulation for attending the
"Shooting" there, as follows : "The next day, if
it be not Sunday, for the Shooting as upon Bartho-
lomews day, but if it be Sunday, the Monday
following."

Defcription of the Fair.—1641. There was publifhed a Tract (a fmall quarto of four leaves) : "Bartholomew Faire, or Variety of fancies, where you
may find, a faire of wares and all to pleafe your
mind. With the feverall Enormityes and mifde-
meanours, which are there feene and acted. London,
printed for Richard Harper at the Bible and Harp
in Smithfield," wherein the author, after giving a
graphic account of the art of picking pockets
there, proceeds :

It is remarkable and worth your obfervation, to
behold and hear the ftrange fights and confufed
noifes in the fair. Here a knave in a Fool's coat,
with a trumpet founding, or on a drum beating,

invites you and would fain perfuade you to fee his
puppets; there a Rogue like a Wild Woodman, or
in an antick fhape like an incubus, defires your
company to view his motion; on the other fide
Hocus Pocus with three yards of tape or ribbon
in 's hand, fhowing the art of Legerdemain to the
admiration and aftonifhment of a company of cocko-
loaches. Amongft thefe you fhall fee a gray Goofe-
cap (as wife as the reft) with a What de ye lack?
in his mouth, ftanding on his booth fhaking a
rattle, or fcraping on a fiddle, with which children
are fo taken, that they prefently cry out for thefe
fopperies; And all thefe together make fuch a dif-
tracted noife, that you would think Babel were not
comparable to it. Here there are alfo your game-
fters in action; fome turning of a whimfey, others
throwing for pewter, who can quickly diffolve a
round fhilling into a three half-penny faucer.

Long Lane at this time looks very fair, and puts
out her beft clothes with the wrong fide outwards,
fo turned for their better turning off; and Cloth
Fair is now in great requeft : well fare the alehoufes
therein ; yet better may a man fare (but at a dearer
rate) in the Pig market, alias Pafty nook or Pie
Corner, where pigs are all hours of the day on the
ftalls piping hot, and would cry (if they could
fpeak) Come eat me ; but they are . . . dear and
the reckonings for them are . . . faucy, &c. &c.

It is clear that the glory of the fair is departing
—Royal Proclamations notwithftanding.

Political Pamphlets.—1647. It feems to have
become the fafhion to defignate fome of the many

political pamphlets of this period " Bartholomew Fairings." One fuch work appeared this year entitled : " General Maffey's Bartholomew Fayrings to Colonel Poyntz." This was afcribed to the famous John Lilburne. It was anfwered in another pamphlet : " Reformados Righted, being an Anfwer to a paltry piece of Poetry entitled, &c." There is nothing in either of thefe throwing any light upon the fair. The fame was not quite the cafe with a quarto pamphlet of the following year : " An Agitator Anatomifed." Here was reference to "a large and beautiful Camel from Grand Cairo in Egypt." Mr. Morley thinks this may have been the beginning of " wild-beaft fhows " in the fair.

This year the Act was paffed againft " Stage plays." It feemed deftined to have an influence on the fair.

1648. Evelyn in his " Diary," under date 28th Auguft this year, notices his coming to London from Say's Court and feeing the " the celebrated follies of Bartholomew Fair." The date here feems to indicate fome change in the date of the fair.

The Commonwealth and the Fair.—1649. This was a year of political commotion. The troubles with the King had terminated on the block. There was iffued in the form of a tract, a book-play entitled : " A Bartholomew Fairing, New, New, New; Sent from the raifed fiege before Dublin, as a preparatory Prefent to the Great Thankfgiving Day. To be communicated onely to Independents." It was publifhed without any printer's name. Its contents throw fome light upon the political events of the period; but thefe have no bearing upon the fair, prefent or future.

It feems indeed to have been anticipated that the advent of the Puritans into power in this the firft year of the Commonwealth might have led to the fuppreffion of the fair.   The fpeech of Zealot-of-the-land Bufy, while fitting in the ftocks at the fair in 1614 ("Bartholomew Fair," by Ben Jonfon) feemed prophetically to hint at this.   Mr. Morley gives the following inftructive picture of the period :

The Puritans did not fupprefs Bartholomew Fair. There were indeed no dramas performed in it by living actors, but the ftate did not condefcend, like Rabbi Bufy, to engage in controverfy with the puppets.   It was for the Corporation of London, if it pleafed, to exercife control, and there was a Lord Mayor, who, as we fhall fee, did make himfelf eminent for an attack upon the wooden Dagons of the Show. Against the fool in his motley none made war; Cromwell himfelf had in his private fervice four buffoons, and had he vifited the fair, true hero as he was, might have been well difpofed to mount a hobby-horfe.   Therefore the clown ftill jefted, and the toyman thruft his baubles in the face of the Roundhead, while the Cavalier's lady, with a con-ftellation of black ftars about her nofe, a moon of ink on her chin, and a coach and horfes—a very fafhionable patch—on her forehead, laughed at the fhort hair under the broad-brimmed hat of the offended gentleman.   Well might fhe laugh at the miferable fcarecrow in plain cloak and jerkin, and

in boots that fitted him : for he had no love
locks and no peaked beard like the gallant at her
fide ; he wore only a little pecked band inftead
of a laced collar, and as for his breeches—not only
did they want ornament and width ; but they even
fhowed no elegant bit of fhirt protruding over them !
Acrofs the Smithfield pavement, Cavaliers in boots
two inches too long, and with laced tops wide
enough to contain each of them a goofe, ftraddled
about; compelled to ftraddle in order that the long
and jingling fpur of one boot, hooked into the ruffle
of the other, might not bring down the whole man
into the gutter. Women I fay might note fuch
things, but the men were in earneft. The dainty
Cavalier in the hiftorical fhirt, embroidered with the
deeds of profane heroes, might glance from the
fpeckled face of his companion towards the clean
cheeks of the Puritan maid in the religious petticoat
worked over with texts and fcripture fcenes ; all
had their vanities, their froth of weaknefs floating
loofe above the ftorm ; all had an eye for the jeft
of the fair, but under it lay in a heaving mafs the
folemn earneft of the time. The fair brought together from almoft all parts of England, men who
had urgent thoughts to exchange, harmonies and
conflicts now of principle and now of paffion to ex-
prefs. The deftiny of fatherland was hidden from
all in a future black with doubt. Men brave and
honeft had their fouls pledged in allegiance to an
earthly king, over whom and againft whom others
as brave and as honeft fet up rights given to them
by the King of kings.

1650. There was publifhed a broadfide and cut, with a " Defcription of Bartholomew Fair: "—

> " Whether this be wit or nonfence, who need care,
> 'Tis like the fubject, which is Bartholomew Fair:
> A mefs of altogether, well enough,
> To get good money, which will make us huff,
> And fwagger bravely, drink a glafs or fo,
> With fome kind fhe-acquaintance which you know,
> Are pretty tempting things, fo much for that,
> I muft now come and tell you plain and flat:
> That in this fong the whole Fair you may view,
> You may believe me when I tell you true."

Set to the tune of " Digby's Farewell." Printed for F. Coles, T. Vere, J. Wright, and J. Clarke. Containing twelve ftanzas of eight lines.

1656. During the Commonwealth feveral attempts were made by the lord mayors to put fome check on the freedom of this fair.[1] One of them, Sir John Deltrich, was knighted by Cromwell foon after the fair-time (viz. 5th Sept.) in 1656 ; and it has been rightly affumed that he was the mayor who preffed hard againft thofe puppet fhowmen and others who had commenced the bufinefs of the fair, as he conceived, twelve hours too foon, and were already at work when he arrived to proclaim the opening. This event appears to have led to a burlefque opening by a company of tailors who met at the " Hand and Shears " already noticed on the

---

[1] The Vagrancy and Mendicity Acts were called into aid. Under thefe, " homelefs beggars " were to be fent to their own parifh. It is probable that the numbers were too great to be dealt with efficiently.

night before the official opening, elected a chairman, and as the clock ftruck twelve, went out into the Cloth Fair, each with a pair of fhears in his hand. The chairman then proclaimed the fair to the expectant mob; and then all formed a proceffion to proceed in tumultuous array to announce the fair to the fleepers in Smithfield, by the ringing of bells and other difcordant manifeftations. The following is the form of proclamation ufed, and contains nothing objectionable.

An unauthorifed Proclamation.—O yez ! O yez ! O yez ! All manner of perfons may take notice that in the Clofe of St. Bartholomew the Great and Weft Smithfield, London, and the ftreets, lanes and places adjoining, is now to be held a Fair for this day and the two days following, to which all people may freely refort and buy and fell according to the Liberties and Privileges of the faid Fair, and may depart without difturbance, paying their duties. And all perfons are ftrictly charged and commanded in His Majefty's name, to help the peace, and to do nothing in the difturbance of the faid Fair, as they will anfwer the contrary at their peril; and that there be no manner of arreft or arrefts but by fuch officers as are appointed. And if any perfon be aggrieved, let them repair to the Court of Pie-Powder, where they will have fpeedy relief according to Juftice and Equity. God fave the King.

This irregular proclamation feems to have been accepted as a legal act by the Lord Kenfington who had become owner of one-half of the tolls of the fair, and it continued down to 1839. It was but a repetition of the double jurifdiction claimed in Sturbridge Fair.

There is in the library of the Britifh Mufeum a doggrel ballad, printed as a broad-fheet, called "The Dagonizing of Bartholomew Fair," which defcribes, with coarfe humour—the groffnefs of which may be attributed in part to the mingled refentment and contempt which underlies it—the meafures taken by the civil authorities for the removal from the fair of the fhowmen who had pitched there in fpite of the determination of the Lord Mayor and the Court of Aldermen to fupprefs with the utmoft rigour everything which could move to laughter or minifter to wonder. Among thefe are mentioned a fire-eating conjuror, a "Jack Pudding," and "wonders made of wax," being the earlieft notice of a waxwork exhibition which I have been able to difcover.—FROST's *Old Showman*, &c., p. 31.

In "A Caveat for Cut-purfes," a ballad of the time of Charles I., there is the following :—

> "The Players do tell you, in Bartholomew Faire,
>   What fecret confumptions and rafcals you are ;
> For one of their Actors, it feems, had the fate
>   By fome of your trade to be fleeced of late."

In another ballad, "Ragged and Torn and True," there is this :—

> "The pick-pockets in a throng
>   At a market or a faire,
> Will try whofe purfe is ftrong,
>   That they may the money fhare."

The Reftoration.—1661. The Reftoration led to

a confiderable reaction from the feverities of the Commonwealth, and the incidents of the fair were affected thereby, as will be feen. The firft noticeable feature is that the period of the fair becomes permanently prolonged from three to fourteen days; with occafional extenfions it is faid to fix weeks' riot and amufement. Another that the pamphleteering continued to be affociated with the fair. There was one " Strange News from Bartholomew Fair " &c. by Peter Aretine, printed for " Theodofus Microcofmus." The contents of this publication are altogether too grofs for detailed mention. There was another tract " News from Bartholomew Fair. Or the World's Mad : being a Defcription of the Varieties and Fooleries of this prefent Age," with Allowance (*i.e.* Licenfed) " Printed for the general ufe of the Buyer, and perticular Benefit of the Seller." It had for motto " Rifum teneatis amici ? " and a frontifpiece reprefenting a modified Puritan, in prefence of Jacob Hall the fafhionable rope-dancer, exhibiting the varieties of drefs !

1663. " Pepys's Diary," that never-failing fource of reference, throws fome light upon the doings of the fair at this period. On the 25th Aug. morrow of St. Bartholomew's Day (new ftyle), Mr. Pepys going at noon to the Exchange, met a fine fellow with trumpets before him in Leadenhall Street, and upon inquiry found that he was " Clerk of the City Market : " three or four men attended him each carrying an arrow of a pound weight in his hand. This was a revival by the Lord Mayor of the old City cuftom of challenging any to fhoot at the

fair. The previous day his lordſhip had attended
to witneſs the wreſtling. On the follewing there
was to be the civic hunting! But the feeling had
ſo far changed (perhaps in conſequence of the event
of 1656) that the Lord Mayor's preſence was not
deſired at this. "The people of the fair cry out
upon it, as a great hindrance to them."

1664. From the correſpondence of the philo-
ſopher John Locke, at this date it is clear he had
elbowed his way with the reſt of the world through
the crowd and made a ſtudy of this fair. Thus
deſcribing the ſights of the city of Cleves (from
whence he writes) to John Strachy at Briſtol, he
ſays " In the principal church at Cleves was a little
altar for the ſervice of Chriſtmas Day. The ſcene
was a ſtable, wherein was an ox, an aſs, a cradle,
the Virgin, the Babe, Joſeph, ſhepherds, and angels,
dramatis perſonæ. Had they but given them
motion it had been a perfect Puppet play, and
might have deſerved pence a piece; for they were
of the ſame ſize and make that our Engliſh puppets
are; and I am confident theſe ſhepherds and this
Joſeph are kin to that Judith and Holophernes
which I had ſeen at Bartholomew Fair."

Plague.—1665-6. There was no fair in theſe
years in conſequence of the Plague viſitation. In
the former of the two years at the uſual fair-time bale
fires were burning in the ſtreets night and day to
purify the air, and they continued until quenched
by heavy rain. In the following year there occurred
during the fair-time (as now extended) the Great
Fire of London, flames two miles in extent and a

mile in breadth, with fmoke extending fifty miles. There would have been a fcene of intenfe confufion if the fair had been gathered; no real danger, per- haps, as the conflagration ended at Pye Corner, on the verge of the fite of the fair. The houfes then fpared here were in exiftence down to Oct. 1809.

In the following year the fair was refumed, and probably was of fome fervice to the City in bringing people and money to it again. Pepys "the im- mortal" records under date 28th Aug. "went twice round Bartholomew Fair, which I was glad to fee again, after two years miffing of it by the plague." It feems patent that Court people and ladies of all qualities were at home in the fair at this period. Pepys records how he took his wife in 1668 "and there did fee a ridiculous obfcene little ftage play called 'Marry Audrey,' a foolifh thing, but feen by everybody; and fo to Jacob Hall's dancing of the ropes—a thing worth feeing and mightily fol- lowed."

Tolls.—1671. The Corporation of London was diffatisfied with the profits of the fair accruing from the arrangement then fubfifting, and referred it to the Comptroller to let the ground for the City and report the tolls to the firft court after the fair. This was done, and appears to have been fatisfac- tory, as the Corporation continued to receive the direct proceeds down to 1685, when the tolls were leafed to the Sword-bearer for three years at a clear rental of £100 per annum. At the expiration of two years it was reported that the tolls had not amounted to more than £68; they were leafed to the Sword-bearer at this rental for twenty-one years.

1674. In "Poor Robin's Almanack" for this year, in a catalogue of jefts upon the purpofes or features of fairs, is the following " Aug. 24 Smithfield for Jack puddings, pigs heads, and Bartholomew Babies."

1678. The " Irregularities and Diforders" of this fair were brought under the notice of the civil authorities ; and the queftion was referred to a Committee " to confider how the fame might be prevented, and what damages would occur to the City by laying down the fame." This is the firft hint of fuppreffion by the City ; " and its arifing," fays Mr. Morley, " is *almoft fimultaneous with the decay of the great annual gathering as a neceffary feat of trade.*" He adds, "There is no year in which it can be diftinctly faid that then the Cloth Fair died. Even at this hour, when the fair itfelf is extinct, there are in the ftreet called Cloth Fair, on the fite of the old mart, one or two confiderable fhops of Cloth-merchants, who feem there to have buried themfelves out of fight, and to be feeding upon the traditions of the fair."

Cloth Trade.—It is in connection with the woollen cloth trade that Bartholomew Fair moft linked itfelf with commerce. It was not fimply the great metropolitan cloth fair, but it was the greateft fair for woollen cloths held in England. For centuries wool had been the great ftaple of this country. Kings had taken its regulation under their own particular charge. The higheft official in the land took his

feat amongſt the peers of the realm literally on a
fack of wool. Cloth ranked firſt amongſt the products of the nation's induſtry. Among the fairs of
the world Engliſh woollen cloth was an important
article of commerce. The centre of this trade for
feveral centuries was located in this particular fair.
Other fairs had other fpecialities. But St. Bartholomew's was the annual trade gathering of Engliſh
clothiers and London drapers. The arms of the
Merchant Tailors were engraved upon a filver yard
—thirty-fix inches in length and thirty-fix ounces
in weight,—with which century after century members of their body were deputed to attend at Weſt
Smithfield during the fair, and teſt the meaſures of
the clothiers and drapers (fee 1609). The " Hand
and Shears " was a famous hoſtelry within the
Cloſe, where the cloth-merchants and the tailors
fraternized. And here, too, the Court of Piepowder
was long held when removed from the Abbey.

It remains to be ſtated in connection with the
events of this year that there was a very grave
queſtion involved as to whether the City had any
legal right to fupprefs the fair. The Cattle Fair was
ſtill very confiderable (fee 1715).

1682. There was publiſhed a new edition of
" Wit and Drollery : Jovial Poems" (1682); there
is contained the following epitome of the features
of the fair (not contained in the edition of
1656) :—

" Here's that will challenge all the fair,
Come buy my nuts and damfons and Burgamy pears !

Here's the Woman of Babylon, the Devil and the Pope,
And here's the little Girl juſt going on the Rope!
Here's *Dives and Lazarus* and the *World's Creation*,
Here's the *Tall Dutch Woman*, the like's not in the nation.
Here is the Booths where the high Dutch maid is,
Here are the Bears that dance like any Ladies;
Tat, tat, tat, tat, ſays little penny Trumpet;
Here's Jacob Hall, that does ſo jump it, jump it;
Sound Trumpet, ſound, for ſilver ſpoon and fork,
Come, here's your dainty Pig and Pork."

It had in faƈt come to this—as Sir Robert South-well truly ſaid in a letter to his ſon in 1685: "The main importance of this fair is not ſo much for mer-chandiſe, and the ſupplying what people really want; but as a ſort of Bacchanalia, to gratify the multitude in their wandering and irregular thoughts."

1688. It had become a cuſtom for the Lord Mayor after proclaiming the fair to call upon the keeper of Newgate, whoſe ſervices were uſually in-volved during the fair, and partake of "a cool tankard of wine, nutmeg, and ſugar." This year Sir John Shorter—natural grandfather of Horace Wal-pole, and of his couſins the Conway Seymours—fol-lowed the uſual courſe, but let the lid of the tankard flop down with ſo much force that his horſe ſtarted; he was thrown to the ground, and died the next day. The praƈtice was diſcontinued during the ſecond mayoralty of Sir Matthew Wood.

In "The Lady's New Year's Gift; or, Advice to a Daughter," publiſhed this year, it is obſerved: "Some women are for merry-meetings, as Beſſus was for Duels; they are ingaged in a Circle of

Idlenefs, where they run round for the whole year, without the interruption of a ferious hour; they know all the Players names & are Intimately acquainted with all the Booths in Bartholomew Fair."

1690. Literature ftill continued to be affociated with the fair. Thus there was publifhed this year: "The City Revels, or the Humours of Bartholomew Fair," by J. G. Gent. Sold by Randal Taylor, near Stationers-Hall, and by moft Bookfellers. Price ftitcht 6d.—not a fingle copy of which is now known to exift. There was alfo publifhed about this date " Roger in Amaze: Or the Countrymans Ramble through Bartholomew Fair. To the tune of: The Dutch Womans Jigg. Printed by and for A. M. and fold by J. Walter," &c. A fheet containing eight fix-line ftanzas. (Library of H. Huth, Efq.)

1691. There was a ftrong feeling fetting in at this period againft the fair. The Corporation ordered a return to the original term of three days, not only as a check to vice, but in order that the pleafures of the fair might not choke up the avenues of traffic. It is clear that this was not effective, for the order was repeated three years later. See 1711.

1697. The Lord Mayor iffued an Ordinance " for the fuppreffion of vicious practices in Bartholomew fair, as obfcene, lafcivious and fcandalous plays, comedies, and farces, unlawful games and interludes, drunkennefs, &c., ftrictly charging all conftables and other officers to ufe the utmoft diligence in profecuting the fame." *Vide* "Poftman" of this date.

Political allufions were very freely made in the amufements of the Fair; and fometimes thefe brought fpeedy retaliation. Thus, in the prefent year William Philips, a Zany or Jack Pudding, was arrefted and publicly whipped for perpetrating in the fair a jeft on the repreffive tendencies of the Government, which the poet Prior has condenfed and preferved for us. The faid clown made his appearance on the exterior ftage of the fhow with a tongue in his left hand, and a black pudding in his right. Profeffing to have learned an important fecret, by which he hoped to profit, he communicated it to the mountebank, in words recorded by Prior thus :—

> Be of your patron's mind whate'er he fays ;
> Sleep very much, think little, and talk lefs :
> Mind neither good nor bad, nor right nor wrong ;
> But eat your pudding, flave, and hold your tongue.

This fame W. Philips is fufpected to have an important hiftory of his own—indeed, to have been fomething befides a clown. He is believed to have been the author of the "Revengeful Queen," publifhed in 1698; alfo of "Alcamenes and Menelippa," and of a farce called "Britons, Strike Home," which was acted in a booth in Bartholomew Fair. Relating to him is alfo fuppofed to have been a book publifhed in 1688, of which nothing but the title-page is now known to exift. This is preferved in the Harleian collection, viz., "The Comical Hiftory of the famous Merry Andrew, W. Phill., Giving an account of his Pleafant Humours, Various Adventures, Cheats, Frolicks, and Cunning Defigns, both in City and Country." A copy of this would now command a large price.

Another of the great fhow characters of this period was Jofeph Clark, the " Pofturer." He is the " whimfical fellow " mentioned by Addifon in the " Guardian," No. 102. He was the fon of a diftiller in Shoe Lane, and was intended for the medical profeffion. This did not fuit his views, nor did the trade of a mercer, to which he was next put. He probably became buffoon in the Court of the Duke of Buckingham. Finally he appeared in the Fair. His performance chiefly confifted in the imitation of every kind of human deformity ; and he is faid to have impofed fo completely upon Molins, the famous furgeon, as to be difmiffed by him as an incurable cripple ! There is a notice of him in the " Philofophical Tranfactions," where it is related that he " had fuch an abfolute command of all his mufcles and joints that he could disjoint almoft his whole body." A portrait in Tempeft's collection reprefents him in the act of fhouldering his leg, an antic which is imitated by a monkey. Froft's " Old Showman," p. 59.

1698. A Frenchman, Monfieur Sorbière, vifiting London, fays : " I was at Bartholomew Fair. It confifts of moft Toy Shops, alfo Fiance, and Picture, Ribbon Shops, no Books ; many fhops of Confectioners, where any woman may commodioufly be treated. Knavery is here in perfection, dexterous Cut-purfes and Pickpockets. I went to fee the

Dancing on the Ropes, which was admirable.
Coming out, I met a man that would have took off
my hat, but I fecured it, and was going to draw my
fword, crying out 'Begar! Damn'd Rogue! Mor-
bleu,' &c., when on a fudden I heard a hundred
People about me, crying, 'Here Monfieur, fee
" Jephthah's Rafh Vow."' 'Here, Monfieur, fee
" The Tall Dutchwoman."' 'See " The Tiger,"'
fays another. 'See " The Horfe and No Horfe,"
whofe tail ftands where his head fhould do.' 'See
the "German Artift," Monfieur.' 'See the "Siege
of Namur," Monfieur;' fo that betwixt Rudenefs
and Civility I was forc'd to get into a fiacre, and
with an air of hafte and a full trot, got home to my
lodgings."

CHAPTER XVIII.

1700.

 TAGE Plays and Interludes.—The Lord Mayor and Court of Aldermen refolved that no booths fhould be permitted to be erected in Smithfield this year; but on the 6th Auguft it was announced that " the leffees of Weft Smithfield having on Friday laft reprefented to the Court of Aldermen at Guildhall that it would be highly injurious to them to have the erection of all booths there totally prohibited, the Right Hon. Lord Mayor and the Court of Aldermen have, in confideration of the premifes, granted licence to erect fome booths during the time of Bartholomew Fair now approaching : but none are permitted for mufic-booths, or any that may be means to promote debauchery." And on the 23rd, when the Lord Mayor went on horfeback to proclaim the Fair, he ordered two mufic-booths to be taken down immediately.

1701. On the 4th June this year the Grand Jury

of Middlefex made a prefentment to the following effect :—

" Whereas we have feen a printed order of the Lord Mayor and Court of Aldermen the 25th June 1700, to prevent the great profanenefs, vice, and debauchery, fo frequently ufed and practifed in Bartholomew Fair, by ftrictly charging and commanding all perfons concerned in the faid fair, and in the fheds and booths to be erected and built therein or places adjacent, that they do not let, fell, or hire, or ufe any booth, fhed, ftall, or other erection whatfoever to be ufed or employed for interludes, ftage-plays, comedies, gaming-places, lotteries, or mufic meetings : and as we are informed the prefent Lord Mayor and Court of Aldermen have paffed another order to the fame effect on the 3rd inftant ; we take this occafion to return our moft hearty thanks for their religious care and great zeal in this matter ; we efteeming a renewal of their former practices at the Fair a continuing one of the chiefeft miferies of vice next to the Play-Houfes ; therefore earneftly defire that the faid orders may be vigoroufly profecuted, and that this honourable Court would endeavor that the faid fair may be employed to thofe good ends and purpofes it was at firft defigned."

In the " Poftman," of September, appeared the following advertifement : " The tiger in Bartholomew Fair, that yefterday gave fuch fatisfaction to perfons of all qualities by pulling the feathers fo nicely from live fowls, will, at the requeft of feveral perfons, do the fame thing this day ; price, 6*d.* each."

There was publifhed this year for R. Hine near the Royal Exchange, "A Walk to Smithfield, or a True Defcription of the Humours of Bartholomew Fair, with the very comical Intrigues and Frolics that are acted in every particular Booth in the Fair, by perfons of all ages and fexes, from the Court Gallant to the Country Clown. With the Old Droll-Players' Lamentation for the lofs of their Yearly Revenues : being very Pleafing and Diverting."

It feems that at this period the principal London theatres clofed during the fair. This was so with Drury Lane in 1702 ; and alfo with feveral of the theatres during May Fair. See 1714.

1703. In the " Obfervator " of Auguft 21 this year was the following :

Does this market of lewdnefs tend to anything elfe but the ruin of the bodies, and fouls and eftates, of the young men and women of the City of London, who here meet with all the temptations to deftruction ? The Lotteries, to ruin their eftates; the drolls, comedies, interludes, and farces to poifon their minds, &c.; and in the cloifters what ftrange medley of lewdnefs has not that place long fince afforded ? Lords and ladies, aldermen and their wives, 'fquires and fiddlers, citizens and rope-dancers, jack-puddings and lawyers, miftreffes and maids, mafters and 'prentices ! This is not an ark, like Noah's which received the clean and the unclean ; only the unclean beafts enter this ark, and fuch as have the devil's livery on their backs !

1707. This year a well-known theatrical managerefs, Mrs. Mynn, produced a new verfion of the "Siege of Troy," reduced from five to three acts, by the aged actor, Settle.   The piece was printed with the following introduction :—

A Printed Publication of an Entertainment *performed on a* Smithfield Stage, *which, how gay or richly foever fet off, will hardly reach to a higher* Title *than the cuftomary name of a* DROLL, *may feem fomewhat new.   But as the prefent undertaking, the work of ten Months' preparation, is fo extraordinary a performance, that without Boaft or Vanity we may modeftly fay,* In *the whole* feveral Scenes, Movements, *and* Machines, *it is noways Inferiour even to any one* Opera *yet feen in either of the* Royal Theatres; *we are therefore under fome fort of neceffity to make this Publication, thereby to give ev'n the meaneft of our audience a full Light into all the Object they will there meet in this* expenfive Entertainment; *the* proprietors *of which have adventur'd to make, under fmall Hopes, That as they yearly fee fome of their happier Bretheren Undertakers in the* FAIR, *more cheaply obtain even the Engroft Smiles of the Gentry and Quality at fo much an eafier Price; fo on the other fide their own more coftly Projection (though lefs Favourites) might poffibly attain to that good Fortune, at leaft to attract a little fhare of the good graces of the more Honourable part of the Audience, and perhaps be able to purchafe fome of thofe fmiles which elfewhere have been thus long the profufer Donation of particular Affection of Favour.*

There was alfo publifhed " The Cloyfter in Bartholomew Fair; or, The Town-Miftrefs Difguif'd."

London, Printed for A. Bancks, near Fleet Street. A Poem. 8vo. 8 leaves.

Limiting the Duration of the Fair.—1708. On the 2nd June this year the Court of Common Council paſſed the following reſolution :—

This Court taking notice that the Fair of St. Bartholomew according to the original Grant thereof, ought to be holden annually three days and no longer. And that by Continuing the ſaid Fair to Fourteen days, as of late hath been practiſed, and the erecting and ſetting up Booths in Smithfield of extraordinary largeneſs not occupied by dealers in Goods, merchandiſes, &c., proper for a fair ; but uſed chiefly for Stage-plays, Muſick and Tipling (being ſo many receptacles of vicious and diſorderly Perſons) Lewdneſs and Debauchery have apparently increaſed, Tumults and Diſorders frequently ariſen, and the Traffick of the ſaid Fair, by the Traders and Fair-keepers reſorting thereto, greatly interrupted and diminiſhed. After long debate, and ſerious conſideration had of the ſame, and being deſirous to put a Stop (ſo far as in them lies) to the further ſpreading of Wickedneſs and Vice, to preſerve the Peace of Her Majeſty's Subjects, and reſtore the ſaid Fair to its primitive Inſtitution, and the Traders reſorting thither to the full enjoyment of their Trades, without any hindrance or obſtruction. And this Court being of opinion, that no ways will be ſo effectual for the end aforeſaid as reducing the ſaid Fair to its ancient time of continuance, doth unanimouſly reſolve, and ſo Order that for the future, the ſaid Fair ſhall be kept Three days only,

and no longer (that is to fay) on the Eve of St.
Bartholomew, that Day and the Morrow after being
the 23rd, 24th and 25 days of Auguft, of which all
perfons concerned are to take Notice and Govern
themfelves accordingly.   See 1750.

On the 3rd July, fame year, the Common Council
confidered certain ftrong petitions for the revocation
of this Order.   The refult is feen in the following
announcement, which appeared in the "Gazette"
of 2nd Auguft :—

The Committee for letting the City's Land in the
Account of the Chamberlain of the City of London
give notice, That the Fair, commonly call'd Bartholomew Fair, annually held in Weft Smithfield in
London is from henceforth to be held three Days
and no longer [days fpecified] and that the faid
Committee will fit every Wednefday at three of the
Clock in the afternoon, to Lett and Difpofe of the
Ground in Weft Smithfield, to perfons reforting to
the faid Fair; of which more particular information
may be had at the Comptroler's Office in the Guildhall of the faid City.

Same year a perfon did penance in the Chapter
Houfe of St. Paul's for publicly fhowing in the Fair
a Blow-Book in which were many filthy and obfcene
pictures.   The book was likewife burned, and the
offender paid the cofts.

The firft travelling *menagerie* feems now to have
appeared in this fair, and attracted confiderable attention.   It ftood near the hofpital gate.   "Sir Hans
Sloane cannot be fuppofed to have miffed fuch an
opportunity of ftudying animals little known, as he

is faid to have conftantly vifited the fair for that
purpofe, and to have retained the fervices of a
draughtfman for their reprefentation." (Froft.)

It may be noted that wild beafts had been kept
at the Tower certainly from 1253 downwards.

1709. There was publifhed "Bart'lemy Fair:
or an Enquiry after Wit; in which due Refpect is
had to a Letter concerning Enthufiafm, To my
Lord * * *. By Mr. Wotton. London Printed
for R. Wilkin, at the King's Head in St. Paul's
Church-Yard." This 8vo. pamphlet of 175 pages
contains no reference to the fair, and probably only
took its title from reference to the difputations there
conducted, and of which I have fpoken.

1710. There was a curious half-fheet octavo
tract, printed this year, entitled "The Wonders
of England, containing Dogget and Penkethman's
Dialogue with Old Nick, on the fuppreffion of
Bartholomew Fair in Smithfield." The title enume-
rates feveral other ftrange and wonderful matters,
as being contained in the book, but, like the fhowman's painted cloths in the fair, pictures monfters
not vifible within; fo there is not a line in the tract
refpecting the fuppreffion of the fair. Yet

"Coming events caft their fhadows before."

1711. It feems probable that in 1691, or 1694,
when the Corporation took fteps to limit the period
of the fair, that a printed ftatement of the reafons
therefor was iffued for the edification of the public
mind. At all events during the prefent year there
appeared: "Reafons Formerly publifhed for the

Punctual Limiting of Bartholomew Fair to thofe
Three Days to which it is determined by the
Royal Grant of it to the City of London. New
reprinted with Additions, to prevent a Defign fet
on Foot to procure an Eftablifhment of the faid
Fair for Fourteen Days. Humbly Addreffed to
the prefent Right Honorable the Lord Mayor to
the Worfhipful Court of Aldermen, and to the
Common Council of the faid City. London Printed
in the year 1711."

1714. It had become the cuftom for the ftars of
Drury Lane, Covent Garden, the Haymarket, Lincoln's Fields, and Goodman's Fields theatres to
enter into engagements to act in the theatrical
booths in Smithfield, and probably alfo in Southwark; and a rich " benefit " they made, fometimes
by acting, but more generally by becoming partners
in a company organized for the purpofes of the
fair. Recruits were brought up from the provincial theatres, and thus became familiar to London
audiences.

1715. In "Dawk's News Letter" it is recorded, "On Wednefday Bartholomew Fair began,
to which we hear the greateft number of black
cattle (Welfh ?) was brought that was ever known."
There was this year at the fair the largeft booth
ever built—it was for the King's players! It had
become the cuftom to reprefent all the great fieges
in which England had been concerned at the fhows
in the fair : hence, perhaps, fomething was done
towards foftering a martial fpirit, not without its
advantages in a national fenfe.

1719. The reftriction of the fair to three days, we are informed, had long been overruled by the public voice. There were this year twenty licenfed dice and hazard tables in the fair.

1730. There was printed in the " Daily Poft " for the 31ft Auguft the following :—

" Thefe are to give notice to all Ladies, Gentlemen and others That, at the end of Hofier Lane in Smithfield are to be feen during the time of the Fair, Two *Rattle Snakes,* one a very large fize, and rattles that you may hear him at a quarter of a mile about, and fomething of Mufick, that grows on the tails thereof; of divers colours, forms and fhapes, with darts that they extend out of their mouths, almoft two inches long. They were taken on the mountains of Leamea. A Fine Creature, of a fmall fize, taken in Mocha, that burrows under ground. It is of divers colours, and very beautiful. The teeth of a dead Rattle Snake to be feen and handled, with the rattles. A Sea Snail, taken on the coaft of India. Alfo the horn of a Flying Buck. Together with a curious collection of Animals and of Infects from all parts of the World. To be feen without Lofs of time."

This feems to have been a very rude attempt at teaching natural hiftory.

1731. The only recorded inftance of *fire* breaking out in the fair occurred this year. The damage refulting was fmall. (See 1810.)

1733. It was about this date that Fielding the novelift commenced public life, by keeping a play-booth in this fair.

The Strolling Player.—The life of a ſtrolling play-manager, attending fairs and ſuch like places of amuſement, was one of much incident, and certainly had its comical ſide. Here is the account of one as given by himſelf :—" I will, as we ſay, take you behind the ſcenes. Firſt then, a valuable actor muſt ſleep in the pit, and wake early to ſweep the theatre, and throw freſh ſawduſt into the boxes; he muſt ſhake out the dreſſes, and wind up and duſt the motion-jacks ; he muſt teach the dull ones how to act, rout up the idlers from the ſtraw, and redeem thoſe that happen to get into the watch-houſe. Then, ſir, when the fair begins, he ſhould ſometimes walk about the ſtage grandly and ſhow his dreſs : ſometimes he ſhould dance with his fellows ; ſometimes he ſhould ſing; ſometimes he ſhould blow the trumpet; ſometimes he ſhould laugh and joke with the crowd, and give them a kind of touch-and-go ſpeech, which keeps them merry and makes them come in. Then, ſir, he ſhould ſometimes cover his ſtate robe with a great coat, and go into the crowd, and ſhout oppoſite his own booth, like a ſtranger who is ſtruck with its magnificence : by the way, ſir, that is a good trick, I never knew it fail to make an audience ; and then he has only to ſteal away and mount his ſtage and ſtrut, and dance and ſing and trumpet, and roar over again." —" Every-Day Book," i. 1243.

1735. The practice had been to grant licences for the fair for fourteen days. The Court of Aldermen now reſolved : That Bartholomew Fair ſhall not exceed Bartholomew Eve, Bartholomew Day, and the next morrow, and ſhall be reſtricted to the ſale of goods, wares, and merchandiſes, uſually ſold in fairs, *and no acting ſhall be permitted therein.* It was known, too, that Sir John Barnard intended rigorouſly to enforce the Licenſing Act. There was in conſequence no theatrical booths, and hence the moſt harmleſs portion of the amuſement was abſent.

1736. Theatrical booths were permitted again this year.

1739. The fair was extended to four days, and more theatrical booths attended in conſequence.

In the " Farrago ; or, Miſcellanies in Verſe and Proſe " [by Richard Barton ?], there is included (pp. 49-58) a piece entitled " Bartholomew Fair," from which we take the following :—

> Round ev'ry booth in face of day,
> Actors a tawdry dreſs diſplay ;
> Their ugly viſors ſeem diſgrace,
> Yet often hide an uglier face.
> The ſun their ſports not to delay,
> Makes haſte to bed, and cloſes day.
> Each wooden houſe then groans, to bear
> The populace that crowd the fair,
> Where Wapping & St. James' unite,
> Pleaſ'd with coarſe objects of delight :
> The chambermaid and counteſs ſit
> Alike admirers of the wit :
> The Earl and footman *tête-a-tête*
> Sit down contented on one ſeat.
> The muſick plays, the curtain draws,
> The peer & 'prentice clap applauſe.

1740. The Prince of Wales viſited the fair—not, indeed, for the firſt time, but with more ſtate than on any previous occaſion. An account of the viſit

was publifhed fome years afterwards in the " New
European Magazine," from which the following
details are drawn :—

The fhows were all in full blaft and the crowd at
its thickeft, when the multitude behind was im-
pelled violently forward; a broad blaze of red light
iffued from a fcore of flambeaux, ftreamed into the
air; feveral voices were loudly fhouting, " Room
there for Prince George! Make way for the
Prince!" as there was that long fweep heard to
pafs over the ground which indicates the approach
of a grand and ceremonious train.   Prefently the
preffure became much greater, the voices louder,
the light ftronger, and as the train came onward, it
might be feen that it confifted, firft, of a party of
the yeomen of the guard, clearing the way; then
feveral more of them bearing flambeaux, and flank-
ing the proceffion; while in the midft of it appeared
a tall, fair, and handfome young man, having fomething of a plump foreign vifage, feemingly about
four-and-thirty, dreffed in a ruby-coloured frock-
coat, very richly guarded with gold lace, and having
his long flowing hair curioufly curled over his forehead and at the fides, and finifhed with a very large
bag and courtly *queue* behind.   The air of dignity
with which he walked; the blue ribbon and ftar and
garter with which he was decorated; the fmall three-
cornered filk hat which he wore, whilft all around
him were uncovered; the numerous fuite, as well
of gentlemen as of guards, which marfhalled him
along; the obfequious attention of a fhort, ftout
perfon, who, by his flourifhing manner, feemed to

be a player—all thefe particulars indicated that the amiable Frederick, Prince of Wales, was vifiting Bartholomew Fair by torchlight, and that Manager Rich was introducing his royal gueft to all the entertainments of the place.

This event gave fafhion to the fair, and, indeed, it had never been confidered derogatory for perfons in the firft rank and fafhion to partake in the broad humour and theatrical amufements of the place. We have already feen that many of the theatrical celebrities of the day " ftarred " in Smithfield, and many who afterwards became famous firft trod the boards here.

The theatrical licences were extended to three weeks and a month at this fair.

1750. Alderman Blackford being mayor, he proclaimed in the middle of July his determination to reduce the fair to its original three days, and to ufe the powers of the Licenfing Act (10 Geo. II.) for the more effectual punifhment of rogues and vagabonds. He herein acted upon the reprefentation of more than a hundred of the chief graziers, falefmen, and inhabitants of Smithfield, who complained that the "infolent violation of the law " by the fair people not only encouraged profligacy, but alfo obftructed bufinefs for fix weeks ! The time occupied in putting up and taking down the booths being a time alfo of great hindrance to the ufual Smithfield marketing and trading. The real fuppreffion of the fair as a fourteen day riot, dates from this time.

1751. The attempted ftrict limitation of the fair

to three days led to confiderable difturbances. Birch, a deputy marfhal of the city, received injuries which proved fatal.

1752. The alteration of the calendar transferred the 3rd September into the 14th. Old Bartholomew's Day ftood at this new date on the calendar. This event very much aided in fhortening the period of the fair. *Vide* " Morley," p. 449.

1753. There was a great demonftration againft the claim of the Corporation to levy tolls upon the goods of citizens, as well as upon thofe of ftrangers, during the time of the fair. Richard Holland, a leather-feller in Newgate Street, had in the preceding year refufed the toll demanded on a roll of leather with which he had attempted to enter the fair, and on the leather being feized by the collector, had called a conftable, and charged the impounder with theft. The fquabble refulted in an action againft the Corporation, which was not tried, however, until 1754, when the refult was in favour of the citizens, and againft the Corporation claims.

While the action was pending Holland's cart was driven through the fair with a load of hay, and was not ftopped by the collector of tolls. The horfes' heads were decorated with ribbons, and on the leader's forehead was a card, upon which the following doggerel lines were written in a bold hand :—

> My mafter keeps me well, 'tis true,
> And juftly pays whatever is due ;
> Now plainly, not to mince the matter,
> No toll he pays but with a halter.

On each fide of the load of hay hung a halter, and a paper bearing the following announcement :—

> The time is approaching, if not already come,
> That all Britifh fubjects may freely pafs on ;
> And not on pretence of Bartholomew Fair
> Make you pay for your paffage, with all your bring near.—
> When once it is try'd, ever after depend on,
> 'Twill incur the fame fate as on Finchley Common.
> Give Cæfar his due, when by law 'tis demanded,
> And thofe that deferve with this halter be hanged.

There was confiderable rioting in the fair. Buck, the fucceffor to the unfortunate Birch, was very roughly handled. The tumult was in fome degree allayed by a ferious accident to the wire-walker, Evans. The wire broke, and he was precipitated to the ground, one of his thighs being broken, and other injuries fuftained.

The Bridewell Boys.—1755. An element in the occafional difturbances at the fair was the conduct of the " Bridewell Boys," a body of youths from the Bridewell Hofpital, diftinguifhed by a peculiar drefs and turbulence of manners. They infefted the ftreets and public places to the terror of the peaceable ; and being allowed the privilege of going to fires with the Bridewell engine, not unfrequently occafioned more mifchief by their audacity and perverfenefs than by their dexterity in fire extinguifhment, refembling in fome degree the volunteer fire brigades which at one time were very prevalent in the United States. On the 13th November this year, at a Court of the Governors of the Hofpital, a memorable report was made by the Committee, who inquired into the behaviour of the boys at the then preceding Bartholomew and Southwark fairs; and, as a confequence, fome of them were feverely corrected and cautioned, and others, after their punifhment, were ordered to be ftripped of their hofpital clothing and difcharged. At a later period the boys were deprived of their diftinguifhing coftume, and a different plan of inftruction was adopted.

1760. The Court of Common Council made a more determined effort than heretofore to put down this fair; but the intereft of Lord Kenfington (fucceffor of Lord Rich) in a portion of the tolls, rendered it impoffible of accomplifhment. See 1827.

1762. Plays were interdicted at the fair this year by the Corporation, and fome hardfhip refulted to thofe who had made arrangements in advance. Strong and fuccefsful meafures were taken to prevent its extenfion beyond the authorized three days.

There was publifhed "A Defcription of Bartholomew Fair" by George Alexander Stevens, whereof the following gives a good idea of the medley life there feen :—

Here was, firft of all, crowds againft other crowds driving,
Like wind and tide meeting, each contrary striving;
Shrill fiddling, fharp fighting, and fhouting and fhrieking,
Fifes, trumpets, drums, bagpipes and barrow girls fqueaking,
" Come my rare round and found, here's choice of fine ware-o ;"
Though all was not found fold at Bartholomew fair-o.

There was drolls, hornpipe dancing, and fhowing of poftures,
With frying black-puddings, and op'ning of oyfters ;

With Salt-boxes folos, and gallery-folks fqualling ;
The tap houfe guefts roaring, and mouthpieces bawling,
Pimps, Pawnbrokers, ftrollers, fat landladies, failors,
Bawds, bailiffs, jilts, jockies, thieves, tumblers and taylors.

" Here's Punch's whole play of the Gunpowder-plot, fir,"
With " beafts all alive," and " peafe-porridge all hot," fir,
" Fine faufages fried " and " the Black on the wire,"
" The whole Court of France " and " nice pig at the fire."
Here's the up-and-downs, " who'll take a feat in the Chair-o ? "
Tho' there's more up-and-downs than at Bartholomew fair-o.

Here's " Whittington's cat," and " the tall dromedary,"
" The chaife without horfes," and " Queen of Hungary ; "
Here's the Merry-go-Rounds, " Come who rides, come who
    rides, fir ? "
Wine, beer, ale, and cakes, fire eating befides, fir ;
The fam'd " learn'd Dog " that can tell all his letters
And fome men, as fcholars, are not much his betters !

1798. There was a ferious propofal made to re-
ftrict the fair to one day. This was only abandoned
from the fear of riot.

1804. There was an action brought in the fair
before the Court of Piepowder on 5th September—
fhowing that the court had fat beyond the prefcribed
three days, which at one time it did not, even though
the fair continued longer—by a fire-eater againft
one of the fpectators of his tricks, who had half
fuffocated him by fuddenly clapping a bundle of
lighted matches under his nofe. The defendant
was fined a guinea by the homage, and the fteward
gave charge to the conftables to turn him out of
the fair if he appeared in it again.

1808. There appeared : " The Hiftory and
Origin of Bartholomew Fair," publifhed by Arlifs

and Huntfman, 37, Bartholomew Clofe (8vo. pp. 26).

1810. A circumftance occurred likely to have been attended with very ferious confequences. Two bands of roughs, who were racing through the fair after their manner, met. In the fcuffle that enfued two ftalls were knocked down, and the falling of a lamp on to a ftove caufed the canvas to ignite, and a ferious difafter was only averted by the prefence of mind of a gentleman who was on the fpot at the moment. In a fimilar rufh in 1812 a child was killed.

In the " Morning Chronicle " appeared the following " Elegy, written in Bartlemy Fair at Five o'clock in the morning," from which I take the principal ftanzas :—

       *   *   *   *   *

Now the firft beams of morning glad the fight,
   And all the air in folemn ftillnefs holds,
Save when the fheep-dog bays with hoarfe afright,
   And brutal drovers pen the unwilling folds.

       *   *   *   *   *

Beneath thofe ragged tents—that boarded fhade,
   Which late difplay'd its ftores in tempting heaps :
There, children, dogs, cakes, oyfters, all are laid,
   There, guardian of the whole, the mafter fleeps.

The bufy call of care-begetting morn,
   The well-flept paffenger's unheeding tread,
The fhowman's clarion, or the echoing horn,
   Too foon muft roufe them from their lowly bed.

Perhaps in this neglected booth is laid
   Some head volcanic, oft difcharging fire !
Hands—that the rod of magic lately fway'd ;
   Toes—that fo nimbly danced upon the wire.

Some clown, or pantaloon—the gazer's jeft,
  Here, with his train in dirty pageant ftood :
Some tired-out pofture mafter here may reft,
  Some conjuring fwordfman—guiltlefs of his blood!

The applaufe of liftening cockneys to command,
  The threats of City-marfhal to defpife ;
To give delight to all the grinning band,
  And read their merit in fpectators' eyes,

Is ftill their boaft ; nor, haply, theirs alone,
  Polito's lions (though now *dormant* laid),
The human monfters, fhall acquire renown,
  The fpotted Negro—and the armlefs maid!

Peace to the youth, who, flumbering at the *Bear*,
  Forgets his prefent lot, his perils paft :
Soon will the crowd again be thronging there,
  To view the man on wild Sombrero caft.

Careful their booths from infult to protect,
  Thefe furl their tapeftry, late erected high ;
Nor longer with prodigious pictures deck'd,
  They tempt the paffing youth's aftonifh'd eye.

But when the day calls forth the belles and beaux,
  The cunning fhowmen each device difplay,
And many a clown the ufeful notice fhows,
  To teach afcending ftrangers—*where to pay.*

Sleep on, ye imps of merriment—fleep on !
  In this fhort refpite to your labouring train ;
And when this time of annual mirth is gone,
  May ye enjoy, in peace, your hard-earned gain !

1825. Bartholomew Day falling on a Sunday the fair was wholly fufpended. Many thoufands of perfons walking for recreation repaired to Smith-field and viewed its appearance. The City officers moſt ſtrictly enforced obſervance of the day : one keeper of a ginger-bread ſtall who plied for cuſtom and refractorily perſiſted was taken into cuſtody, and held in priſon till he could be carried before a magiſtrate on the following day, when he was fined for the offence.—Hone.

Hone's Survey of the Fair.—It was on the morning following this day that Hone made his memorable viſit to the fair, which he has recorded at large in his " Every Day Book " (i. cols. 1168-1251), and from which I take the following condenſed deſcription of the extent and nature of the exhibition :—

There were ſmall *uncovered* ſtalls from the Skinner Street corner of Giltſpur Street beginning with the beginning of the churchyard, along the whole length of the churchyard. On the oppoſite ſide there were like ſtalls from Newgate Street corner. At theſe ſtalls were ſold oyſters, fruit, inferior kinds of cheap toys, common gingerbread, ſmall wicker baſkets, and other articles of trifling value. They ſeemed to be mere caſual ſtandings taken up by petty dealers and chapmen in ſmallware, who lacked means to purchaſe room and furniſh out a tempting diſplay. Their ſtalls were ſet out from the channel into the roadway. One man occupied upwards of twenty feet of the road lengthwiſe with diſcontinued woodcut pamphlets, formerly publiſhed weekly at two pence, which he ſpread out on the ground and ſold at a halfpenny each in great quantities; he had alſo large folio bible prints at a halfpenny each, and prints from magazines at four a penny. The fronts of thefe ftandings were towards the paffengers in the carriage way.

Then with occafional diftances of three or four feet for footways from the road to the pavement began lines of *covered* ftalls, with their open fronts oppofite the fronts of the houfes, and clofe to the curb-ftone, and their enclofed backs to the road. On the St. Sepulchre's fide they extended to Cock Lane, and from thence to Hofier-lane, and along the weft fide of Smithfield to the Cow-lane corner. In John Street they were refumed and ran thitherward to Smithfield bars, and there on the weft fide ended. Croffing over to the eaft fide, and returning fouth, thefe covered ftalls commenced oppofite their termination on the weft and ran towards Smithfield, turning into which they ran wefterly towards the pig-market, and from thence to Long-lane. Again on to the eaft fide to the great gate of Cloth Fair, and fo from Duke Street on the fouth fide to the great front gate of Bartholomew hofpital; and then refumed to Giltfpur Street and fo reached the uncovered ftalls.

Thefe covered ftalls thus furrounding Smithfield, belonged to dealers in gingerbread, toys, hardware, garters, pocket books, trinkets, and articles of all prices, from a halfpenny to a half fovereign. The gingerbread ftalls varied in fize, and were confpicuoufly fine from the Dutch gold on their different fhaped ware. The ufual frontage of the ftalls was 8, 10, 12 feet, but fome as large as 25 feet. They were 6 feet 6 inches or 7 feet high in front and from 4 feet 6 to 5 feet at back : and all

formed of canvafs tightly ftretched on light poles.
The fronts were to the pavements. The houfes of
bufinefs in the ftreets had their fhutters up, and
doors clofed.

The *Shows* of all kinds had their fronts towards
the area of Smithfield, and their backs clofe againft
the backs of the ftalls. The centre of the area was
thus entirely open, and from the carriage way
through it all the fhows might be feen at one view.
Againft the pens at the fide there were not any
fhows. No carriages or horfemen were permitted
to enter the fair on account of the crowded maffes
of people prefent. . . .

It has to be noted that there was an unufually
large affemblage of fhows at the fair, including
feveral menageries.

1826. The "Mirror of the Months" contained
the following graphic anticipation of the fair to be
held this year:—

Another year arrives, and fpite of Corporation
"refolutions," and references to "the Committee,"
and "Reports" and "recommendations" to abolifh
the fair, it is held again. Now arrives that fatur-
nalia of nondefcript noife and nonconformity "Bartlemy Fair;" when that prince of peace-officers the
Lord Mayor changes his fword of ftate into a fix-
penny trumpet, and becomes the lord of mifrule and
the patron of pick-pockets; and lady Holland's
name leads an unlettered mob inftead of a lettered
one; when Richardfon maintains, during three
whole days and a half, a managerial fupremacy that
muft be not a little enviable even in the eyes of Mr.

Ellifton himfelf; and Mr. Gyngell holds, during the fame period, a fcarcely lefs diftinguifhed ftation as the Apollo of maid fervants; when the incomparable (not to fay *eternal*) *young* Mafter Saunder's rides on horfeback to the admiration of all beholders, in the perfon of his eldeft fon; and when all the giants in the land, and the dwarfs too, make a general mufter, and each proves to be according to the moft correct meafurement at leaft a foot taller, or fhorter, than any other in the fair, and in fact the only one worth feeing, —"all the reft being impoftors!" In fhort, when every booth in the fair combined in itfelf the attractions of all the reft, and fo perplexes with its irrefiftible merit the rapt imagination of the half-holiday fchool boys who have got but fixpence to fpend upon the whole, that they eye the outfides of each in a ftate of pleafing defpair, till their leave of abfence is expired twice over, and then return home filled with vifions of giants and gingerbread nuts, and dream all night long of what they have not feen.

The fair was fmall, and one of its principal features was the bookftalls, which occupied the whole of the weft fide of Giltfpur Street.

1827. The fair was again large, and for the firft time I am enabled to prefent a return of the cafh returns of the various places of amufement there affembled. The refult will be ftartling to thofe who have hitherto failed to realize the importance with which the fair was regarded : Wombwell's menagerie, £1,700; Richardfon's theatre, £1,200; Atkins's menagerie, £1,000; Morgan's menagerie,

£150; exhibition of " pig-faced lady," £150; ditto,
fat boy and girl, £140; ditto, head of William
Corder, quaker, who was hanged at Chelmsford for
murder of Maria Martin—the crime being revealed
through a dream of the victim's mother, £100;
Ballard's menagerie, £90; Ball's theatre, £80;
diorama of the battle of Navarino, £60; the Chinefe
jugglers, £50; Pike's theatre, £40; a fire-eater,
£30; Frazer's theatre, £26; Keyes and Line's
theatre, £20; exhibition of a Scotch giant, £20.
The comparative attractiveness of the different fights
affords room for reflection.   Of course these entertainments only reprefent a portion of the cafh tranfactions of the fair.

Lord Kenfington at length intimated that confidering the corrupt ftate of the fair, and the
nuifance caufed by it in the neighbourhood of
Smithfield, he would now throw no obftacle in the
way of its abolition.   His fhare of the tolls was
from £30 to £40 a year; the eftimated value of
thefe was from £500 to £600.   The Corporation
accordingly bought up thefe tolls, and henceforward
the fole rights and intereft in the fair became vefted
in the City.

The End.—1839. The London City Miffion,
having pointed out to the Corporation the moral
pollution fpread by the retention of the fair, the
matter was again referred to the City Lands Committee, who referred the queftion to Mr. Charles
Pearfon the then able City Solicitor; and he fpeedily
difcovered a rational mode of dealing with it : he
advifed *an abfolute refufal to let ftandings for fhow-*

booths in a fair that was created in the firſt inſtance for the purpoſes of trade!

The Markets Committee had in the meanwhile been working in the direction of largely increaſing the tolls for ſtalls, &c. The effect being that in 1836 they had increaſed to £162, 1838 to £284 ; this year £305. The ſmaller the number of booths the more each ſeemed able to pay, ſhowing that the popular patronage of the fair was ſtill conſiderable.

New Bartholomew Fair.— In 1843 the City authorities prohibited the aſſembling of " ſhows " of any and all kinds in Smithfield; but with this prohibition was the announcement that arrangements had been made for the ſtanding of ſuch ſhows as deſired on a large piece of ground adjoining the New North Road, called Britannia Fields, near the ſite of the Britannia Theatre, in the pariſh of Hoxton.

In this ſtep it may have been thought to preſerve the income from tolls by a bodily transfer of the fair to another locality. I doubt if the original Charter would have ſupported ſuch a courſe; but the influence of the City would have obtained the authority of Parliament for the change. But even Parliament cannot change the ſentiments of the people in regard to their amuſements, or divert the channels of commerce from the time-honoured channels in which they have been wont to flow ; and the project for the new Bartholomew Fair fell dead very early in its inception ; but for two or three years ſhows did congregate there.

1855. *The end had come!* The old ceremony of
ftate proclamation had been difcontinued in 1840.
In 1850 the Lord Mayor (Mufgrove) having walked
quietly to the appointed gateway with the neceffary
attendants, found there was no fair to proclaim!
After that year the Lord Mayor attended no more
for the purpofe. The laft Bartholomew Fair was
proclaimed this year (1855). The City indeed
ftill pays to the Rector of Bartholomew the Great
the annual fee of 3*s*. 6*d*. in refpect of the proclamation no longer made. The live Cattle Market
was difcontinued the fame year—removed to Ifling-
ton. The Meat Market opened in 1868 has
obliterated all traces of a ftate of things which had
continued for feven centuries.

1859. Mr. Henry Morley publifhed " Memoirs
of Bartholomew Fair," " infcribed with friendfhip
to his friend John Forfter." In his preface he fays
" When I firft refolved upon the writing thefe
memoirs, I knew fimply that Bartholomew fair was
an unwritten portion of the ftory of the people.
Bound once to the life of the nation by the three
ties of Religion, Trade and Pleafure, firft came a
time when the tie of Religion was unloofened from
it; then it was a place of Trade and Pleafure. A
few more generations having lived and worked,
Trade was no longer bound to it. The nation ftill
grew, and at laft broke from it even as a pleafure
fair. *It lived for feven centuries* or more, and of its
death we are the witneffes. Surely, methought,
there is a ftory here; the memoirs of a Fair do not
mean only a bundle of handbills or a catalogue of

monfters. And then the volume was planned which is now offered to the reader, with a lively fenfe of its fhortcomings." Thus launched upon the world it was and is a book fuited to the companionfhip of all lovers of objeᴄ́ts of antiquity. I am glad to have been able to fupplement its record with fome details of intereſt.

FAIRS OF FRANCE.

CHAPTER XIX.

T is to France that we muſt look if we would fully comprehend alike the ſplendour and importance of the fairs of Europe. Even here, as elſewhere, they are now to be regarded as things of the paſt; but of a paſt that is full of inſtruction.

In the eighth and ninth centuries hardly any trade was known in France, other than that carried on in markets and fairs; theſe were, therefore, almoſt the only places for providing oneſelf with neceſſaries. Artificers and dealers lived apart, diſperſed in the country; the towns were chiefly inhabited by the clergy and ſome handicraftsmen, with few or no monks or nuns, the far greater part of the monaſteries being either in the open country or the neighbourhood of the cities. The nobility lived on their eſtates, or attended the Court. The *Pote* people were ſo far under their Lord's power as not to quit the place of their birth without his leave; the villain was annexed to the eſtate, and

the flave to the mafter's houfe or land. Such a dif-
perfion was little promotive of trade, which loves
large and policed communities; *and it was to
remedy this inconvenience that its Kings eftablifbed
fo many fairs. Vide* " Extracts translated from New
Hift. of France," 1769, i. 65.

There feem to have been three grades of fairs.
—1. *Free fairs*, to which all might come without
reftriction of toll or other limitation. 2. Fairs
having their franchifes reftricted by fome local right
or ufage. 3. Common fairs, without any fpecial
franchifes whatever. I fhall mainly confine myfelf
to a notice of thofe falling under the firft of thefe
definitions—free fairs.

CHAMPAGNE AND BRIE.

I may fpeak of the fairs of thefe provinces col-
lectively. They were not only amongft the moft
celebrated of France or of Europe, but poffefs the
charm of great antiquity. They are believed to
have been founded by the earls of thofe provinces.
Sidonius Apollinaris alludes to them, A.D. 427.
They were held in feventeen of the chief cities—
fome of which had as many as fix yearly, others
four, none lefs than two.

I have already given (in the firft chapter in this
book) fome account of the commercial importance
of thefe fairs in Europe, and need not re-traverfe
that ground. They have a great intereft from an
Englifh point of view for reafons which will prefently
appear.

Thefe diftricts were not indeed provinces of France at the early date above named. They only became fo in 1284, and fo far from their fairs gaining any additional luftre by the annexation, the very reverfe appears to have been the fact. The domination of the crown of France fpread awe inftead of confidence into the minds of their wealthy traders!

The truth I fufpect to be that charges and reftrictions previoufly unknown were impofed. This view indeed finds direct fupport in the fact that in 1349 Philip de Valois granted letters patent confirming ancient franchifes, and fuppreffing the new impofitions. By means of this document we learn precifely what the ancient privileges were. The patent confifted of thirty-fix articles, but the more material may be grouped under five heads, viz.:

1. *The Franchifes.*—All foreign dealers their factors and agents to have free liberty under the Royal protection, to refort to thefe fairs with their goods, provided however that thefe fame goods were defigned to be fold or exchanged there; or failing this were to be removed within the appointed time for the duration of the fair. They were exempted from all dues, impofitions, &c., according to the good and ancient ufages, cuftoms, and liberties of the faid fairs. No favours or letters of refpite might be granted againft the faid dealers, or the cuftoms and liberties of the faid fairs—all fuch, if obtained, being null. No dealers reforting to or returning from, fhould be ftopped or molefted, without fpecial warrant from the wardens of the

confervation, and for obligations made truly and really in the fair.

2. *Wardens of the Privileges.*—Thefe were judges appointed during the fair, to fee that the franchifes were preferved, and to take cognizance of contefts that might arife between traders there. Every fair was to have two wardens, one chancellor to keep the feal, two lieutenants, forty notaries, and 100 ferjeants. The wardens and chancellors were fworn in the Chamber of Accounts, Paris, *where they were yearly to make their report of the ftate of the fairs.* No judgment might be given during the fair but by the two wardens, or when one was unavoidably abfent, by one warden and the chancellor.

3. *How goods were to be brought within the franchife.*—The drapers and traders of the feventeen cities of Champagne and Brie frequenting the fairs —that is to fay thofe of the cities in which one of thefe feventeen fairs was held—might not fell their cloths or other ftuffs, wholefale or retail, within or without the kingdom, *unlefs firft fent to one of the fairs and expofed for fale from the firft day appointed for the fale of cloth until the fixth following,* on pain of forfeiture ; they being, however, at liberty to difpofe of them as they pleafed, if not fold in that time.

Farmers, curriers, &c., muft bring their leather to the fair, and expofe it all together from the firft of the three days, without referving any for the laft days, *or felling in any other place than that defigned for the fale of leather.*

Horfe-dealers, both fubjects and foreigners, muft

have their ftables in the faid fairs from the third day of the cloths (*i.e.* fixed for the fale of cloth) until the fair ended.

In like manner all other wares brought into the fair were to remain on fale, fome for fix days, others for three days only, according to their nature and quality.

4. *Infpections.*—Thefe were of two kinds, one by the wardens confervators, and the other by examiners chofen out of the trading companies frequenting the fair. The wardens' infpection was at the opening of every fair, to fee that the dealers had all fuitable convenience and fecurity—the infpectors being properly qualified judges of the character of the goods brought, with authority to ftop and feize all that were of inferior quality; but this not without appeal to fix, five, or four perfons experienced in the particular trade.

5. *Payments, Bonds, and Exchanges.*—All tradefmen, alike French and foreigners, might agree in their contracts for payment of goods fold in the fair—to be paid in gold and filver current at the time of making the contract, notwithftanding any ordinance concerning money to the contrary. Intereft for loans, and goods fold on credit at fairs, might not exceed fifteen per cent. The intereft might not be added to the principal in renewing bonds made at fairs. Nor might bonds made at any other time run in the ftyle of thofe ufed at fairs, as if made there.

All letters, acts, contracts, &c., relating to fairs, to be null *unlefs under the authenticated feal of the fairs.* None unlefs he had actual refidence in fairs might ufe the feal or other obligations, or enjoy the privileges thereof.

The re-eftablifhment of thefe privileges—many of which were obvioufly made in the intereft of merchants attending to buy—had the effect of re-ftoring the fairs of thefe provinces to their former greatnefs. Again multitudes of traders came from Germany, Italy (particularly from Florence), Lucca, Venice, and Genoa, with gold, filver, and filk ftuffs, fpices and other goöds of their country, or of the Levant, taking in exchange cloths, leather and other commodities, not only the produce of the provinces, but brought from other parts of France.

I fpeak of the fair of *Troyes* feparately hereafter, on account of one of its diftinguifhing features.

Mr. Morley has pointed out that before the eftablifhment of free fairs in France, the rights of *falutaticum*, *pontaticum*, *repaticum*, and *portulaticum*, abforbed one half of a foreign merchant's goods upon their firft arrival and debarkation. Afterwards traders came exempt not only from imperial taxation, but from many of the ordinary rifks of travel.

One great element of intereft in thefe fairs centres in the circumftance of the following correfpondence between the Wardens of the fair and the Lord Mayor of London concerning dealings in thefe fairs in the thirteenth century. They have been carefully preferved amongft the records of the City for fix centuries—and now for the firft time gain the glory of printer's ink. They reveal a feature in the comity of nations ; and prefent a proof of the cofmopolitan interefts of commerce which can fcarcely be excelled. Hence I propofe to give them entire :

1. *Letter directed to the Mayor by the Keepers of the Fairs of Champagne and Brie, dated September* 1299.

To the venerable man, the provident, wife and difcreet Warden of London, or to his vicegerent, Peter de Fremeville, knight, and Robert de Champagne (*de Campaniis*), keepers of the fairs of Champagne and Brie for our moft illuftrious Lord the King of the French, increafe of all good with greeting and fincere affection. Whereas heretofore, by our letters patent fealed with the feal of the fairs of Champagne, we have entreated you to compel, or caufe to be compelled, the burgefs Fauberti, a citizen of Florence and horfe-dealer (*mercatorem equorum*), together with Guido Fauberti, Nutus (or Nuto) Fauberti, brothers of the faid burgefs, Mafter Gerald de Galaiòn phyfician, [and] James fon of the faid Nutus, affociates of the faid burgefs, by the fale of their goods and the feizure of their bodies, fending them back to us, to yield and pay to Pucheus de Pré (*de Prato*), formerly horfe-dealer in the faid fairs, Martin de Burgo novo, brother of John de Burgo now deceafed formerly horfe-dealer, and John de Burgo novo, nephew of the faid John deceafed and of Martin aforefaid, or to the bearer of our faid letters for them, one thoufand fix hun-

dred petits livres Tournois with fufficient damages
and expenfes ; and to fatisfy us concerning the faid
King's amends for default of the fairs. In which
fum of money they are held effectually bounden,
and every of them in the whole, for the body of the
fairs of Bani (*Bari*) *fuper Albam* from the year of
Our Lord 1292, as well by reafon and becaufe of
certain pledges made and committed in and upon
the body of the faid fairs, as by reafon and becaufe
of the reftitution of more fureties and more cofts
and damages, which by default of the faid burgefs
and his affociates before mentioned in and upon the
body of the faid fairs they had and were faid to
have incurred : as in certain open letters of definitive fentence fealed with the feal of the faid fairs is
faid to be contained. Upon which things Tolnetus
[elfewhere Nicholas] called Conceffe, our fworn fervant in the faid fairs, by word of mouth related to
us that he in the year of Our Lord 1293 prefented
to you our aforefaid letters (as he fays), which
deprecatory letters of ours directed to you if for-
footh you received, yet you willed not to demand
due execution of the fame, or to write back any
anfwer to us, although at the end it was duly contained that what you fhould do therein, you would
will and deign by your letters to write back, and
although in prefence of many truftworthy perfons
you were fo requefted by our faid fervant; on the
ground that war was begun and raifed between the
moft excellent princes, the King of France and
King of England : as our faid fworn fervant on oath
has related all thefe things to be true, whereat we

moſt greatly marvel, if it is ſo and we hold our-
ſelves not contemned, ſince this is to the no mean
damage and grievance of the ſaid creditors, and
prejudice and contempt of the government of the
ſaid fairs committed unto us, becauſe on account of
the war aforeſaid you were by no means bound to
keep back our ſaid letters deprecatory demanding
due execution.   Wherefore as much as we can with
diligence on behalf of our moſt excellent lord, John
by the grace of God, King of France and Navarre,
Lord of Champagne and Brie, and on our part, by
the tenor of theſe preſents, we move your providence to be entreated, that you do cauſe all the
goods of the aforeſaid burgeſs Fauberti and his
aſſociates before named and of the ſaid company to
be ſolemnly proclaimed for ſale, and to be ſold and
divided without delay to the uſes and cuſtoms of
fairs, or ſo much of them that out of the price of
the ſale the ſaid creditors (or, for them, the bearer
of theſe preſents) as to the aforeſaid ſum of money
with ſufficient damages and expenſes, and we, as to
the amends of our ſaid lord the King, be wholly
ſatisfied ; and that the body of the ſaid burgeſs
Fauberti together with the bodies of his aſſociates
aforenamed—if they can be found in your juriſdiction, and if the ſale of goods does not ſuffice for
the premiſes—you do ſend back to us to the fairs
in ſure and faithful cuſtody to pay among them the
charges of the creditors, and to clear themſelves
before us in this matter as to the uſes and cuſtoms
beforeſaid.   If, however, you wiſh to put forward
any thing contrary to the report of our ſaid ſervant,

and believe your own interefts to be concerned, be prefent in perfon before us, or, for yourfelf, fend at a fitting day which the bearer of thefe prefents fhall caufe to be named to you, to fay what fhall feem to you expedient.   Otherwife, we fhall then hold the faid report to be faft and firm, you doing thereupon, on account of the reverence and honour due to our aforefaid lord the King and the intervention of our prayers, becaufe we are bounden to you and yours in all manner of favours deferved, fuch and fo much as you would wifh us to do for you in the like or a greater cafe.   What you fhall do herein, have a care to fignify to us by the bearer of thefe prefents in your letters patent together with the prefent letters demanding execution fent back, notwith- ftanding that they fhall not be prefented to you by the fervant of the fairs.   Given in the year of Our Lord one thoufand two hundred and ninety-nine in the month of September.

J. DE SANCTO NABORE.

2. *Letter fent to the Keepers of the Fairs of Cham- pagne and Brie, dated March* 19, 1299-1300.

To the noble men and difcreet lords Peter de Fremeville knight and Robert de Champagne keepers of the fairs of Champagne and Brie for the lord the King of France, Elias Ruffel, Mayor, and the Citizens of London, Greeting and continual in- creafe of fincere affection.   Whereas you lately wrote unto us that we fhould compel the burgefs Fauberti &c. [named as before] as well by fale of

their goods as by feizure of their bodies and alfo
fending them to you, to render to Pucheus de Pré
formerly horfe-dealer, Martin de Burgo novo and
other creditors in your letters comprifed, or to the
bearer of your faid letters, 1,600 petit livres Tournois together with damages and expenfes, and alfo
the amends of the Lord the King for default of
fairs; in which fum of money the aforefaid dealers
(*mercatores*), and every of them in the whole, are
bound by their letters made in the fairs of Bari
fuper Albam, by reafon of divers contracts between
them before had from the year of Our Lord 1292,
as in your letters thereupon to us directed more
fully is contained: We willing, fo far as the laws
and cuftoms of England permit, by mutual interchange to comply with your prayers, have caufed
to come before us, in the prefence of John de
Flekers your fervant and bearer of the prefents, the
aforefaid burgefs and Nutus, dealers, to anfwer to
your faid fervant concerning the faid debt according
to the form of your letters, which faid dealers afferted that they are quit of all the aforefaid, becaufe
of them all they fufficiently fatisfied the faid creditors, and therein proffered a letter of Gencian de
Paris, baker (*panetarii*) of the King of France, and
Robert de Champagne, keepers of the fairs of
Champagne and Brie fealed with the feal of the fairs
of Champagne, in which it is contained that the
faid burgefs, for himfelf, his brothers, and affociates,
in the fairs of Bari fuper Albam in the year of Our
Lord 1293, appeared in perfon before the faid
keepers, and fpoke with the faid Pucheus and com-

pounded with him under fuch form that the faid
Pucheus held himfelf as paid by the faid burgefs,
his brothers and affociates abovefaid, by reafon of
the faid compofition, as the faid Pucheus before the
faid keepers acknowledged and wholly affented to
the faid compofition for himfelf and his affociates.
And becaufe by the letters aforefaid it appeared that
the faid burgefs and his affociates by the faid compofition are totally quit of the debt aforefaid, we
could not by your mandate lawfully compel them
to pay the faid money. Given at London on
Saturday next before Mid-Lent in the year of Our
Lord 1299.

3. *Second letter* [of the Keepers] *of the Fairs of
Champagne and Brie for the burgefs Fuberti to the
Lord Mayor, dated May* 1300.

To the provident men, the venerable and honorable Mayor and Citizens of London, or their vice-
gerents, or one of them, Peter de Fremville, knight,
and Robert de Champagne, keepers of the fairs of
Champagne and Brie, continual increafe of fincere
affection with greeting. Whereas we, by our letters
patent fealed with the feal of the faid fairs, have
many times (*pluries*) prayed and requefted you to
compel and caufe to be compelled the burgefs Fouberti, citizen of Florence and horfe-dealer by feizure
of his body and goods, and alfo by the fale of the
goods of Guido Fouberti &c. [as before], to fatisfy
Pucheus de Pré formerly in the faid fairs horfe-
dealer, Martin &c. [as before], on and of the fum

(that is to fay) of 1060 [for 1600] petits livres Tournois with moderate damages and cofts, in which fum of money the faid burgefs Fouberti together with his affociates aforefaid is held bound to the beforenamed Pucheus, Martin and John, as debtor, concerning the body of the paft fairs of Barri *fuper Albam* in the year of Our Lord 1293, as well by reafon and becaufe of certain pledges made and committed in and upon the body of the abovefaid fairs, as by reafon and becaufe of the reftitution of more fureties and more cofts and damages which by default of the faid burgefs and his affociates beforementioned in and upon the body of the faid fairs they had and were faid to have incurred, as in certain letters of definitive fentence fealed with the feal of the fairs of Champagne is faid to be contained: upon which, firft, you would make no anfwer to us, or for our faid letters deprecatory demand any execution, as Nicholas called Conceffe our fworn fervant, bearer of our faid letters (as he faid), reported to us on oath by word of mouth ; but upon the tenor of our fecond letters which you caufed to be detained with you—as John de Flichers our fworn fervant, bearer of the fame (as he fays) related to us with his own mouth—upon thefe things with certain clofed letters you wrote back, that you caufed to come before you in prefence of the faid John de Flichers the aforefaid burgefs and Nutus, dealers, according to the form of our letters to anfwer to our faid fervant concerning the faid debt. Which faid dealers afferted they were quit of all the abovefaid, becaufe of all thefe they duly fatisfied the faid creditors &c. [reciting what was faid in the laft]. By the courfe of thefe prefents we thus hereupon notify to you that the faid fum of money has not yet been in any way fatisfied, as Dignus de Pré, fon and heir (as it is faid) of Pucheus deceafed, has given us to underftand. And affuredly, moreover, as foon as the faid burgefs on account of the things aforefaid appeared before you, and alleged the things contained in your anfwer, you ought to have taken into your hand his goods and thofe of his faid affociates, and to have fixed a certain and fit day for him before you, as in our letters abovefaid was contained ; for the cognizance of what relates to fairs belongs to no judge, but to us only by reafon of the government of fairs committed unto us. Wherefore, on the part of our lord the King of France and on our own part, we again afk your providences to caufe without delay fo much of the goods of the faid burgefs and his affociates aforefaid to be taken, fold, and divided to the ufes and cuftoms of fairs that the aforefaid Dignus de Pré may be fully fatisfied of the whole fum of money aforefaid with damages and expenfes, and we, of the amends ; and the body of the faid burgefs, if the fale fhall not fuffice for the cofts of the faid complainant, left on account of your default *it behove us to inhibit the land and fairs of Champagne and Brie to all your fubjects and their goods*. What you fhall do herein, have a care to fignify to us in your letters patent by the bearer of thefe prefents, fending back the prefent letters together with our other letters aforefaid detained with

you, as has been faid.   Given in the year of Our
Lord 1300 in the month of May.   J. de Sancto
Nabore.

I have placed a paffage in italics, as indicating the
fact that the merchants of London attended thefe
fairs.

4. *Letter from the Lord Mayor of London in anfwer
   directed to the Keepers of the Fairs of Champagne
   [and Brie] dated* 20 *Aug.* 1300.

To the difcreet and honourable men, if it pleafe
their moft dear friends, the lords Peter de Fremville, knight, and Robert de Champagne, Wardens
of the fairs of Champagne and Brie for the illuftrious King of France, Elias Ruffel, Mayor of
London, and the Citizens of the fame City, Greeting and continual increafe of fincere affection with
health.   Whereas heretofore you wrote to us that
we fhould compel the burgefs Fuberti, Citizen of
Florence, horfe-dealer &c. [naming the others as
before], as well by fale of their goods as by the
feizing of their bodies and fending them to you, to
render to Pucheus de Pré, formerly horfe-dealer,
Martin de Burgo novo, and other creditors in your
faid letters comprifed, or to the bearer of the faid
letters, 1600 petits livres Tournois together with
damages and expenfes, and alfo amends of the Lord
the King for default of the fairs; in which fum of
money the faid burgefs and his affociates, by their
letters made in your fairs beforefaid, are bound by
reafons of divers contracts between them had be-

longing to the year of Our Lord 1293 ; as in your
letters thereupon to us directed more fully is contained : We, as much as in us lies, and as the
customs and rights of the Realm of England permit
us to do, willing to comply altogether with your
prayers and requests, have made to come before us,
in the presence of your servant the bearer of the
presents, the said burgefs and Nutus whom we
found in our jurisdiction. Nevertheless we sequef-
tered their goods in the presence of your servant
putting upon them concerning the said debt, as is
contained in your letters aforesaid. And your
letters being heard and understood, the said traders
(*mercatores*) afferted that they are not bound of right
to answer to your said letters, because in your letters
secondly to us directed (as you affert) it was contained that the said burgefs and his affociates before
you in your fairs in the year of Our Lord 1292
bound themselves, upon which obligation they proffered a certain letter of fatisfaction of the said debt,
sealed with the seal of the fairs of Champagne and
Brie. In which said letter it was contained that the
said burgefs before you compounded with the said
Pucheus, to which composition he the said Pucheus
affented ; and in these your letters now to us directed
it is contained that the said burgefs and his affociates
in the year of Our Lord 1293 bound themselves
before you in your fairs : at which writing we
marvel. Moreover, at the time in which your said
letters were directed unto us, our lord the illustrious
King of England was in his war of Scotland with
whom at present we have not been able to confult,

nor are the faid burgefs and his affociates of the
liberty of our City of London: on which account,
without the fpecial mandate of our Lord the King
of England we dared not move a hand toward the
feizing of their bodies, or fend the faid burgefs and
others out of the Realm of England.   Therefore
we requeft and earneftly entreat your lordfhips that
at prefent in this charge you will hold us excufed
from the actions abovefaid, and deign to write to
our Lord the illuftrious King of England upon the
aforefaid debts and requefts; and thofe things which
fhall be commanded us for the advantage of the
faid creditors, and for your good pleafure, we will
difpatch without delay, and to the utmoft of our
power.   Farewell in Him who is the falvation of
all men.   Given at London on Saturday next after
the feaft of the Affumption of the Bleffed Virgin
Mary in the year of Our Lord 1300.

CHAPTER XX.

OTHER FAIRS OF FRANCE.

 HAVE now to notice fome of the other great fairs of France. And here it has to be remarked that while the later fovereigns—certainly down to Louis XV.—adopted the regulations already reviewed, for their model in the government of fairs, yet that there were fome neceffary deviations, according as time, place, and other circumftances demanded. The chief of thefe deviations will be noted in the following fummary, wherein I review the provincial fairs firft, and afterwards thofe in and around Paris.

Poftlethwayt, in his " Dictionary of Trade," from which fome of the preceding and following details are drawn, remarks, not with entire clearnefs : " Though it be not effential to thefe meetings of traders to have comedians, rope-dancers, and the like, yet there are few confiderable ones without enough of them; and, perhaps, is what greatly contributes to the trade of them—the nobility and

country gentry greatly flocking to them, more for
their diverfion than what they buy there, which
might be had, perhaps, better and cheaper at home.
It is well known how the nobility of Languedoc
flock to the fair of Beaucaire, and thofe of Normandy to that of Guibray; but it is nothing in com-
parifon to the affembly of German princes and
nobles at the three fairs of Leipzic, and the two of
Frankfort-on-the-Main." He was writing in the
firft half of the laft century. Things are now much
changed.

BEAUCAIRE (in Languedoc).—An important town,
whofe manufactures confift of filks, red wines, taf-
fetas, olive oil, and pottery. But its trade is chiefly
due to its great fair, held annually between 1ft and
28th July, the fite extending from the Rhône to
the bafe of the Caftle Rock. This fair was eftablifhed in 1217 by Raymond VI., Count of Tou-
loufe, and was for many ages attended by merchants
and manufacturers from all countries in Europe,
and even from Perfia and Armenia. Arthur Young
vifited it in 1788, and records ("Travels in
France") that the bufinefs tranfacted at it reached
10 million livres—£439,000. So late as 1833 it
drew together 60,000 perfons, and the amount of
its tranfactions were ftated to be 150 millions of
francs—£6,000,000 ! This would appear to be an
over-eftimate.

I believe the fair now only lafts one week, namely
from 22nd to 28th July inclufive. It is a rule that
all bills muft be prefented on the 27th, and protefted

if neceſſary on 28th—laſt day of the fair. The trade in linen and cloth is very large.

Besancon.—This ancient city, a great centre of warfare and of trade from the days of the Cæſars, had once a fair of great celebrity. At a later period it was chiefly notable for carrying on the buſineſs of exchange. This buſineſs had been perfected at the fairs of Lyons, from whence it paſſed here. On the firſt day of the fair the merchants of a certain ſtanding announced the terms on which they were willing to exchange with different countries, and on the ſecond day an authoritative declaration was made of the fair terms of exchange with any foreign country. For this purpoſe, with the conſtant fluc-tuations in all actual coinage, it was neceſſary to have a unit which ſhould be common to all lands, and free from the poſſibility of depreciation. Hence everything was reckoned by means of an imaginary unit—*ſcutus marcharum,* or money of account : ſo that the form which the buſineſs took was not that of buying bills, but of exchanging theſe fictitious coins, made realizable in one town, for quantities of actual coinage of another country, according to the authoritatively declared rate, which took account of the difficulty of tranſport, and of various riſks. A ſcutus marcharum was worth in Genoa 67$\frac{1}{3}$ ſoldi of the actual coinage of the place. The queſtion to be ſettled was what, at this time, ſhall be paid in Piacenza for a ſcutus marcharum in Genoa ? This was the fair rate of exchange, and the announce-ment of it was intended to exclude the operations of private fpeculators (in which it was not entirely fuccefsful), and to fecure a divifion of the advantage among each of the parties tranfacting bufinefs. *Vide* Cunningham's "Englifh Induftry and Commerce," 1882, p. 278.

BORDEAUX.—This city has or had two fairs annually—one commencing on the 1ft March, the other on the 15th October ; they each continued fifteen days. The October fair was generally the more confiderable.

The chief commodities difpofed of were wines and brandies, and it was no unufual fight to fee feveral hundreds of veffels beyond the ufual average number in the port, fome of thefe being of un- ufually large tonnage.

The fairs had the fame privileges with thofe of Champagne, Lyons, Paris, and Poictou. The con- fular judges performed the office of confervators, with the fame jurifdiction as thofe of Lyons.

CAEN (Normandy).—This free fair was once very famous. It begins the day after Low Sunday, and lafts fifteen days, of which the firft eight were defignated the "great week," the other portion the leffer, becaufe formerly the franchifes lafted only the firft eight; and becaufe the concourfe of ftrangers was much greater during the early week of the fair.

The merchants dealt in merchandife of all kind, but woollen manufactures were the great fpeciality. The fhops in which the dealers expofe their goods here are defignated " Lodges." A confiderable number of horfes and of cattle were brought to it from the provinces of Normandy. This fair was regarded as next in importance to that of Guibray.

It feems that in 1433 there was an attempt to defpoil this fair, by an attack of 700 horfemen, of which I find the following brief record :—" Whereupon they fent the Lord Ambrofe de Lore with vii. c. horfemen, to robbe and fpoyle the poore people, commynge to the faier, on the daye of Sainct Michaell the Archangell, kepte in the Suberbes of the toune of Caen."—*Hall*, Hen. VI. ann. ii.

During the year feveral fmaller and ordinary fairs are held for the fale of horfes, cattle, butter, and poultry.

DIEPPE.—This is a free fair of comparatively modern date, faid to be the laft authorized in France, having been founded by letters patent in 1696. It was firft opened on 1ft December that year. It continues for fifteen days. All foreigners are at liberty freely to trade here, and goods declared to be for the fair are not liable to feizure while the fair lafts ; nor were they liable to infpection by the wardens—a relaxation of practice apparently not quite in the intereft of the buyers.

Its franchifes and privileges are, that all goods brought into the port of Dieppe during the fair, and there fold or bartered, are exempt from one moiety of duties inwards and outwards. And merchandife imported and not fold during the fair may be carried out free of cuftoms.

GUIBRAY (Lower Normandy).—A fair of very confiderable importance, lafting from 10th to 25th Auguft, was held here. Arthur Young, of agricultural fame, defcribes in his "Travels in France" (1788), a vifit to it on 22nd Auguft, and records as follows : " At this fair of Guibray merchandife is fold, they fay, to the amount of fix millions (£260,500) . . . I found the quantity of Englifh goods confiderable, hard and queen's ware ; cloth and cottons. A doz. of common plain knives, 3 livres ; and 4 livres for a French imitation, but much worfe." It was a feature of this fair that the refident gentry for long diftances around came here to make their purchafes.

LYONS.—It has been fuppofed that the ancient fairs of this city were founded on a fpecial privilege granted by the Roman conquerors. They are four in number—the firft is that of the *Epiphany*, which always begins in January, the Monday after the twelfth day ; the fecond is *Eafter* fair, beginning on *St. Nifier's* day in April ; the third in Auguft, which begins on *St. Dominick's* day in that month ; and the fourth is the fair of *All Saints*, beginning on St. Hubert's day, in November. The fituation of this city, at the confluence of the Saône and the Rhône, render it unrivalled for the facilities of water carriage through fome of the richeft parts of France.

Thefe fairs were of the higheft mercantile repute, and at a very early period bills of exchange were brought into requifition in the adjuftment of the accounts for merchandife purchafed there. It feems alfo that bills refulting from commercial dealings in many other parts of Europe were made payable at the Lyons fairs.

Fixed days for payment followed each fair. The ceremonies attending thefe days were as follows : The chief magiftrate came to the lodge of the Exchange, accompanied by his regiftrar and fix fyndics, viz., two French, two Italian, and two Swifs or Germans; and there, after a fhort difcourfe to the affiftants, recommending probity in trade, and obfervance of the laws, cuftoms, and ufages of the place, the laws, cuftoms, and ufages were read *in extenfo ;* and the clerk drew up a procefs verbal of the opening of the "payment." The next day they met at the City-hall, and by plurality of voices *fettle the courfe of exchange for all cities with which Lyons had any commercial correfpondence.* This cuftom prevailed for fome centuries; and even when the ftrict regulations here defcribed were frequently departed from, the regulations were capable of being enforced on appeal.

When bills were drawn to be paid at one of thefe appointed times at Lyons, which had not then begun, the drawer faid " pay this my firft of Exchange, &c., in the next Epiphany (or other) payment ; " but if the payment had already begun, the bill had to be drawn payable " in this current or prefent payment of Epiphany " (or other term).

The bills fo drawn were to be accepted in the firft fix days of the payment they were made payable in; and the perfon on whom they were drawn was not obliged to declare whether he would or not accept until the fixth day. But after that day the bearer might proteft them for non-acceptance, though he might detain them during the whole time of that " payment," to fee whether any one offered to difcharge them. The proteft, however, was immediately forwarded to the remitters; and if any one paid a bill in the time of the payment before the fixth day (or that being a feaft day, the day following) it was at his own rifk.

The bearers of bills not fatisfied by the laft day of any " payment" were to proteft them on the third day after the payment finifhed, otherwife they loft their right as againft the drawers; but if this were done in form, and in the time prefcribed, the holder might afterwards refufe payment from any one that offered it, and take his reimburfement upon the drawer, alike for principal and charges. And the faid holders of bills were obliged to take their reimburfement on the drawers or indorfers in a time limited, viz., for all bills drawn from any part of *France*, in two months; thofe which were from *Italy*, *Switzerland*, *Germany*, *Holland*, *Flanders*, and *England*, in three months; and thofe which were drawn from *Spain*, *Portugal*, *Poland*, *Sweden*, and *Denmark*, in fix months, to be counted from the date of the proteft; or in default thereof they loft their rights againft the drawers and indorfers. See *Befançon*.

The general reader muft pardon thefe details, which are of commercial fignificance. It was cufto-mary at an early period to make the bills drawn from Amfterdam and elfewhere on the " payment " of Lyons, in " golden crowns of the fun ;" but when this fpecie became decried in France, the ufage of exchange came to be to draw for the payment of Lyons (as was practifed in France generally), viz., in crowns of fixty fous, equal to the prefent Englifh half-crown. Thefe practices may be compared with the ufages of Nuremburg, Frankfort, and Leipzig fairs.

The franchifes of the fairs of Lyons in the early half of the laft century had this fpecial feature : that all goods intended for foreign countries, fent out of this city during the fifteen days of either fair, paid no cuftoms outwards, provided the bales and parcels were marked with the city arms, and had certificates of franchife properly made out. To enjoy this privilege the merchandife had to be fent out of the kingdom before the firft day of the following fair, unlefs fpecial permiffion for delay had been obtained.

There is reafon to believe that a confiderable trade in books was tranfacted at thefe fairs during the fixteenth and feventeenth centuries.

These fairs have a great hiftory, which cannot be followed up here, and. there is the lefs need to make the attempt becaufe the inquiry is already in competent hands, thofe of Mr. Chancellor Chriftie, of Darley Houfe, Matlock. The authorities which may be confulted are the following :—

1. "Ordonnances et priviléges des Foires de Lyon, et leur antiquité avec celle de Brie et Champagne et la confirmation d'ialles par fept roys de France." Printed at Lyons in 1560, and fubfequently.

2. " Cat. de la Bib. Lyonnaife a M. Cofta redige par Aime Vingtrifme." (Lyon, Brun, 1853.) Pp. 458-61. Nos. 10,353-10,415.

3. A Memoir addreffed to Charles VIII. in 1485, and prefented by M. Pericaud ainé in his privately printed " Notes et documents pour fervir a l'hiftoire de Lyon, 1483-1546 " (Lyons, 1840).

4. In the " Proces de Bandiction de la Maifon Neuve Accufé d'herefia à Lyon 1534," printed by Fick, Geneva, in 1873.

MONTRICHARD (in Touraine).—This fair was famous for the great concourfe of traders to it from all the provinces of the kingdom ; but particularly for the great trade in woollen ftuffs, amounting on an average to fome 12,000 pieces at each fair.

RHEIMS.—This city had formerly four fairs; it has now two only, May and October—the great fair on St. Remigius' day. Thefe were all free fairs, two of the original fairs lafting eight days, the others but three days. Their franchifes were mainly the fame as thofe of Champagne. A very large commerce was in early times tranfacted at thefe.

ROUEN.—This ancient trading city had two fairs;

the one called Candlemas fair, beginning on the 3rd February, and the other called Pentecoſt fair, opening the day after the feſtival. They each continued fifteen days, and were much frequented by foreigners, particularly the Dutch, Britiſh (Engliſh and Scotch), and thoſe of other northern nations; its advantageous poſition for trade, by reaſon of facilities of water carriage, offering great inducements to the concourſe of foreign traders.

Goods ſold and exchanged at theſe fairs, and carried out of the city during the fifteen days, paid but half dues outwards.

TOULON.—This town—the Plymouth of France —has a fair, not deſignated " free," which commences on 3rd November, and continues "fifteen working days." Its franchiſes, granted in 1708, were that no goods while it laſts are ſubjeĉt to any duties; and all traders, alike French and foreigners, enjoy the franchiſes and liberties granted to the fairs of Lyons, Brie, Champagne, Rouen, and other cities. Theſe underwent ſome modifications in the following year, at the inſtance of the farmers-general of the revenues of France.

TROYES.—This town (one of the cities in Champagne) was noted in the middle ages for its great fairs, of which there were two—one being fixed to the Monday after the Second Sunday in Lent; the other commencing on 1ſt September. Philip of Valois granted the privileges of theſe fairs.

A laſting record of the importance of the deal-

ings thereat is handed down to us in the form of
" Troy (Troyes) weight," ufed in connection with
dealings in the precious metals. It is faid that this
fyftem of weights was brought from Cairo by the
crufaders, and was firft and permanently adopted as
the ftandard of weight in the dealings of the fairs
of Troyes. Hence it may be inferred that the
trading was largely in the precious metals, in fpices,
and in drugs.[1]

Goods fold at thefe fairs were exempted from all
cuftoms outwards, local dues excepted, under certain reftrictions.

It is recorded efpecially of thefe fairs, that they
had a ftaff of notaries for the atteftation of bargains,
courts of juftice, police officers, fergeants for the
execution of the market judges' decrees, and vifitors
—the *prud'hommes*—whofe duty it was to examine
the quality of goods expofed for fale, and to con-
fifcate thofe found unfit for confumption. The
confifcation required the confent of five or fix reprefentatives of the merchant community at the
fair.

Sifmondi, in his " Hiftory of the Italian Re-
publics," writing of the events of the thirteenth
century, fays :

The Tufcan and Lombard merchants however
trafficked in the barbarous regions of the weft, to
carry there the produce of their induftry. Attracted
by the franchifes of the Fairs of *Champagne* and of

---

[1] James VI. of Scotland adopted Troy-weight in 1618 ;
but curioufly the Troy-weight (Scots) coincided more nearly
with Avoirdupois.

Lyons, they went thither, as well to barter their goods *as to lend their capital at interest to the nobles, habitually loaded with debt;* though at the risk of finding themselves suddenly arrested, their wealth confifcated by order of the King of France, and their lives too fometimes endangered by fanctioned robbers, under the pretext of reprefling ufury. Induftry, the employment of a fuperabundant capital, the application of mechanifm and fcience to the production of wealth, fecured the Italians a fort of monopoly through Europe: they alone offered for fale what all the rich defired to buy ; and notwithstanding the various opprefſions of the barbarian kings, notwithstanding the loffes occafioned by their own oft-repeated revolutions, their wealth was rapidly renewed.

Infpectors of Fairs.—In the courſe of the preceding notices of the chief fairs of France various references have been made to the infpection of goods, as forming part of the regulations of fuch fairs. Thefe infpectors were appointed by the ftate. It was their bufinefs to attend at all fairs where there was any confiderable trade in woollen and other textile fabrics ; to infpect and mark them ; and if deficient or not conformable to the authorized regulations, to feize them. Such examination it is obvious required to be made with great circumfpection and referve, and at hours fuited to the convenience alike of buyers and fellers. The infpectors were ufually accompanied, in the performance of their duties, by the judge of the police of manufactures, and the wardens and jurats of trades in the respective places.

Some free fairs had their own judges and particular jurisdiction.

An examination of M. Bottin's "View of the Fairs of France" goes to show that they took place mostly on the frontiers of the kingdom, or on the marches of ancient provinces; or at the foot of high mountains, or at the beginning or end of the snow season, which for months shuts up the inhabitants in their valleys; or in the neighbourhood of the famous cathedrals or churches frequented by flocks of pilgrims; or in the middle of rich pasture tracks. But there are some marked exceptions to these rules.

The establishment and abolition of fairs—with the exception of cattle markets and the markets of the metropolis—are now generally left to the discretion of the departmental prefects.

CHAPTER XXI.

THE FAIRS OF PARIS.

HE City of Paris had fairs in great variety, fome of which I now proceed to notice.

St. Denis or *Lendit Fair.*—One of the earlieft, perhaps the firft, was the mercantile fair of St. Denis, chartered early in the feventh century by Dagobert "in honour of the Lord and to the glory of St. Denys at his feftival." This fair, by reafon of the privileges granted, became known under the name of the *forum idictum*—whence *l'indict*, and its corruption to *landit* and *lendit*. To it came the iron and lead of the Saxons, the flaves of the northern nations, the jewellery and perfumes of the Jews, the oil, wine and fat of Provence and Spain, the honey and madder of Neuftria and Brittany, the merchandife of Egypt and the Eaft.

The fair, which lafted ten days from the 10th of October, was opened by a proceffion of monks from the Abbey of St. Denis; and in later times it was ufual for the Parliament of Paris to allow itfelf a holiday, called Landi, in order that its members might take part in the great marriage-feaſt of commerce and religion : juſt as the Engliſh Parliament uſually finds relaxation in horſe-fleſh and mammon on the " Derby day " at Epſom !

Engliſh merchants frequented this fair in the ninth century, *vide* Cunningham's " Engliſh Induſtry and Commerce," 1882, p. 82.

But St. Denis had another fair, at one time famous, to which tradition has accorded the following origin. The Paris Cathedral received from Conſtantinople, in 1109, ſome fragments of the croſs, regarded as authentic. The populace could not find room in the church where they were depoſited in any one day ; hence the biſhop carried them in great pomp to the plain of St. Denis, where there was room enough for the vaſt concourſe of worſhippers who aſſembled to contemplate and adore. This ceremony and proceſſion were renewed at ſtated periods. The ſchools of the cloiſter of Notre Dame had early taken part in the proceſſions ; and finally the ſtudents of the Univerſity of Paris claimed it as a patron feſtival, which it certainly was not.

In proceſs of time a mart or fair became eſtabliſhed on the recurrence of this Church feſtival. The ground was regarded as conſecrated for the purpoſe. On each 12th of June (the day after the feſtival of St. Barnabas) the proceſſion took place. It was at a later period called the " Feaſt of the Parchment."

Early in the morning of the day of proceſſion, the ſtudents, attired in their beſt, aſſembled on horſeback at the top of Mount St. Geneviève, to accompany the Rector of the Univerfity, who, arrayed in his fcarlet cloak, and wearing his doctor's cap, proceeded on a mule or hackney, accompanied by the deans, proctors and myrmidons, to the plain of St. Denis, where the market for the fale of parchment was already opened. The rector upon reaching the fair caufed to be put afide as much parchment as would be required by the Univerfity for the coming year, and received from the fellers a donation equivalent to £100 of the prefent day. This I affume was the toll paid for the right of holding the fair.

After this the ftudents alighted from their horfes, and inftead of forming part of the proceffion back to Paris, amufed themfelves at the fair. This invariably led to riot and diforder, and not a year paffed without blood being fpilt. Thus from the fifteenth and fixteenth centuries the decrees of parliament againft the carrying of arms or fticks, which were continually being renewed and always neglected, teftify to the gravity of the evil, and to the difficulties of putting an end to it.

At laft, in 1566, the fair was transferred from the plain to the town of St. Denis, and at about the fame period paper began to fuperfede parchment even for public documents. The rector, therefore, ceafed getting a fupply of parchment at the fair, and the ftudents having no further pretext for attending, it fpeedily fell into difufe. By the beginning of the feventeenth century the only veftige of it left was the general holiday which the rector

granted to the ſtudents of the Univerſity upon the
firſt Monday after the feaſt of St. Barnabas, *vide*
Lecroix's "Science and Literature in the Middle
Ages," pp. 34-36.

St. Germain.—This fair was held in a large permanent building ſpecially provided, conſtituting
ſomething like twin market halls, elegantly con-
ſtructed of timber, and long regarded as models of
conſtruction.   The two halls embraced nine ſtreets
in line interſecting each other and divided into
twenty-four ſections or aiſles ; the ſhops having
little rooms or ſtore-houſes over them, and behind
ſome of them were open ſpaces, with wells—regarded as of importance in caſe of fire, although
not proving of much avail when the event occurred.
The ſtreets were diſtinguiſhed by the names of the
different trades conducted in them—as Goldſmiths'
Street, Mercers' Street, &c.

The fair was opened the day after Candlemas
Day.   It was greatly frequented by traders from
Amiens, Beaumont, Rheims, Orleans, and Nugent,
with various ſorts of cloth and textile fabrics.   The
goldſmiths, jewellers, and toymen of Paris made a
fine diſplay of their wares.

There were brought to this fair, one year with
another, ſome 1,400 bales of cloth and other woollen
ſtuffs, of which the inſpector of manufactures at the
Cuſtom-houſe, Paris, was required to keep a particular regiſter.   Two inſpectors of the fair were
required to be preſent at the opening of the bales of
goods.   There was alſo a further inſpection made

by the Mafters and Wardens of the Guilds of Drapery and Mercery.

I find a graphic account of this fair in Lifter's "Travels in France," 1698, which I here tranfcribe:

We were in Paris at the time of the fair of St. Germain. It lafts fix weeks at leaft; the place where it is kept, well befpeaks its antiquity; for it is a very pit or hole, in the middle of the Faubourg, and belongs to the great abbey of that name. You defcend into it on all fides, and in fome places above twelve fteps; fo that the city is raifed above it fix or eight foot.

The building is a very barn, or frame of wood, tiled over; confifting of many long allies, croffing one another, the floor of the allies unpaved, and of earth, and as uneven as may be: which makes it very uneafy to walk in, were it not the vaft croud of people which keep you up. But all this befpeaks its antiquity, and the rudenefs of the firft ages of Paris, which is a foil to its politenefs in all things elfe now.

The fair confifts of moft toy-fhops, and Bartholomew=fair ware; alfo fiance and pictures, joiner's work, linen and woollen manufactures; many of the great ribband fhops remove out of the Palais hither; no books; many fhops of confectioners, where the ladies are commodioufly treated.

The great rendezvous is at night, after the play and opera are done; and raffling for all things vendible is the great diverfion; no fhop wanting two or three raffling boards. Monfieur, the

Dauphin, and other princes of the blood come at leaſt once in the fair-time to grace it. Here are alſo coffee-ſhops, where that and all ſorts of ſtrong liquors . . . . are ſold.

Knavery here is in perfection as with us; as dexterous cut-purſes and pick-pockets. A pick-pocket came into the fair at night, extremely well-clad, with four lacqueys with good liveries attending him : he was caught in the fact, and more ſwords were drawn in his defence than againſt him ; but yet he was taken, and delivered into the hands of juſtice, which is here ſudden and no jeſt.

I was ſurprized at the impudence of a booth, which put out the pictures of ſome Indian beaſts, with hard names ; and of four that were painted, I found but two, and thoſe very ordinary ones, viz. a leopard, and a racoun. I aſked the fellow, why he deceived the people, and whether he did not fear cudgelling in the end: he anſwered with a ſingular confidence, that it was the painter's fault; that he had given the racoun to paint to two maſters, but both had miſtaken the beaſt; but however (he ſaid) though the pictures were not well deſigned, they did neverthelefs ſerve to grace the booth and bring him cuſtom.

St. Laurence (or *St. Laurent*).—So called from its ſituation near St. Laurence's Church. It is ſo ancient that no date can be even approximately fixed for its origin. Its chief traders were goldſmiths and mercers, picture-painters, ſempſtreſſes, lemonade-ſellers, toymen, earthenware people, gingerbread bakers, &c. &c. To it came people from Amiens, Beauvais, Rheims, and other places of Picardy and Champagne, with light fabrics, both plain and ftriped, and camlets of all forts.

The fair feems originally to have lafted but one day; but the period gradually became extended to two months, commencing the day after St. James's day and ending at Michaelmas. It was proclaimed by found of trumpet.

Thefe two rival fairs had this peculiarity: they were always open as bazaars. They were not fairs in the ufual fenfe of the term for more than three months in the year. The St. Germain fair was held in the winter, and the St. Laurent in the early part of the fummer. The former never recovered its popularity after the fire which deftroyed the wooden conftructions ufed during the fair (1763), though by the erection of new galleries, more elegant than the old ones, there was added to the attractions of a fair a dancing-faloon, the Winter Wauxhall, which was well attended for a time.

The St. Laurent fair was held in the upper part of the faubourg of that name, was larger and more elaborately decorated than the St. Germain fair, but it had no Wauxhall, and the only amufements for the frequenters of its Chinefe Redoubt were fwings and other foreign games.

The St. Ovide Fair.—This was eftablifhed in Auguft, 1764, and was held in the very centre of Paris, upon the Place Vendôme, then bounded on one fide by the church and convent of the Capucines. It was held there for fome years, and then transferred to the Place Louis XV., where it did not laft long, although it had originally been made fafhionable as the *Gingerbread Fair.* It was at this fair that Nicolet, previous to eftablifhing his theatre *des grands danfeurs du Roi,* difplayed the wonderful ftrength and agility which gave rife to the proverb " *de plus fort en plus fort, comme chez Nicolet.*" —Lacroix, " The Eighteenth Century," p. 356.

Onion Fair of Notre Dame.—This fair is held in September, commencing with the feaft of Notre Dame, and continuing till the end of the month. It is held on the Ifle of Notre Dame, along the Quai Bourbon. A prodigious quantity of black and red onions are brought into the city at this period, the citizens laying in a ftock for the whole year.

Pork or Bacon Fair.—This "fair for gammons" is held on the Tuefday in Paffion Week in the ftreet of Notre Dame, lafting but the one day only. There is fold at it immenfe quantities of hams, flitches of bacon, and other falted pork. Many amufing articles have been written concerning it.

HORSE AND CATTLE FAIRS.

The horfe and cattle fairs of France were and are very numerous. I fhall give but a brief outline of the chief or more remarkable. Thofe of *Chénerailles* (a great town of Auvergne) are chiefly famous for their fat cattle, brought for the moſt part to Paris. The fairs are held the laſt Tueſday in every month. The fairs of *Guibray* and *Caen* are amongſt the chief for horſes. That of Fontenay, in Poiċtou, for the horſes bred in that province. It is held 24th June, and is one of the moſt noted in France. The fair at Niort, on 1ſt December, is chiefly for foals. At *Nogent-ſur-Seine*, is a conſiderable horſe fair, the 11th Auguſt. There are three annual cattle fairs at *Braiſne-le-Comte*, near Soiſſons, viz. on 6th May, 14th September, and 14th December. The greater part of the ſales are for Paris. The fairs of *Nangis* and *Crecy* in Brie, on 4th July and 29th September reſpeċtively, are very conſiderable, and from theſe the graziers and butchers in the Iſle of France are ſupplied. *Montely* is a fair chiefly for cows, great numbers of which are brought by the farmers and peaſants about Paris and all the Iſle of France. It is held 9th September. There are alſo ſeveral fairs for pigs held in the villages around Paris, and innumerable other cattle and horſe fairs of leſſer note, not calling for any particular mention.

FAIRS OF RUSSIA.

CHAPTER XXII.

THE SMALLER RUSSIAN FAIRS.

HE modern growth of Ruffia is greater than that of any other European country. Its fairs have done much to facilitate that growth. It feems as if its people were paffing through thofe ftages of commercial building up which the other nationalities have long left in the dim vifta of the paft. The greateft fair held in Europe at the prefent time is that of *Nijni Novgorod;* yet that is not greater, relatively, than was Sturbridge in England, or thofe of Lyons, or of Bari (Italy), or of Bruges, in Flanders. There are feveral other large fairs, of which I fhall alfo give the beft details available. They are chiefly in fouthern Ruffia. The fair of Riga is an exception. The fair of Kiakhta is in Afiatic Ruffia, as are alfo thofe of Irbit and Yekaterinburg. I fhall firft notice the fmaller fairs, and finally that of Nijni.

BERDICHEFF (in the government of Volhynia,

fouthern Ruffia).—This town has long been famous for its fairs. King Staniflaus Auguftus permitted the holding of ten in the year. Five either now are or recently were held, viz. in January, March, June, Auguft, and November. Thofe of June and Auguft are the moft confiderable. Thefe fairs have given rife to the commercial importance of the town. The chief trade of the fairs is in grain, wine, honey, wax, leather, and horfes and cattle ; while cotton and filk goods, glafs-ware, hardware, falt, fifh, and beetroot fugar are becoming of increafing importance. The value of the goods fold is efti-mated at £800,000 ; the Jews are the chief pur-chafers. At the principal horfe fair there is fome-times a fhow of 40,000 horfes. The nobles of the country with their families attend the fairs, and remain encamped in the neighbourhood of the town during the three weeks they laft. At the January fair, 1883, a circus was burned, and about three hundred lives were loft.

ELIZAVETGRAD (fouthern Ruffia).—This town, formerly defignated " Fortrefs of St. Elizabeth," with its " Great Perfpective," and boulevard of white acacias, has four annual fairs, the moft im-portant of which is that of St. George, held on 23rd April (old ftyle). The value of the goods brought into the fair in 1863 was over £300,000. The chief commodities of the diftrict are tallow and grain. The goods brought into it are thofe manu-factured at Odeffa, Wilna, and Berdicheff. There is alfo a daily market held here, with tranfactions of confiderable magnitude, efpecially after harveft.

Jitomir (or Zytomiers), chief town in the province of Volhynia, weftern Ruffia, has two annual fairs—one in July, the other in Auguft. Apart from the trade at thefe, which is confiderable, the ordinary commerce of the town is fmall. There are three markets weekly.

Karkoff.—This town, fituate in the adminiftrative province of the fame name in fouthern Ruffia, is a place of very confiderable importance. It has four fairs, the " Kreftchenfkaya " or Epiphany fair, opened 6th January, being one of the moft important in the empire. In 1863 goods to the amount of from two and a half to three millions fterling in value were brought to that fair, the textile fabrics alone reprefenting a value of about one million fterling. Cattle and wool conftitute the local produce. The wool fales take place exclufively at the Trinity fair in June. Bazaars and markets are alfo held on Sundays, Wednefdays and Fridays. Thefe are particularly active immediately before Chriftmas and Eafter. This is one of the moft pleafant diftricts of Ruffia. The vine and the mulberry, with other fruits, thrive here.

Kasan (Kazan).—This, while an independent ftate, had a confiderable fair, one of the greateft in Europe; but John the Terrible prevented Ruffian merchants from attending it. In 1552 Kafan was conquered by this fame Ivan, and annexed to Ruffia. See *Makariev* and *Nijni Novgorod.*

KORENNAYA, fouthern Ruffia, twenty-feven verfts from Kurfk.—Two very large fairs are held, viz. on the ninth Friday after Eafter, and on the 8th Sept. in each year. The cathedral within the famous monaftery of Bogoroditfky-Znamenfky (*Apparition of the Virgin*) contains a holy image held in great veneration—that of the apparition of faid Holy Virgin, after whom the monaftery is named. Immenfe crowds follow the proceffion of the holy image every year, at a period coincident with the firft fair. The monaftery was founded in 1597.

KREMENCHUK.—An important town in fouthern Ruffia on the Dnieper, in which fairs are held at end of January for fourteen days, on 24th June for eleven days, and on 1ft September (all old ftyle) for ten days. The bufinefs tranfacted is not large, particularly having regard to the favourable fituation. In 1862 the fales of thefe fairs amounted to £85,000, and the value of the goods brought to about £110,000.

KURSK.—A town in fouthern Ruffia, on the river Tufkor. Two fairs are held here—one in April, the other in the tenth week after Eafter. There are alfo two weekly markets—Mondays and Fridays. See alfo *Korennaya.*

MAKARIEV.—The monks of the monaftery of St. Macarius (after which the town feems to be named) by virtue of their charter eftablifhed a fair here in 1641, after which annually in the month of July for a fpace of three weeks the few wretched huts, built on a fandy defert, were replaced by thoufands of fhops erected with a promptitude peculiar to the Ruffians. Taverns, coffee-houfes, a theatre, ball rooms, a crowd of wooden buildings painted and adorned with tafte, fprung up. People from many nations thronged here in great multitudes: Ruffians from all the provinces of the empire, Tartars, Tchuvaches, Te-heremiffes, Calmuks, Bucharians, Georgians, Arme-nians, Perfians and Hindus; and in addition Poles, Germans, French, and Englifh. Notwithftanding the confufion of coftumes and languages, the moft per-fect order prevailed: all were there for the purpofes of commerce. The riches which were gathered there within the fpace of two leagues were faid to be incalculable. The filks of Lyons and Afia, the furs of Siberia, the pearls of the Eaft, the wines of France and Greece, the merchandife of China and Perfia. Thefe were brought in contraft with the moft ordinary articles of everyday life, in true Eaftern fafhion. This fair was in truth one of the developments of *Nijni Novgorod,* which fee.

OREL.—An important town in fouth-weftern Ruffia founded by John the Terrible, about 1565, for the defence of the Grand Duchy of Mofcow againft the Tartars. The town has a large trade in tallow and hemp, alfo in linfeed oil, wheat, cattle, timber and falt. This commerce has two outlets— the one by land; the other by water down the Oka, to Kaluga, Serpukhof, Kolomna, Murom, Nijni-Novgorod, Rybinfk, and St. Peterfburg. There are three fairs annually—between 6th and 20th January, during the fifth and fixth weeks after Eafter, and from 8th to 31ft Sept. (O.S.) The firft is the leaft confiderable of thefe. The market or bazaar days are Fridays and Sundays. After harveft as many as 10,000 carts enter the town daily, laden with wheat and other produce.

POLTAVA, fouthern Ruffia, on the river Vorfkla, long famous for the leeches found in its pools and moraffes, and which are largely and widely exported. The importance of the trade of the town is chiefly due to its fair (Ilyinfkaya) held on 10th July, and lafting a month. The average value of the goods carried to this great commercial gathering is efti-mated at about three and a half millions fterling. The number of carts engaged in bringing the pro-duce from Mofcow, Odeffa, Kharkoff, Kurfk and Voronej is upwards of 20,000. Ruffian manufac-tures are much fold, but wool is the great ftaple of trade. Horfes, cattle, and fheep are likewife bought and fold in great numbers. There are two other fairs—one on the feaft of the Afcenfion.

RIGA (the capital of Livonia, Baltic Provinces) had feveral centuries fince, two confiderable fairs, one held in May, the other in September, very much frequented by Englifh, French, Dutch, and other merchants. At the period of thefe fairs the town wore a very commercial afpect, and the port was thronged with fhips. The local cuftoms were peculiar, and gave rife to difficulties. The townfmen had priority in the ſelection of warehouſes, and in the ſale of commodities, and as a reſult the veſſels of foreigners were unduly detained, and the ſelection of the produce made in advance of their opportunities. Hence it was recorded in the middle of the laſt century that theſe fairs were on the decline.

ROSTOF, on the river Don, near its mouth in the ſea of Azof (Lake Nero), and famous for its manufactures of white lead, vermilion, and other mineral and chemical ſubſtances ; alſo for its linen manufacture. Large fairs are held twice a year, when very conſiderable numbers of cattle and horſes change ownerſhip.

VORONEJ, on the Voronej river, near its confluence with the Don ; one of the moſt flouriſhing towns in ſouthern Ruſſia. Its trade is in grain, linſeed, tallow. Four fairs are held annually, the larger being thoſe of 9th May and 29th Auguſt (O.S.). Markets are held three times a week.

CHAPTER XXIII.

NIJNI-NOVGOROD.[1]

THIS may now be pronounced the great mercantile fair of the world. It probably bears a greater refemblance (but on a larger fcale) to that of Sturbridge in its beft days, than any other of paft or prefent times. It is almoft the laft remaining type (in Europe) of the mediæval form of commerce. The origin and early hiftory of this fair are fomewhat obfcure. Authentic records atteft that mercantile gatherings were held at Nijni fo early as 1366; and tradition points to a ftill earlier origin. Before Kafan was conquered by Ivan the Terrible in 1552, Ruffian merchants were prohibited from attending fairs in that province. A confiderable fair then held was the precurfor of the prefent.

The Ruffians held a fair at another place on the Volga. In 1641 the monks of the monaftery of St. Macarius, by virtue of their charter, founded a

---

[1] The name fignifies *Lower New Town,* to diftinguifh it from Novgorod the Great on the Volkhof, North-Weftern Ruffia.

fair at *Makariev*, feventy-one miles below Nijni. Of this fair I have already given fome account. " The monks of the monaftery (fays Michell) very cleverly made Nijni a place of religious as well as commercial refort, and levied taxes on the trade which they foftered." Up to 1751 the tolls had ftill been collected by thefe monks; but in that year the fair became the property of the State. In 1824 it definitely fixed at Nijni-Novgorod. It was probably removed here temporarily in 1816, when the town of Makariev was deftroyed by fire.

The fituation of the town oppofite the confluence of the Volga (having a courfe of 2,320 miles) and Oka (with 900 miles of navigation) rivers, is preeminently fuitable for the purpofe of commerce, of which thefe rivers indeed, prior to the introduction of railways, conftituted the great arteries. The town of Lower Novgorod was founded as early as 1222, and was in 1237 occupied by the Tartars. When it was taken from them, they declared perpetual warfare againft it, and facked it more than once. By means of the two large rivers named—which extend, with their contributory ftreams and canal communication with the Baltic, over a confiderable portion of northern, eaftern and fouthern Ruffia—an eafy communication is maintained with the richeft agricultural and manufacturing provinces. The Kamma, a tributary of the Volga, alfo affords water communication with the remote provinces of Ural and parts of Siberia. The productions of China are carried during the month of September over the Baikal Lake, and in fpring reach the Volga along with the

Siberian caravans. The productions of Aftrakhan, Perfia and Bokhara afcend that river, while thofe of Peterfburg, Germany, England, and France defcend it: fo that the merchandife of the eaft and the weft meet as in a common centre here. And this line of commerce dates back into far diftant ages, promoted and fhared in by thofe trading monks who took fo leading a part in founding the great Hanfeatic League.

It is an interefting hiftorical fact that the firft veffel of war ever built in Ruffia was launched at Nijni by a company of merchants from Holftein, who obtained permiffion in the feventeenth century to open a trade with Perfia and India by way of the Cafpian fea. The veffel was called the Friedrich. The travels of Olearius were in connection with this undertaking, of which there is a great hiftory, to be recounted on fome other occafion.

The town has many fine modern buildings. In the ordinary way, the beft view to be had of it and the furrounding country is from the " Otkos " or terrace built by order of the Emperor Nicholas.[1] It is faid to be one of the beft views in Europe. As far as the eye can reach extends the vaft alluvial plain, rich with culture, and occafionally dotted with forefts; whilft the Volga, flowing down from Tver,

---

[1] This terrace is locally known as Mouravieff's Folly, in confequence of a tower built by him, upon which he defigned to place a facfimile of the famous Strafburg clock, but on fo gigantic a fcale that the hours and minutes, the moon's phafes, and planets, cycles, &c., fhould be diftinctly vifible from every locality of the town and fair!

looks like a broad blue ribbon ftretched over the country from one extremity of the horizon to the other. Much of the plain below is inundated in fpring by the overflowing of the river, leaving a fertile depofit which confiderably enhances the value of the land. The ftationary population of the town does not exceed 30,000 or 40,000, but during the fair the inhabitants fwell up to confiderably over 200,000 ; and this quite irrefpective of prodigious numbers of cafual vifitors. The ancient Kremlin, with its low arched gates, whitewafhed towers, and crenellated walls, is one of the fights of the place. The thick green foliage of the gardens and the gay refidences of the inhabitants all blend into a very picturefque whole.

Site of the Fair.—We muft next take a glance at the fite of the fair, which is outfide the town, and can hardly be feen from the gates. Turn then from the Volga, or Afiatic direction, and there, acrofs the Oka (here about a quarter of a mile broad), is a low, almoft inundated flat, of triangular fhape, between the two rivers. This was regarded as the moft convenient fite. Great difficulties were prefented by the fwampy nature of the foil. Deep fewers vaulted over were conftructed through the morafs ; thefe being connected by canals with the rivers. The buildings for the bazaars were raifed on piles, and the whole boggy furface of the plain was covered to the depth of fome feet with gravel and clean fand. Through this the ordinary furface water and the inundated flow percolates, and leaves clean paffages or roads. In the midft of the plain

is the great bazaar—an immenfe rectangular market-
place—divided by lanes or paffages, interfecting at
right angles into fixty-four fquare groups of ware-
houfes, or blocks of ftone-built buildings, two
ftoreys high, with projecting verandahs, fo as to
fhelter goods and paffengers from the fun or rain ;
containing, befides fome public offices in the centre,
2,522 large ftores for merchandife, to each of which
is a fmall chamber for the merchant.

The connecting ftreets are fome thirty or forty
yards wide ; and the centre avenue is yet much
wider, and planted with trees. Thefe ftreets much
refemble thofe of Cairo, Smyrna, and other oriental
towns. In the centre of that block of permanent
buildings is located the official refidence of the
governor during the fair, as alfo all the bufinefs offices
for the adminiftration. It was in this official refidence
that the Duke of Edinburgh ftayed during his vifit
to the fair a few years fince. It is equivalent to the
royal pavilion of fome of the early Englifh fairs.
The principal avenues of the fair are connected with
fome ten miles of wharves or river frontage ; and
during the fair bridges are erected fo as to give
eafy accefs from the town to the fair. The coft of
preparing the fite and the principal buildings was
forty millions of roubles—£1,670,000 fterling. The
fair, however, has long outgrown the original
limits, and miles of temporary ftructures fpring into
exiftence for the occafion. It extends over fome
feven or eight fquare miles !

Unloading.—As the period of the fair approaches,
the ordinary defolation of the location paffes rapidly

away. The rivers, bufy indeed at all times when navigation is poffible, now become almoft blocked by traffic. A perfect foreft of mafts is vifible. All diftinct trace of the ordinary bridge of boats feems loft. The 400 or 500 fteamers, built mainly in England and Belgium, which in the ordinary way are trading on the 1,600 miles from this to the Cafpian fea, all feem concentrated here. They dart about like ftraws on thefe mighty rivers. But more ftriking-looking are the quaint mediæval-looking barges, coming as they do from the moft diftant parts of the empire, piloted through canals and rivers in order to find their appointed place here. Thefe are all being rapidly difcharged of their cargoes by an army of ragged Tartar labourers. Here will be found merchandife from every quarter of the globe; merchandife which has in fome cafes been feveral years on its way hither; merchandife which comes from localities fo remote as not to be brought into voluntary affociation with this fair. Centuries ago, we are told by the hiftorian of Genoa, the Genoefe merchants built larger fhips than were required for their regular trading operations, fhips calculated to withftand the terrors of the Bay of Bifcay, and the ftorms of the German Ocean, in order to make voyages to the Hanfeatic towns, to Wifburg and Gotland, as alfo to the coaft of Ruffia in order to participate in this great fair (Bent's " Genoa," 1881, p. 107).

The Fair.—And now we arrive at the fair itfelf. Round the public offices in the centre are ranged the European wares, the French millinery, and

Englifh broadcloth. Next follow the Armenians, a
numerous and diftinguifhed clafs in every commercial affemblage throughout the Eaft. Near thefe
the Bokharians ufually range themfelves, and they
are eafily diftinguifhable from other Afiatics by their
fquat corpulent figures and dark complexions.
Nearly a whole fide of the bazaar is occupied by the
Chinefe market, in which the fhops are all laid out
in Chinefe fafhion. Tea is the chief article of the
Chinefe trade; and on this portion of the fair I fhall
fpeak later. Beyond the ftone buildings of the
bazaar commence the rows of wooden booths in
which the motley Siberian and Tartar tribes eftablifh themfelves with their furs and peltry; the
moft remarkable to a European eye, though not the
leaft common of their wares, being the dark moufe-
coloured hide of the wild horfe, with black mane
and ftreak along the back, much prized by the
Bafhkirs and other tribes for its warmth as well as
beauty.

The wine trade has never conftituted a great
feature of the fair, although wine fkins from the
Caucafus may be feen; and many of the brands of
fouthern Ruffia may be found on application.

Moft of the ftreets of the fair have elegant light
arcades on each fide, fupported in front by caft-iron
columns, where purchafers can walk about, well
fheltered in all kinds of weather. The ftalls are
generally very handfome, and in fome inftances extend from ftreet to ftreet, fo as to leave two fronts.
They prefent nothing of the confufion of an ordinary fair; the goods of every kind are as neatly

ranged as in the ſhops of a city. To facilitate
buſineſs there is a ſeparate quarter ſet apart for each
different and important claſs of goods. One
quarter contains groceries, of which the value ſold
is very great. In another, dried fiſh and caviar are
expoſed in moſt fragrant variety, of which great
quantities are ſold, amounting to about £60,000 in
value. I may here remark that the annual value
of the ſturgeon alone taken in the Volga is eſtimated
at two and half millions of roubles; and above
30,000 barrels of caviar have been diſpatched from
Aſtrakhan in a ſingle year. A third quarter contains leather articles of every kind, which may be
bought exceedingly cheap; boots and ſhoes are diſpoſed of in very large quantities. Morocco leather
is alſo ſold wholeſale to a very large amount. A
great deal of it comes from Aſtrakhan, where, as in
other parts of European Ruſſia, goats are kept for
the uſe of their hides to make this leather, more
than for their milk or fleſh. The pleaſant ſoap of
Kaſan is ſold in large quantities. One is glad to
find that it is in ſuch demand.

The iron and iron-ware ſtored in the mile of
ſhops where nothing but this metal is ſold, has been
brought at immenſe expenſe from Siberia; yet much
of it in its original crude ſtate probably came from
Tula, not a great diſtance from where it is now, in
its highly finiſhed form, expoſed for ſale. Weapons
and glittering arms of all kinds occupy conſpicuous
places in the hardware ſtores. There is, as a ſet-
off, a very conſiderable ſupply of holy images and
prieſtly veſtments!

The cloth range is large and well ftocked. One quarter contains ready-made clothes of all defcriptions. The cloaks alike for men and women are made from ftuffs with moft fingular patterns. Some of the figured works from Afia are really beautiful. The value of the woollen goods (Ruffian and foreign) fold annually is feldom lefs than three millions of roubles—£375,000. The quarter for fancy articles—gloves, handkerchiefs, ribbons, &c.,—is always crowded with purchafers, attracted by the graces of the fair occupants from Rue St. Honoré. The divifion for cotton goods is fully ftocked. The mills of England are largely drawn upon for thefe; but they are not in the hands of Englifhmen at this fair. The value of cotton goods fold here averages about twenty-two million roubles—£2,750,000! A grand difplay is made by the filks and fhawls, chiefly of oriental manufacture, and hence in very brilliant colours. The manufactured filks difpofed of here yearly are eftimated at ten and half millions of roubles, or £1,312,000; while of raw filk there is fold over 300,000 lbs. The furniture fhops conftitute a great feature of the fair; and one can but be furprifed to fee coftly carved tables, chairs, fofas, and ftill more large and valuable mirrors from France and St. Peterfburg. Glafs and cryftal articles, mainly from Bohemia, conftitute a very attractive difplay, while the jewellery alike of Europe and of Afia is always a fource of confiderable attraction, and the means of creating a large expenditure of cafh. The precious ftones from Bokhara and other parts of Central Afia are placed in the moft tempting prominence and profuſion. But beware of taliſmans and turquoiſes that appear to be cheap; they will probably be found equally cheap and much more ſatisfactory nearer home. The malachite and lapis-lazuli ornaments and other ſtones from Siberia are ſometimes good inveſtments; but ſome expert knowledge is required. Curious belts of ſilver may be purchaſed, but not without long bargaining. The hall-mark is repreſented by the number 84. There is a ſtall for the ſale of ornaments in gold and ſilver, ſet with Siberian and Perſian ſtones. Beware! But it is impoſſible to recount in any detail all that may be purchaſed or ſeen.

The Tea Quarter.—One of the moſt ſingular ſights of the fair is the tea quarter, which occupies the greater portion of an immenſe diviſion ſtanding by itſelf, and diſtinguiſhable by its Chineſe architecture. The Chineſe ſuperintend this buſineſs themſelves, or rather formerly did ſo. Along the wharves enormous pyramids of cheſts of tea are heaped upon the ground, covered only with matting made from the inner bark of the birch tree. Theſe cheſts of tea, called "tſibiki," are ſo packed as to be impervious to rain or damp. Outſide the ordinary wooden cheſt is a covering of wickerwork of cane or bamboo, round which, at Kiakhta, raw bullhides are tightly ſtretched, with the hair inwards. Theſe cheſts arrive at Nijni from China, having been received in barter, at Kiakhta or Maimatchin, on the Chineſe border of Ruſſia. The Ruſſians, who are great tea drinkers, are accuſtomed to the higher qualities of tea grown in North China; but thefe are now quite as eafily obtained from Canton as from *Kiakhta* (which fee), and it is faid (contrary to former belief) that the fea carriage has no deteriorating effect whatever. Here may be feen fome kinds of tea which fcarcely ever enter into the Englifh trade, viz. yellow and brick, the former of a delicious fragrance and very pale, but injurious to the nerves if taken very frequently ; it is handed round after dinner, in lieu of coffee, in Ruffia. The brick tea is confumed by the Kalmucks and Kirghizes of the Steppe. The beft yellow tea fells for about 35*s.* per pound. The tea trade of the fair has fhown a tendency to decreafe.

Outfkirts of the Fair.—To the cafual vifitor the outfkirts of the fair are almoft more interefting than its centre, for obfervation and ftudy. The conftant fucceffion of carts in long ftrings; the crowds of labourers ; the knots of earneft-looking traders with long beards; the itinerant vendors of liquid refrefhments and white rabbit-fkins; the greafy flovenly monk collecting kopecks of thofe who fear to withhold their charity left their tranfactions be influenced by the Evil One ; the frequent beggars, pleading for the moft part that they have been burned out, and fhowing the moft dreadful-looking fores as evidence of their veracity; all thefe go to make up the great affemblage, the unique *tout enfemble* of the great fair of Nijni-Novgorod as it has been, and is to-day. How long will it remain ?

Adminiftration of Fair.—The adminiftration of the fair is carried on under the fupervifion of the Governor of the Province; the arrangement of all commercial matters and adjuſtment of difficulties being entruſted to a committee of gentlemen called the "Fair Committee," choſen from among the aſſembled merchants. This committee conſiſts of a preſident, three aldermen, and three committee-men, beſides the manager of the fair-office and the mayor of the town of Nijni. The management of all Government property is in the hands of this committee. The letting of ſhops and ſtorehouſes and the erection of bridges and all temporary works comes alſo within their province. The conditions on which the ſhops and ſtores built by Government are let to merchants and dealers are exceedingly liberal, and this rent is the ſole profit made by Government on the tranſactions of the fair. No im-poſts of any kind are levied in the ſhape of licences or duties. Shops are let to the firſt applicant, the ſole reſervation being that the occupier of the previous year has a prior claim. In order to pro-mote competition, each row of buildings is devoted to a certain kind of merchandiſe, thus obliging the merchants to endeavour to underſell one another. To prevent monopolies or over-ſpeculation, no mer-chant is allowed to hire more than three conſecutive ſhops, nor is he allowed to occupy more than one ſhop unleſs they adjoin each other. The number of ſhops let in 1874 was 6,086, and their total rent amounted to ſomething over £28,000.

The fair laſts ſix weeks—the really buſy period being from the 18th to 27th Auguſt, when the height is reached. Some fifteen days beyond are allowed for the ſettlement of accounts. The uſance of the fair is twelve months credit, *i.e.* from one great fair to the following; but fometimes, in dull times, and under fpecial circumftances, as much as two years credit is given. This was particularly the cafe in 1849.

Trade of the Fair.—The annual trade of the fair has been the fubject of various conjectures; but I believe the Government of the Province has caufed careful eftimates to be made from time to time. In 1697 the trade of the fair was eftimated at £12,000 per annum—evidently far too low. In 1790 it was ftated to be £4,500,000!

The following are the details of the principal branches of the fair in 1849, which were underftood to be lefs than the tranfactions of the preceding year: money being fcarce, and there was a ftagnation in the grain trade. The total eftimate of the Ruffian produce offered for fale was £7,916,016, of which there were fold raw produce £1,917,940; provifions £858,684; home manufactures £3,981,716—total £6,758,340, leaving £1,157,675 unfold. The value of the foreign goods and produce was eftimated at £2,430,191; of thefe Afiatic articles fold to the extent of £1,329,131; European raw materials £493,955, and manufactured goods £204,888—leaving £402,217 unfold. So that the total merchandife at the fair was eftimated at the value of $10\frac{1}{2}$ millions fterling, of which about nine millions were fold.

In Murray's "Handbook of Ruffia," written by Mr. Michell, the then well-known Britifh Conful, and publifhed in 1868, it is ftated that the aggregate ſale and purchaſes at the fair repreſented about ſix-teen millions ſterling; which dealings were con-ducted by from 150,000 to 200,000 traders from the various countries of Europe and Aſia.

Mr. Doria, ſecretary of the Britiſh Embaſſy at St. Peterſburg, reported that the trade of the fair had increaſed from about ſix millions ſterling in 1847 to over £20,000,000 in 1874 (165 millions of roubles), when upwards of 6,000 ſhops were let. The iron ſold in various forms amounted to 5,557,800 pouds of 36 lbs.—the value being £2,193,812. Tea of the value of about £1,200,000 was ſold.

At the fair of 1879 the iron trade figured largely, and the following facts were obtained regarding the ſupplies. The Ruſſian ironmaſters ſent 15,130,498 pouds (1 poud = 36 lbs.) of wrought iron, ſteel, and metal work, of the value of 7,528,350 roubles. A conſiderable amount was alſo imported into the iron ports of the Volga, viz. at Laïchev, 1,337,541 pouds; Kaſan, 16,474; Simbirſk, 22,066; Saratov, 92,361; Roſtov, on the Don, 67,762. Caſt iron was not in great force, there being only 530,488 pouds, of the value of 412,475 roubles. One of the largeſt contributions was ſent from the works of Count Strogonof, being 6,725,588 pouds.

Revenue of the Fair.—The fair conſtitutes a ſource of State revenue. When in 1751 the fair firſt be-came the property of the State, its tolls or revenues were farmed at about £150 per annum. In the reign of the Emperor Paul (end of laſt century) the farmer of the tolls engaged to build a new bazaar, and to pay £4,500 a year into the exchequer. In 1824 a new governor's houfe, bazaar, and fhops were erected, already defcribed, and an annual fum of £8,000, part of the rental of thefe, was appropriated to pay the coft of thefe buildings. The rental, as we have feen, is now approximating to £30,000.

A "charity dormitory" was fitted up by Count Ignatieff, with accommodation for fome 250 houfe-lefs vagrants; but if all of this clafs who are prefent were to apply for admiffion, probably accommodation for 20,000 would be needed!

The mode of eftimating the number of perfons attending the fair is peculiarly ingenious. The bakers are required to make daily returns of the quantity of bread they fell, and in this manner an approximation is arrived at. Of thofe prefent at the fair, only about one in a hundred are female.

It may be remarked that there is an excellent reftaurant under the governor's houfe in the fair. Some of the refrefhment booths in the fair prefent a remarkable fight, and, we may fairly add, fmell! The "Armenian kitchen" is one of the fights. Excellent horfe-flefh may be had at the Tartar reftaurants!

The paffport fyftem has been abolifhed as to perfons attending the fair, the governor finding it impoffible to examine, or indeed even to open the 40,000 documents per day that were formerly fent in. Befides, identification is out of the queftion; and the pickpocket fraternity ufe to purchafe, or more appropriately fteal, the authorization they required under the old fyftem.

Sanitary Arrangements.—The ſanitary arrangements of the fair conſtitute by no means an unimportant feature. To a ſometimes tropical heat there is the uſual accompaniment of clouds of finely pulverifed duſt. The Eaſterns aſſembled are not proverbial for habits of perſonal cleanlineſs. There is indeed an aroma unmiſtakable. The ſewers are fluſhed feveral times a day by means of water drawn from Lake Meſtcherſki, giving a fall of ſix yards into the river Oka. Round the central bazaar is a ſmall canal, provided in caſe of outbreak of fire, and found valuable on many occaſions. Smoking is prohibited within the limits of the fair under a fine of twenty-five roubles. The fair is guarded by a ſpecial ſervice of Coſſacks and police.

Amongſt the amuſements are a theatre with a very good ballet, for which latter Ruſſia is famous.

There is a belief that the glory of the fair is departing. Wallace, in his " Ruſſia," 1877 (ii. 196-7), ſays :—" I went to the great fair—and was diſappointed. All the deſcriptions of it which I have read are much too highly coloured. ' The motley crowds of Orientals, repreſenting every country in the Eaſt,' is not viſible to the naked eye of a proſaic obſerver. A few Georgians, Perſians, and Bokhariots may be ſeen ſitting at their booths or ſtrolling about; but they are neither very pictureſque nor very intereſting in any way. There is a ' Chineſe Row' where tea is ſold, and where the roofs of the booths ſhow traces of the influence of pagoda architecture ; but I find there no children of the Celeſtial Empire. As to the various kinds of merchandife, they may all be feen to much better advantage in the fhops and bazaars of Mofcow. Altogether, I fhould advife the traveller not to go very far out of his way to vifit this great annual gathering, which is commonly fpoken of by Ruffians —efpecially by thofe of them who have never feen it—as if it were one of the feven wonders of the world." This is in conformity with the general depreciatory ftyle of the entire work.

I ought not to omit mention of a little privately-printed book, "The Great Fair of Nijni Novogorod, and How we got there." By William Forfyth, Q.C. (1865.) He too was difappointed with the fair.

Two fmaller Fairs.—Beyond the great fair which I have now defcribed as fully as fpace would permit, there are two other fairs at Nijni, which, however, are little vifited by foreigners. The one held in January on the ice, at the mouth of the Oka, is devoted to the felling of wooden wares, fuch as boxes and toys. Great numbers of people come to this fair from the neighbouring villages. In January, 1864, the ice on which the booths and inns were conftructed gave way, and a confiderable number of men, women, children, and horfes miferably perifhed by drowning. Since then this winter fair can hardly be faid to have revived.

The other fair held on 6th July (N. S.) is for the fale of horfes.

CHAPTER XXIV.

FAIRS OF ASIATIC RUSSIA.

RBIT, in the government of Perm, in Afiatic Ruffia.—The town is fmall, with a population of little more than 1,000. It is enclofed with palifades, and contains two churches and a market-place furrounded with fhops. Here in paft times a noted fair was held annually, attended by Ruffian merchants on their way to Kiakhta. In more recent times it has been fuperfeded by the fairs of Yekaterinburg and Nijni.

KIAKHTA (fometimes defignated Maimatchin, the depot for commerce).—This town is fituated in Afiatic Ruffia, in the government of Irkutfk, on the Chinefe frontier. The fair appears to have been eftablifhed by treaty between China and Ruffia towards the latter part of the fixteenth century. The mode of bufinefs is after the fafhion of thofe early barter marts, which fairs originally were. The reafon for this ftate of things here is that the Ruffians are prohibited from exporting their coin, and there is no rate of exchange or other facilities for bills of exchange between the two countries. The Russian commodities are transported by land from St. Petersburg and Moscow to Tobolsk. From thence the merchants and merchandise may embark upon the Irtish down to its junction with the Oby; they can then work up the last-named river as far as Narym, where they enter the Ket, which they ascend to Makoffskoi-Osteog. At that place the merchandise is conveyed about ninety versts on land to the Yenisie. It is then necessary to ascend that river, the Tunguska, and Angara to Irkutsk, cross the Baikal Lake, and go up the river Selenga almost to Kiakhta. On account of the labour of working up so many rapid rivers, and of the incessant transhipments—which can hardly be accomplished in one summer—many prefer to go overland altogether. They make as a general rendezvous the town of Irbit, where a considerable fair was formerly held. From thence the progress is in sledges during the winter to Kiakhta, which is usually reached in February— the season in which the chief commerce is carried on with the Chinese. The Russian merchants purchase on their way all the furs they can find in the small towns, where they are brought from the adjacent countries. When they return in the spring with the Chinese goods, chiefly tea, occupying great bulk, the water route is preferred. Formerly the woollen cloths of Prussia were conveyed to this fair in large quantities—to the value of some £1,500,000—by the Russian merchants. The manufactories of Poland and Ruffia now furnifh the cloth taken to China.

The mode of procedure in the dealings is this : The Chinefe merchant comes and examines the goods he requires in the warehoufe of the Ruffian trader. When the price is fettled, the goods are fealed in the prefence of the Chinefe. Both parties then repair to the Mai-ma-tfhin, where the Ruffian choofes his commodities, and leaves behind him a perfon of confidence, who remains in the warehoufe until the Ruffian goods are delivered. About 8,000,000 lbs. of tea, of which two-thirds are of fuperior quality, were formerly taken into Ruffia as the proceeds of this barter. There is a fmall duty levied on the produce of each country. The trade has fallen off fince fea-borne tea became prevalent. Much of this now goes to Odeffa through the Suez Canal.

YEKATERINBURG (or Ekaterinburg or Jekaterin-burg), in the government of Perm in Afiatic Ruffia, forming the capital of the mining diftricts of the Ural. It is a modern place, and a confiderable fair has fprung up, fuperfeding that formerly held at Irbit.

INDEX.

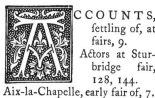